BEDFORDSHIRE
HISTORICAL RECORD
SOCIETY

ISBN 0 85155 042 8

Printed and Typeset by Advance Offset (Hitchin) Ltd.

THE PUBLICATIONS OF THE BEDFORDSHIRE
HISTORICAL RECORD SOCIETY
VOLUME 60

The Bedfordshire Farm Worker
in the
Nineteenth Century

by

NIGEL E. AGAR

PUBLISHED BY THE SOCIETY   1981

CONTENTS

Abbreviations

B.H.R.S. Bedfordshire Historical Record Society
C.R.O.   Bedford County Record Office
BPP   British Parliamentary Papers

This volume has been published with the help of a grant from the
Bedfordshire County Council

HAROLD OWEN WHITE

The Society in 1965, when Harold White became Secretary, was in some
straits. Within three years it had lost by sudden death the Treasurer and
Secretary who in two post-war decades had revived it to vigorous activity. To
replace F. J. Manning as Treasurer had not been easy; how was it possible to
find a successor to Charles Freeman as Secretary? When Harold White's name
was suggested, it hardly seemed feasible to hope for a man already so involved
in business and public work (as so sensitively described by John Dony in a
recent issue of the *Bedfordshire Magazine*), yet he accepted at once. He was
much more than an efficient Secretary. His expert knowledge and his sensible
advice were always at the Society's service; while his moral support of the by
now elderly editor was unfailing. His wife Marjorie was always with him at
the Annual General Meeting. He was one more exemplar of the dedication
which for 70 years the Society has been fortunate to receive from its officers.
In a wider context, yet relevant here, his total support of Bedfordshire history through all his life has the affectionate gratitude of this Society.

J.G.

PREFACE

Until recently farm workers have attracted little historical interest compared with other working class groups. Much of what is ostensibly labour history could be better described as trade union history, for historical work on the working class has been concerned primarily with the evolution of working class organisations, and farm workers made less impact on the development of the organised labour movement in Britain than groups such as miners or dock workers. Rural workers are traditionally far more difficult to organise than urban workers, but even so their efforts to form a union in the 1870's were more widespread and determined than is generally realised.

Farm workers, however, are suitable as a subject for labour history if seen in the context of their communities. In the early years of the last century their way of life was inextricably bound up with the poor law, whose reform was one of the earliest and most important of the major reforms of which nineteenth century England was so proud. Throughout the century domestic industry in the form of lace-making in the north of Bedfordshire and straw-plait in the south, had a more profound effect on rural society here than in any other comparable county.

The volume is based on a PhD thesis submitted to the School of Social Studies of the University of East Anglia in 1979, of which a copy is available at the County Record Office. In this connection I should like to acknowledge the advice and support of my supervisor, Dr. Richard Wilson, and his colleague, Dr. B. A. Holderness, both of the UEA, and also of Miss Pamela Horn of the Oxford Polytechnic, who examined the thesis. I owe a debt too to Dr. W. A. Armstrong of the University of Kent at Canterbury, who first drew my attention to the farm workers as a possible subject for study.

The documents printed here include two main categories of material: first, extracts from British Parliamentary Papers taken from the Blue Books of the period, and secondly, documentary material at the Bedfordshire County Record Office. Neither the original thesis nor this present collection would have been remotely possible without the assistance of Miss Patricia Bell, the County Archivist, and her colleagues, in particular Mr. James Collett-White. I must acknowledge here also the importance of the work on the administration of the Old Poor Law done by Mr. Peter Grey of the Bedford College of Higher Education.

A final accolade of respect should be paid to the subject of this study, the nineteenth century farm worker himself, without whose patience, endurance and skill England would be a very different place.

March 1981   Nigel Agar

THE BEDFORDSHIRE FARM WORKER IN THE NINETEENTH CENTURY

Although nineteenth century England was the world's first industrial society, agriculture remained the largest single male occupation at mid century and farm workers formed the largest occupational group. As long as industry was powered by steam, it was confined largely to the midlands and north. The population of an inland, rural county like Bedfordshire remained almost entirely dependent on agriculture and the most typical Bedfordshire man was one who earned his living on the land.

It is not always realised that societies where most of the working population are engaged in cultivating the land in return for wages, are, historically speaking, rather rare. Most agrarian societies in the past have either been based on some form of serfdom or slavery or have been peasant societies where the typical countryman cultivated the land on his own account with the help of his family. Even within the British Isles during the nineteenth century, peasant communities were the rule in Scotland, Wales, Ireland and some remote parts of England. Only in the progressive, prosperous south and east of England was most of the land cultivated by farmers who employed labour on a considerable scale.

In lowland England, the peasantry had long disappeared by the nineteenth century. In an arable county like Bedfordshire, rural society had become divided into three classes — landowners great and not so great who drew a rent; farmers (some owners, others tenants) who managed the land in return for profits from the sale of produce; and a much more numerous class of wage-dependent labourers. It is with this last class that this book is concerned.

Bedfordshire is an appropriate county in which to make a study of the Victorian farm worker. Being one of the corn-growing counties of the eastern half of England, the classic pattern of landlord, farmer and labourer was highly developed and accepted with little interchange or social mobility between classes. The farm-labouring way of life in Bedfordshire was relatively undistorted by outside influence. North of the Trent, farm-workers' wages were influenced favourably by the presence of industry and coalfields; in the pastoral counties of Wales and the west there was less rigid distinction between master and man on the land; while further south the influence of London made itself felt in terms of higher wages and greater opportunities.

Although the Bedfordshire labourer was an underprivileged member of society, this does not imply that agriculture was necessarily a backward sector of the economy. Throughout the nineteenth century, Bedfordshire was in the van of technical progress in English farming. Woburn had become established as a centre of excellence, and commentators such as Batchelor in 1808 with his "General View" or Evershed writing in a Royal Agricultural Society Prize Essay in 1864 testified to the skill of Bedfordshire farmers.

Indeed, in the Victorian phase of the agricultural revolution, Beds and Herts had taken over much of the lead hitherto associated with East Anglia during the eighteenth century. In this early period much of the progress had been concerned with getting the most out of existing resources by crop rotations, animal breeding and land enclosure. During the nineteenth century a second agricultural revolution was to take place with an emphasis on new inputs such as artificial fertilisers (for example superphosphate), on guano, on pipe-drainage and on new brick-built farmsteads. Rothamstead, over the Herts border, and Woburn became centres of these developments.

An important prerequisite of most forms of farm improvement was land enclosure. In Bedfordshire enclosure took place largely by local act of parliament between about 1750 and 1840. It was believed at one time that the process of enclosure itself destroyed a self sufficient peasantry and brought into being a class of landless labourers. This theory is not widely held today and in Bedfordshire the majority of those who worked on the land were already wage-dependent labourers who might have been affected by enclosure but who had no opportunity to influence the course of events.

Parish enclosure of the commons removed a valuable resource from those labourers who happened to possess common rights or who had managed to obtain *de facto* use of them to gain access to grazing or firewood. In some villages the number of small farmers went dramatically down in the decade after enclosure but there is insufficient evidence to warrant the assumption that such people inevitably became labourers themselves. Possessed as they had been of small but real resources they are more likely to have swelled the ranks of the class of petty entrepreneurs, cottage proprietors and shopkeepers who possessed a status between the farmer and the labourer in the village community.

Once a village was enclosed, however, most landlords preferred to let their estates in substantial units to tenants who possessed working capital. This tendency by itself would tend to make it difficult for anyone in the labouring class who wished to break into farming. To that extent the gaps in the social hierarchy were both widened and made more difficult to cross.

The abject condition of the employed farm worker needs some explanation, considering that there were times when agriculture was prosperous and that the farm worker possessed skills that were essential to a farming economy. The farm workers remained illpaid and they stayed at the bottom of the social hierarchy not because their skills were insufficient but because their skills were too widely diffused. Even the very skilled farm worker was not to be compared with an urban industrial worker who had served an apprenticeship and possibly had a union behind him to exploit some bargaining power. Farm workers were too numerous – at least in the earlier years – and were trapped in a village with little alternative but to face an employment oligopoly of farmers who had no intention of breaking a tradition of low pay. Furthermore, farm work was highly seasonal, particularly in an arable district, and, although this meant that the superior workman could on occasion earn more by organising a temporary or informal gang system, it also meant that there were long periods when employment was slack.

To better himself a skilled farm worker could only move off the land into the towns where he could earn higher wages doing less skilled work as a labourer or a van man. Outside the market garden district he had little prospect of setting up for himself on a farm and, in a county with little industry, other forms of local employment were minimal. Wages on the land varied from time to time but one can distinguish three periods – one from early in the century to the reform of the poor law in 1834 when wages were closely linked with poor law relief, secondly a period of improvement in the period of 'high farming', and thirdly a period of stagnation and decline following the agricultural depression which began in the 1870's.

In the first period – the 'Speenhamland' era – farm workers' wages in Bedfordshire as in many other southern counties were inextricably involved with the system of parish poor relief. This seems to have started as an expedient adopted first in Berkshire but spreading over much of the rural south to enable farm workers and their families to survive the price inflation of the French wars. Thanks to widespread distress after Waterloo, local wage subsidies continued after the wars were over and a high proportion of the rural wage earners were technically paupers deriving part of their income from parish funds.

The actual administration varied considerably between parishes. According to a select committee of the Lords in 1824, nearly all Bedfordshire districts admitted to paying allowances in aid of wages. Some parishes, like Ampthill, had an elaborate system of parish doles, while others, like Wilden, operated a system of 'labour rate' by which farmers could choose between employing labour or paying a rate. The roundsman system by which underemployed labourers went round the parish in search of work while their wages were made up by the parish overseer, was in use in some areas. This had been officially discouraged by order of the magistrates in 1819 as inefficient and wasteful but still seems to have survived until 1834.

The whole system of parish poor relief came under severe criticism from the currently fashionable utilitarian school of economists and when a wave of rioting spread through rural England in 1830, the government set up a Royal

Commission to examine the whole question of the Poor Laws.

The Royal Commission into the Poor Laws investigated conditions in a series of parishes selected from those counties which happened to come first alphabetically on a list of English counties. This included Bedfordshire and data from Bedfordshire parishes was included in the final report.

The Report condemned the old poor law and action was taken at once to reform the whole poor law system. Under the new Act discretion was taken from the individual parishes which were henceforward grouped into Poor Law Unions which had the duty of maintaining Union workhouses within which all aid to the indigent would henceforward be administered, as far as that was possible. Outdoor relief in the form of cash handouts was from now on to be very strictly controlled and confined to aged sick. There was to be no more subsidising of wages nor provision of parish employment in hard times.

In Bedfordshire, as elsewhere, there was some resistance to the new Act culminating in a riot at Ampthill in May 1835. It is possible to show however that special circumstances applied there. It is undeniable that the new poor law divided opinion in Bedfordshire as elsewhere — it was welcomed by the property-owning classes as it promised to reduce the burden of poor rates, but it was viewed with apprehension by the wage earners. Rioting broke out in Ampthill partly because the district had never entirely settled down after the Flitwick riots of the Swing year 1830, but in addition Ampthill had possessed a very well administered system of parish doles before 1834, while the villages around had been noted for corruption and chaos.

Whatever the immediate causes of the riots, the incident put Bedfordshire under the limelight again and when another royal commission was appointed to investigate the working of the new act, both figures of the establishment and members of the radical opposition collected evidence from Bedfordshire villages.

In the course of the investigation men like Daniel Adey, an assistant Poor Law Commissioner, and Thomas Overman, an overseer, gave evidence to the effect that the new poor law was working and was not only much more economical but that the poor were at least no worse off than before, while witnesses like James Turner and Mark Crabtree, who had come from the rising anti-poor-law movement in the north, asserted that Bedfordshire labourers were now in a state of desperation, and gave extensive evidence from the village of Westoning to support their contention.

Farm workers were now entirely dependent on wages for their income with little or no outdoor relief to fall back upon. Much of the standard of living debate therefore turned upon the amount of employment available. Without parish relief there was a considerable moral obligation on the part of the more prosperous employers to provide winter work if at all possible on such projects as land drainage and improvement. It is therefore more to the point to examine the amount spent overall on labour by typical farming employers, rather than the actual wage scale in use when labourers were fully employed.

Wages did in fact marginally improve in the fifties and sixties as agriculture became more prosperous with increasing urban demand for food, but wages on the land never competed effectively with urban wages nor even with other forms of employment becoming available in country districts. During the period of high farming in the mid-century decades, farm labourers were leaving the land, some to go to the towns, others to seek employment in the police, on the railways and in the building and brickmaking trades.

In Bedfordshire, only the widespread practice of domestic industry – lace making in the north of the county and straw plait in the south – enabled families to survive economically by providing employment for women and children.

Realising that a persistent flight from the land would leave farming bereft of labour, employers and landowners cast around for some incentive for members of the labouring classes to stay in the rural community. They were unwilling to raise wages except by a very small amount, but hoped to provide some kind of alternative by fringe benefits such as the provision of village education, building better cottages (sometimes let at uneconomic rents) and by the provision of allotments.

At the end of the sixties it became evident that these expedients were not enough and, when farm workers' trade unions were organised in other parts of the country, there was immediate interest in Bedfordshire. As a result, wages were forced up to a nineteenth-century peak in the early seventies, but shortly afterwards an economic recession began to hit agriculture as cheap American grain and Australian and New Zealand meat started to enter the country. Farming as a whole then went into a deep recession from which it had not recovered by the end of the century. Unable to protect its members against this new threat, the union collapsed in the county, wages went into decline, and the flight from the land became a flood.

To make matters worse, the standby of domestic industry was also under pressure for similar reasons. Cheap Chinese and Japanese plait began to be imported in larger quantities from about 1870 and, while this seems to have benefited the Luton hat-making industry, it undermined the prosperity of the female village plaiters; the lace makers could not complete with machine-made lace. One of the more beneficial aspects of this development was that at least some of the pressure was now removed from labourers to set their children to work just at the time when it became compulsory to provide village schools under the 1870 Education Act.

The growing disparity between urban and rural wages in the mid century decades was reflected in the population statistics of Bedfordshire communities. While the county as a whole increased in population in every decade in the century, much of this increase was to be found in the disproportionate growth of Bedford and Luton and to a lesser extent the smaller market towns. Even before 1851 some village communities had gone into decline. In the intercensal decades 1861 – 71 and 1871 – 81 about half the village parishes of Bedfordshire went into population decline with a tendency for the more remote and the smaller communities to be worse affected.

The poor law itself imposed some distortions on the growth of communities. After 1834, the administration of relief under the poor law was carried out by a new local government unit the 'poor law union' of parishes. Individual parishes were however still assessed for their poor rates according to the 'burden' of paupers who claimed settlement within them even if this relief was only available in the form of residence in a union workhouse.

There was, therefore, an incentive on the part of landowners to minimise the liability of a parish to pay poor rates by carefully restricting residence within the parish to those who could be assured of employment. This was done most effectively in those parishes where either one landowner controlled the parish or where a few landowners could get together to carry out a policy of exclusion. This created what was known as a 'close' parish – not to be confused with an 'enclosed' parish in the sense of land enclosure. According to Robert Wheale, a poor law inspector, about twenty Bedfordshire parishes could be regarded as 'close' parishes, although oddly enough he excludes both the Russells' Woburn and the Whitbreads' Southill.

Two different sorts of community began to emerge. In the close parishes where residence was something of a privilege, the villagers might benefit from the landowner's benevolence in the form of better cottages, possibly a school and possibly access to allotments, but at the price of tight social control, absence of variety of employment and many services, and of course extreme deference to the powers that be.

In the other or 'open' parishes a wider distribution of landed property led to the emergence of a class of petty property owners – cottage proprietors, tradesmen and craftsmen. There can be no doubt that the small scale cottage proprietors exploited their position with regard to the pressure on housing caused by farm workers being excluded from the tightly controlled 'close' parishes, and put up inferior houses let at extortionate rents. They relied on labouring families being able to make up their income from strawplait and so be in a position to pay the rent. Open parishes developed into the larger, rougher villages with a more anarchic outlook but with more employment opportunity. Some of these communities – Toddington was an often quoted Bedfordshire example – acquired widespread reputations for rowdyness and anarchy. Most Bedfordshire villages came into an intermediate category of semi-open villages where an accepted upper echelon held most of the power and property with little challenge from below, but a fringe of petty proprietors managed to let in a shifting clientele of itinerants and the socially mobile.

Moving to the open village was often one step towards urbanisation for the farm worker and the move was sometimes continued to the back yards and slums of the country towns, many of which contained a considerable population of farm workers in the nineteenth century.

Access to housing was but one of the ways in which the gentry sought to retain labouring families on the land. Another was the provision of village education. An account of education in the villages of Bedfordshire is to be the subject of a separate volume in the *Bedfordshire Historical Record Society* publications, but it is worth noting that although the initiative usually came from vicars and squires, there is evidence of direct demand for education from the labourers themselves. Secondly, whatever the good intentions of the more generous of the propertied classes, the provision of education often had to take second place to economic pressures on labouring families, who had to sacrifice their children's education to the demands of the straw plait or lace dealer.

A third benefit to the labouring classes was the provision of independent access to cultivatable land of their own. In spite of land enclosure this had never entirely disappeared in this county. Even the applicants for poor relief contained a minority of people who had access to their own land. Allotments were seen as a means of social control in times of unrest. This could cut both ways – at the time of the 1830 riots the larger estates made allotments available to labourers in an attempt to ease local distress, while later during the years of the Farm Labourers' Union in the 1870s one landowner (Smyth of Quickswood) took away allotments of labourers in Sharpenhoe who had joined the trade union. Meanwhile, a leading Bedfordshire land steward, Henry Trethewy, the Cornish-born agent of the de Grey estates at Silsoe, took the lead in advocating allotments for the labourers both as a means of improving working classes diets and as a means conducive to social stability. With the onset of depression in the 1870s the old dream of radical land reform reasserted itself – a splinter of the farm labourers' union revived small holdings in place of wages as an economic aim, and the Rural Labourers' League assisted Bedfordshire villagers to obtain allotments by petition to local authorities in the 1880s and 1890s.

Apart from sporadic outbreaks of unrest, the Bedfordshire farm workers were typical of rural working class in the rest of England in being patient acceptors of their lot. They appeared to be the last major group in nineteenth century society – at least among the adult, male population – to have no collective political ambitions. It was all the more surprising then when farm workers' trade unionism appeared first in Warwickshire and parts of the eastern counties, and then over all the hitherto quiescent rural south and midlands of England in the period between 1872 and 1875.

In fact the suddenness was more apparent than real. Rural protest had never entirely been absent in the county. It is true that the Swing riots of 1830 and the poor law riots of 1835 had been extremely localised in this county, but unrest at the village level had never been entirely absent for long. Men and women were indicted for riot and affray in one village or another on several occasions in the first two decades of the century. It is true there was no repeat of the poor law riots at Ampthill in 1835, but the practice of rick burning and farm sabotage and similar forms of covert violence remained endemic through the thirties and forties.

Although Bedfordshire had been a moderately active Swing county it was virtually non-existent as a Chartist county. There was very little Chartist activity in the Borough of Bedford itself and none in the countryside as far as is known. This is hardly surprising — Chartism did not catch on in rural areas unless there was some special factor involved such as a tradition of dispossessed rotten boroughs or decayed industry — conditions that often went to-gether in parts of East Anglia and the English West Country where Chartism was found in a rural context.

The difficulties of organising an effective trade union among farm workers or for that matter among any kind of rural workers are obvious enough. It is hardly surprising that the first effective trade unions in Britain represented the urban skilled worker in the 1850s. The farm workers, including those in Bedfordshire, were, however, prompt to organise themselves in the course of the second wave of British trade union activity — the so-called 'new unionism' of the 1870s when trade unionism spread to the unskilled, to the women and the white collar workers from its base in the urban proletariat.

Once they became organised the farm workers had some natural advantage. They had large numbers, close knit communities and a certain amount of public sympathy. They even had some natural leaders drawn mainly from nonconformist lay preachers, although in Bedfordshire two of their most effective allies were middle class Anglicans — Henry Taylor a Luton schoolmaster and borough councillor who became their Bedfordshire leader, and H. H. Havergal, the vicar of Cople, who was secretary to his village branch. The often cited disadvantage of being employed in small units was perhaps less marked in the nineteenth century, when farms in Bedfordshire often employed twenty or thirty men — as many as some industrial firms in that era.

Nevertheless it must be admitted that farm workers' trade unions operated in what was a very hostile environment with all the levers of power in the hands of their oppressors. They were lucky to get more than a very guarded sympathy, and that only from exceptional members of the influential classes.

It has been suggested that farm workers' trade unions only flourished where there was a definite set of pre-conditions present in the rural social structure. These were large farms, arable farms and the practice of farm workers living in their own cottages not in farmers' own houses. All three conditions applied to Bedfordshire, and one might add a third, in that it appeared necessary to be in reasonable range of a large borough from which the organisers could operate, in this case Bedford and Luton, although some Bedfordshire parishes were affiliated to a Huntingdonshire district organised from the village of Brampton in that county.

When the National Agricultural Labourers Union (NALU) was organised in 1872 two districts were set up in Bedfordshire. The most successful was the South Beds and Herts District run from Luton which established branches in an area from Ampthill south to St. Albans in Hertfordshire — an area roughly commensurate with the straw plait district. A second area was organised from Bedford itself with branches in the Ouse valley villages. Together with a few parishes along the Hunts border they amount to about two thirds of the county having branches in the period 1872 to 1875.

The extreme north along the Northamptonshire border and the extreme east near Cambridgeshire seem to have had no union activity.

NALU had much immediate support and some degree of practical success. Wages were forced up by a shilling to a nineteenth century peak in 1874. The union promoted migration of labourers, and they organised opposition to unpaid overtime. When the inevitable backlash occurred among the farmers at a meeting in Dunstable, which resolved not to employ union labour, a farmer in Barton-in-the-Clay complained that it was already too late — all the men in his village were already members of the union.

By 1874 the NALU was numerically the largest union in the county and its leader Joseph Arch was assured of mass attendance when he came to speak in the county which he did on 28 March and 10 October 1874 at meetings in Bedford and Eversholt. Although the lock-out of that year spread in some degree to the county, there was not the dramatic confrontation that there was in East Anglia. Nevertheless the union went into steep decline as it did elsewhere in England and had vanished by the end of the decade.

The reasons were various. In the summer of 1875 the NALU split after a conference in Birmingham. Matthew Vincent, editor of the *Labourers Union Chronicle*, the successful and well-produced union weekly paper, broke away to organise a splinter union, the National Farm Workers Union, with its main object the achievement of land reform and small holdings. The Bedfordshire branches withheld their subscriptions from both factions for a short time but then seem to have rallied to the original organisation of NALU. Nevertheless the damage seems to have been done. Charges of peculation were widely believed, economic recession on the land had made farmers even more reluctant to maintain the modest gains that the labourers had made in wages, and indeed neither the wage policy of NALU nor the land reform objectives of

the NFWU remained credible. As the recession began to bite the more ener-
getic and mobile of the farm workers left the land in ever increasing numbers.
The brief success of NALU had merely served to enable labourers to win
some of the benefits of what was to be the last era of prosperity for English
agriculture for many years to come. In the last years of the century only one
area of the county was to remain prosperous — the market gardening region
of the Ivel Valley where wages were relatively high, but as a result of special
skills and intensive agriculture, and owing little to collective bargaining, and
where the union had never been strong. The brief success of the union did
have one result — it sowed the seed of political aspiration which was to bear a
harvest with the labourers' vote in 1884.

NIGEL AGAR
March 1981

1. GENERAL VIEWS

Three general views of the life of the farm worker in nineteenth century Bed-
fordshire provide a background for the other sections.
    The first is taken from the account, published in 1808, of the county's
agriculture written by Thomas Batchelor, the Lidlington farmer and author. It
is one of a series edited by Arthur Young, then secretary of the Board of
Agriculture.

Batchelor 1808
Chapter XIV. Rural Economy: Labour, Servants, etc.
The greatest part of the business of husbandry is performed by day-labourers
in every part of the county. It is common, however, on most farms of considerable size, to retain annual servants in the capacity of horse-keeper, cowman, shepherd, and kitchen-maid, though the great advance in the price of
provisions has apparently contributed to diminish the number of domestic
servants of every description.
    It seems generally agreed, that the horse-keeper ought to attend his horses
at four o'clock in the morning, to allow them a sufficient time to feed, and
get them properly geared for their work before he takes his breakfast. The
team is taken to work as soon as it is light in the winter; at six-o'clock, or the
time when the day-labourers come, in the spring; and about five, or as soon as
convenient, in harvest. About ten o'clock, an interval of a quarter of an hour,
or more, is allowed for the servants to feed. This is called *beaver time;* but
when the business of ploughing is performed by day-labourers, who have no
mess in the house with the servants, they sometimes delay their breakfast till
nine, which generally occupies half an hour.
    It is common to finish ploughing from one to two o'clock. The horse-
keeper attends his horses in the afternoons, and frequently does not entirely
leave them for the night till eight o'clock.
    I find the prices stated under the names of horse-keeper, head ploughman,
second ploughman, &c. from ten to seven guineas per annum, and it is presumed an able man would for the former price undertake the management of
six horses, and with the assistance of a boy, two or three more; but there is
great variety in this species of management.
    The business of cow-man is, with the exception of dairy farms, generally
allotted to a day-labourer, who must of course finish the milking in proper
time to attend the teams, or other business of the farm.

A shepherd, where the flock is large and valuable, seldom attends to any other business. Mr. Bennet, of Tempsford, who has a flock of five or six hundred of New Leicesters, gives as much as fifteen guineas per annum. I have reason to believe this is not the highest price that is given in the county, though there are many more at twelve, and even as low as five guineas.

The wages of a common servant-maid of *all work*, varies from four to seven guineas, according to the quantity of labour, &c. About five guineas seems the most usual price, though it may be rather below the average of the straw-plait districts in the south-east of the county. Where the farms are large, the business of the dairy becomes more troublesome to the mistress, and as the calls of necessity are less distinctly heard, a more expensive class of servants makes its appearance, under the names of laundry-maid, dairy-maid, &c. whose wages rise as high as nine or ten guineas per annum.

In some places a wheat-barn tasker is hired by the year, who agrees to thrash one load of wheat *per diem*, with an allowance for extra work; but the late unfavourable seasons have contributed to diminish their number, from the great hazard attending any bargain of that kind. Boys of various ages are hired at from two or four or five guineas per annum; and the general time of service commences, or at least concludes, with Old Michaelmas-day, in all cases.

It is common for the servants to dine at the same table as their master, wherever the farms are not very large: some little distinction is made occasionally; but the servants seldom look forward with eager expectation to the pleasures of a separate table.

The breakfast and supper of men-servants consists in general of a *mess* of milk. In addition to this, bread and cheese, and sometimes meat is allowed.

In respect to female servants, tea in the morning and afternoon, is of late years, become nearly a general practice; and the custom of employing them in milking the cows, is fallen into general disuse.

Day-labourers are expected to work as long as the light is sufficient, in the winter; and from six o'clock in the morning till six at night, in summer. Of this nearly an hour and a half are consumed in meals.

The weekly pay of labourers varies from eight to nine shillings, in the west and northern parts of the county. In the south and eastern district, the wages are in general rather higher; as from nine to ten shillings in the greatest part of the district included between Eaton-Socon, Dunstable, and Luton.

There seems no precise distinction between the pay of winter and summer. Small beer is generally allowed; but customs differ with respect to giving the labourer in addition to his pay a *mess*, that is, a common dishful of milk, *crumbed* with bread, or boiled milk only. In these cases, the former is valued at 2d and the latter at 0½d per day.

With respect to the hay-harvest, customs are very various. Sometimes a distinct set of mowers and haymakers are employed. The former is about 2s 4d per acre, with a quart of ale: the latter from 9s to 12s per week, who generally leave work at six in the evening, unless when carrying the hay, in which case they are generally allowed some ale, or perhaps a supper, when they have finished. There are others who hire their men for a month, allowing them food and three half-pint *horns* of ale, perhaps twice a day; and in this case the hours of labour are usually from five in the morning to seven at night, and their weekly pay is eight shillings.

The labourers which are necessary for the business of harvest, are generally hired by the farmers who employ them, previously to Holy-Thursday, in the towns near Ampthill, as the market held on that day is much resorted to, by such as have not provided situations, or harvest-servants. In other parts of the county, certain markets, and fairs, which happen nearer the time of harvest, are attended for the same purpose, and one shilling, or sometimes a dinner, or supper, is given by way of earnest, or to bind the bargain.

The hours of labour extend in harvest, from sunrise to sunset, or when carrying the corn, as long as the day-light permits.

In the vicinity of Ampthill and Woburn, two guineas and 1s earnest, is generally given for a month in harvest, and wood-carting is probably worth 10s more on the average.

In the eastern, and some other parts of the county, larger prices are often given, but these are frequently to men who come from distant parts, and consequently cause no expense by wood-carting, &c. At Bromham the harvest month is stated at £2 7s with wood-carriage; at Souldrop 50s ditto; at Eaton Socon £3 to £3 3s; at Luton 50s; at Sundon 52s 6d; at Stotfold 49s and two loads haulm straw to burn; at Biggleswade 50s to 63s with a little haulm.

A pair of coarse gloves is generally given to the men, which they wear when binding the wheat into sheaves; and on the whole, the average expense of the first month in harvest may be stated at 48s or 2s per day, exclusive of food, liquor, and wood-carting or other equivalents.

The mode of living, or the kind of food provided for the men, varies considerably in different places.

With some it is customary to give seed-cakes and ale for breakfast, as well as at wheat harvest-home, &c.; but in general, meat is allowed three times a day, which consists of pork, bacon, &c. with from one-fourth to one-third of butchers' meat, and in general plum-puddings; and three meals on each of the four Sundays in the month. It is customary to allow three pints and a half of ale per day, viz. in the morning, at eleven o'clock, and at four in the afternoon; but in some places, the allowance of ale extends to four or five pints, and one pint per man on a Sunday. The evening of the harvest-home is, as is usual in most places, a scene of festivity, when the harvest men, their wives, and children, and other helpers and neighbours, compose a numerous and expensive assemblage. When the month is finished, the plum-pudding disappears, and daily pay is reduced about Lidlington, &c. to 1s but remains in some places as high as 15d and even 18d with food and beer as before.

In the eastern part of the county many instances are met with, where the harvest-men are hired from *first to last*, as it is termed. It is similar to other kinds of piece-work; the men may be expected to exert themselves to the utmost in their power, but the work may be expected to be less carefully performed, the corn may not be ripe, or sufficiently dry, to carry when it is most convenient, and if wet weather ensues, the master has to chuse whichever he may deem the least of two evils, viz. either to feed a number of men who will do no work out of the field, or to pay and discharge them, and hire others to finish the harvest.

This practice, however, seems much on the decline, in the district where it has been fashionable, and another practice occasionally makes its appearance, which consists in allowing the harvest-men a kind of board-wages, amounting to £5 5s for the month, with small beer, and three pints of ale per diem, and perhaps a harvest-home supper, and wood-carting. I conceive that this practice has a tendency to dissolve the bond of union which ought at that time to subsist between a farmer and his labourers: their mode of living, as well as every other attendant circumstance, tends to repress their spirit and activity. The origin of this practice, may be often traced to certain domestic declamations on the trouble and expense of cookery, &c. an argument which it is obvious, will not be attended to, except on very large farms; and it may be safely inferred, will never make a figure among the advantages attendant on such occupations.

Family circumstances furnish the means of tracing the price of labour as far back as the year 1741; at which time, day-labourers received 8d per day from one month after Michaelmas to Lady-day, which is twenty-one weeks, and 1s per day through the rest of the year, with the addition of their food in the time of harvest. The year's earnings were of course £13 10s in money, with the addition of a meal perhaps once a week, and a mess of milk with bread every morning, and about five weeks' food in harvest.

Soon after this period, an alteration took place with several farmers in Lidlington, and 9d per day was the regular wages, exclusive of hay-time and harvest. About 1751, the pay in hay-time appears to have been 8s per week, with little ale, or food; and the harvest month 31s with food and some ale. The modern prices have been before-mentioned.

From 'General View of the Agriculture of the County of Bedford' by Thomas Batchelor, London, 1808.

The second view is taken from the report of a Royal Commission into the Employment of Women, Young Persons and Children in Agriculture for which evidence was collected in 1867 by George Culley. Like most of the investigators for this Commission, he interpreted his frame of reference very widely in terms of education, housing and domestic industry during the period of mid-century prosperity.

Culley 1867

...

10. The cost of labour paid in wages, according to the evidence given to me, varies with and is generally about equal to the rent, being highest where crops of all kinds can be best grown, and lowest where a bare fallow is considered the best preparation for a good crop of wheat. The lowest payment per acre for labour, as stated to me, was 24s, and the highest 38s, the latter figure being much higher than in the case of farms most closely resembling it in the north of England, but lower than in several cases of which I received evidence in Bucks.

I do not think that the farmers in Bedfordshire, who are an industrious and intelligent class, can afford to add much to the cost of cultivation as far as payment in wages is concerned. On an average, as will be seen from the evidence, where farms consist, as they generally do in Bedfordshire, of three-fourths arable land there would be required for the cultivation of a farm of 400 acres of such land capable of growing all kinds of crops a staff of 14 men and eight lads, and the cost in wages would be nearly as follows:—

	£	s	d
3 men at £37 14s each	113	2	0
11 men at £35 2s each	386	2	0
8 lads, averaging £13 each	104	0	0
Total cost in wages of regular staff	603	4	0

As nearly as may be 30s 2d per acre. Compare this cost of labour with that on a farm of the same size and nature and under the same course of husbandry in North Northumberland, and let us see how the different systems affect the labourers, farmers, and landowners.

The corresponding wage account on such a farm in Glendale would be —

	£	s	d
8 men at £38 12s each	308	16	0
8 women at £14 each	112	0	0
3 lads at £13 each	39	0	0
Total cost in wages of regular staff	459	16	0

As near as may be 23s per acre.

Some part of this reduced cost may be due to management, some part is due to the employment of a class of women almost equal to the ordinary run of Bedfordshire male labourers, and the remainder, which is no very small part, is due to the fact that the northern hind at a slightly higher wage is a much cheaper article.

11. The difference of the result of these systems to the labourers is, that whereas in one case the tolerably certain income arising from employment in agriculture amounts to £603 4s to be divided amongst 14 families, giving about £43 1s 9d to each, in the other it amounts to £483 16s (adding £24 as the annual value of eight cottages), to be divided amongst eight families, giving £60 9s 6d to each, the difference of upwards of £17 having to be made up to the southern family by the far less certain earnings of one grown up daughter in lace making or straw plaiting and the chance of having children employed younger in farm labour than would be the case in the North; if "plait was good" the Bedfordshire girl of 18 would probably make the £17, but how much of it would go to the family purse? and, unhappily, plait is not always good. . .

In Bedfordshire female farm labour had largely died out due to the alternative female employment provided by lace making in the north of the county and straw plait in the south.

12. It is not, however, the custom to employ women in farm labour in Bedfordshire. In the north of the county the females of the labouring class are engaged in lace making, and in the south and more populous part of the county in plaiting straw; straw plait, especially when the trade is good finding employment also for a good many boys and men. When plait is "good" straw plaiters, both male and female, are able, so I was constantly informed, to earn higher wages than persons of the same sex employed in agriculture, but during the time I was in the county plait was very "bad", and many families were in consequence in great distress. I shall never forget the scene I witnessed when accompanying the relieving officer on one of his usual weekly visits to Toddington (a large "open" village in the plait district, to which I shall refer afterwards), where, according to evidence which cannot be gainsayed, a large portion of the male population of so-called workmen expect the female plaiters to maintain them throughout a great portion of the year. At the time of my visit one-third of the entire population of the parish were receiving relief, and it seemed altogether to puzzle the relieving officer to account for the manner in which one half of the remainder lived.

Farm workers were hired on a weekly basis.

13. The hiring throughout the county is a weekly hiring, the weekly wage (exclusive of additional payments for piece or extra work and allowances, such as

beer) varying from 11s to 14s per week, 11s being the lowest weekly wage for a regular able-bodied farm labourer, and 14s the highest, where the labourer's duty involves Sunday attendance. In Bedford Union the weekly wage for an ordinary labourer is 12s; in Woburn Union, and in the plait district generally, the weekly wage is 11s. It will be my business afterwards to endeavour to show how far this nominal wage is increased by piece work, extra wages in hay time and harvest, and other allowances, when referring to the evidence on the earnings of labourers and their families.

Housing. Most labourers live in the cottages in the villages rather than on or near to the farms.
14. The labourers' cottages, except in a few cases where blocks of two, three, or four cottages have been built attached to the steadings on larger farms (a custom which is, however, extending), stand in villages pretty thickly scattered over the county, and in few instances have the labourers to go far to their work.

Gang work was rare except in the market gardening districts around Sandy and Biggleswade.
. . .
26. It will be seen from the evidence that employment in private gangs exists only to a very limited extent in either Bedfordshire or Bucks, and is usually confined to the employment of from 10 to 20 boys between 8 and 13 years of age under a steady labourer or foreman; in only one instance was a return made to me of such a gang where both girls and boys are employed, and in that case it consisted of five boys and five girls, all under 13 years of age, occasionally employed in twitching, weeding, &c. (See evidence of Mr. T. T. Hine, of Knotting, in Summary of Circular Questions.)

In only one case is a gang such as I have described employed throughout the whole year, viz., the Woburn Park gang, consisting of 16 boys between 10 and 13 years of age employed under a skilled workman in such light work as is suited to their age; their hours of labour are 11 hours in summer and nine hours in winter, including 1½ hours for meals, and there is a rule that every boy must be able to read and write before entering the gang. (See Mr. Stephenson's evidence in Summary of Circular Questions.)

I had several opportunities of seeing these boys during my stay at Woburn, and I think that if children are to be continuously employed in farm labour between 10 and 13 years of age they could not be employed in a manner better calculated to make them efficient labourers without overtaxing their strength than that in which the boys composing the Woburn gang are employed. The Melchbourne Park gang consists of 10 boys between 8 and 10 years of age employed in light work during spring, summer, and autumn. The Aston Clinton gang is composed of 15 boys whose average age is 10½, and of these the Rev. C. W. W. Eyton says, "there is nothing injurious to the health of these boys arising from the nature of their employment, nor are they ill treated in any way."

The same remark would, I think, apply to all the boy gangs in these two counties, and, putting aside the educational part of the subject, it appears to me that children are better employed in such gangs or parties than when mixed up with adult labourers or draggling after their parents in piece work.

27. There is one return under the head of employment in private gangs which, though referring to what is not strictly employment in agriculture, should, I think, be noticed here; it is a return of women and children employed for from eight to 12 weeks during each year in peeling onions for the market gardeners in the neighbourhood of Biggleswade; it will be seen from the evidence that 339 females are so employed in the parish of Sandy, of these 93 are married women, 108 young women and girls over 13 years of age, and 138 girls under 13 years of age; in the return from Sandy no mention is made of boys so employed, but from the Beds general evidence, 47 (d,e,f, g,h) it appears that boys up to 12 years of age assist their mothers in onion peeling; the work is done in sheds on the gardens under a foreman whose business is to measure the onions, peeling being done by the piece. Women working from 7 a.m. till 6 p.m., with an hour's rest, can earn from 1s to 1s 6d per day, and children of 12 about 6d. per day. I heard of no complaint concerning this mode of employment except that it prevented the mothers from attending properly to their household duties, and helped to make the children's attendance at school very irregular after 7 years of age.

CHILD LABOUR AND EDUCATION Small boys up to 10 – 13 years of age were however of importance in more normal arable farming by their work as ploughboys. As ploughing went on throughout most of the year this made it difficult to introduce compulsory education even in the off season without disrupting agricultural work.
...

30. The services of the ploughboy being required throughout the whole year, becomes the chief difficulty as far as these counties are concerned, of applying to boys employed in farm labour regulations for school attendance somewhat similar to those under the Printworks Act. It may be that as economy in the management of horses becomes better understood the system of "driving" teams will disappear and the driver be set free to attend school during the winter months, as nearly all other boys under 13 years employed in farm labour could do; at present, however, on most of the arable farms in both counties the ploughboy is expected to crack his whip in November and December as frequently as in March or April, and the only way of catching him would be to insist upon his stopping work when the horses do, at 2 p.m. so as to give him time to rest and prepare himself for an evening school.

31. The usual hours of work for boys employed in farm labour, except in some parts of Bucks, where they are employed with and have the same hours as women, are the same as for men, in Bedfordshire from 6 a.m. to 6 p.m. in summer, and from light to dark in winter with one and a half or two hours allowed for meals; in Bucks from 6 a.m. to 5 p.m., with one and a half hours allowed for meals, except in the north-east of the county where the hours of labour are the same as in Bedfordshire.

By this date many farm children were attending local elementary schools voluntarily.

. . .

35. The tables of school returns will sufficiently illustrate the answers given to circular question iv. 43, which asks for a return of the approximate number of children of the agricultural labouring class in attendance at elementary schools. In some cases the returns given include all the children in attendance at the school for which the return is made. In most it is confined to the children of the class intended, and in one instance (Woburn) it is confined to the children of agricultural labourers; as a whole, however, the returns may be fairly taken to represent the school attendance of the agricultural labouring class, being most accurate in the case of rural parishes where the population consists almost exclusively of that class.

36. Table A, Beds summary, contains returns from all the elementary schools in Woburn Union, and the account amounts to this, that in a union containing 29,603 acres, and, according to the census of 1861, 11,682 inhabitants, most of whom belong to the class in question, there are in average attendance at elementary schools —

In summer .399 boys under 10 years of age.
74 boys between 10 and 13.
289 girls under 10 years of age.
77 girls between 10 and 13.

Total number of children under 13 in
average attendance 839
Total number of such children on the
registers of schools 1,100

Supposing that 80 per cent. of the population belong to the class (labouring class) for which the returns are made, it would appear that there is one child under 13 years of age on the register of some elementary school for every 8½ persons, and one in average attendance for every 11 persons nearly. Of the children under 10 years of age there are about 25 per cent. more boys than girls in average attendance, whereas of the children between 10 and 13 there are 4 per cent. fewer boys than girls. It will be remembered that these figures related to a union where straw plait or lace making, but chiefly straw plait, are the only occupations of females of the labouring class.

37. Taking the returns from seven parishes in Ampthill Union, four parishes in Biggleswade Union, and one parish in Luton Union (see Beds summary of school returns C, D, E, excluding Biggleswade, there being no return from the large boys' British School there), in all of which parishes, except Cranfield, straw plait is the usual occupation of females. We have again (allowing the same proportion of inhabitants not to belong to the class for which the returns are made), one child under 13 in average attendance at school for every 11 persons. Here, however, the boys under 10 years are only 12 per cent; in excess of the girls under 10, and the boys between 10 and 13 exceed the girls by about 20 per cent., (the attendance of girls between 10 and 13 being very small in the parish of Sandy, where there is the attraction of onion peeling as well as straw plaiting.)

Evening School had begun to make an impact
. . .

46. Eight of the 16 parishes in Woburn Union have evening schools, with a total average attendance of 165 scholars, from a population of 11,682, or about 1 in 54 of the labouring population, the number on the register of such schools is about 1 in 45 of the labouring population, making the same deduction from the whole population as I did in the case of day schools. Out of 50 parishes in the county of Bedford, for which returns were made, having an aggregate population of 44,378, 29 have evening schools, with a total average attendance of 546 scholars, and 952 names on the register, giving an average attendance for the labour class (supposing that all these scholars belong to that class) of rather more than 1 in 65 persons, and of names on the register of schools, of about 1 in 37 persons.

Not surprisingly in view of the dependence of market gardening on child labour it was the P.L.U. of Biggleswade that opposed any legislative interference in child labour.
. . .

51. In Bedfordshire . . . the Bedford, Ampthill, and Luton Boards decided in favour of such legislative interference; the Woburn Board, while deprecating any compulsory scheme of education, expressed an opinion that no boy should be employed in farm labour under 10 years of age; the Biggleswade Board objected altogether to legislative interference. . . .

HOUSING In the 1860s landlords had come to realise that higher wages in the towns would draw labourers away from the land unless something was done to balance the disadvantages of low rural wages by improving the quality of rural houses. Some parishes had stood to gain – others had lagged behind. Generally speaking the villages with a resident agricultural landowner were better provided for than those without.

. . .

73. Of the villages which I visited in Bedfordshire those in which the cottages are best and the poor most cared for are Husborne Crawley, Tingrith, Biddenham, Cardington, Cople, Melchbourne, Oakley, Turvey, Silsoe, and Southill; in Bucks they are Aston Clinton, Halton, Chilton, Botolph and Middle Claydon, Shalstone, Great Brickhill, and Chenies, all of them villages in which the cottages belong to the landowners, and all of them, except three, lying, as it were at the door of the owner.

74. Of the villages which I visited in Bedfordshire I saw the worst specimens of cottages in Salford, Sheeplane (Potsgrove), Tilsworth, Toddington, Sharnbrook, Swineshead, Thurleigh, and Biggleswade; in Bucks, in Cublington, Oving, Ickford, Long Crendon, Oakley, Shabbington, Stewkley, Winslow, Maids Moreton, Ivinghoe, Great Missenden, Burnham, and Hitcham. There are cottages in these 21 villages, in some of them many, quite unfit for human beings to live in; in five of them, viz., Salford (where the cottages belong to All Souls College, Oxford), Tilsworth, Sharnbrook, Swineshead, and Maids Moreton, as bad specimens as any to be found belong to the landowners; in five of them most of the bad cottages are built on the waste; and in the remaining 11 they belong to small freeholders and speculators. . . .

The different housing policies of various Bedfordshire landowners was described.

. . .

77. On the Duke of Bedford's estate the occupants of the cottages I am now speaking of hold direct from the landowner, who gives a power of nomination to the farmer. On Lady Cowper's and Sir Harry Verney's estates these cottages are let with the farms, the farmer having entire control over them and their occupants. Mr. Trethewy, agent to Lady Cowper, in speaking to me of this arrangement, said that he considers this supply of cottages necessary as a substitute for the old plan of having a certain number of single men living in the farmer's house; that the horsekeeper, cowkeeper and shepherd on a farm are or ought to be in the same position as a groom or domestic servant; and that he has never known any evil result to the labourer from his being brought more under control of the farmer. . . .

ALLOTMENTS Apart from housing, allotments were considered as a means of providing the low paid farm worker with a fringe benefit. In this Bedfordshire had given a national lead.

. . .

80. In obedience to your instructions, I obtained as much evidence as I could on the subject of allotments and their value to the labourer. Examples of the

systems adopted on the Duke of Bedford's, Lady Cowper's, Lord St. John's, Lord Dynevor's and Mr. Whitbread's estates, are given in Beds evidence, Nos. 88 to 92; and on Mr. Henley's and the Dorton estates in Bucks, evidence 128 and 129; in Beds evidence, No. 89, will be found extracts from a very able paper on this subject, read by Mr. Trethewy, agent to Lady Cowper, at a meeting of the Central Farmers Club, in which the advantages of an allotment of a moderate size to a farm labourer are very clearly stated; what this moderate size should be is still a moot point; on the Duke of Bedford's estates, in these two counties, nearly 1,400 allotments of about 20 poles each, are provided at rents varying from 2d to 4d per pole, 20 poles being considered sufficient for the spade husbandry of a farm labourer in his leisure hours. On Lady Cowper's, Lord St. John's, Lord Dynevor's, and Mr. Whitbread's estates, the common allowance is 40 poles, and as in all these cases, the sole object in granting the allotment is to confer a benefit on the labourer, it would appear that the experience of the owners of these estate where the allotment system has been long established (since 1829) is that an allotment, to be of real benefit to the ordinary farm labourer, should not exceed 40 poles, and it is a question whether even that is not too much; I had the pleasure of hearing this question discussed by Messrs. Trethewy and Bennett, who have under their care the largest systems of allotments in these counties, and accepting the position that the allotment is intended to take the place of a garden, and is injurious to the farm labourer in regular employment as soon as it induces him to neglect his legitimate work, or to grow crops which can be produced by the farmer at a much cheaper rate, I am inclined to think that the best quantity to allow, if the quantity must be invariable, lies nearer 20 than 40 poles, that 20 poles is a perfectly safe allowance to make is I think shown by the fact, that many farmers themselves allow that quantity to their labourers in cases where there is no such provision by the landowner; that the poor themselves fully appreciate the advantage of having a "bit of land", is too well known to require any reference to evidence on the subject, the desire is so great that landowners and their agents have taken advantage of it to overcome the lawless habits of the inhabitants of such villages as are found in the west of Buckinghamshire, by a rule that a conviction before a bench of magistrates carries with it a forfeiture of the allotment. On this subject, Mr. Golding, agent for the Dynevor estate in Bedfordshire, says, "the men would suffer anything rather than forfeit their allotment". The man who showed me the allotments in Oakley and Shabbington parishes summed up his account of them by saying, "You see, Sir, Oakley were a wild blackguard place, and Mr. Henley have done it to cure the place." It is evident that an allotment system, which should be confined to, say, 30 poles in a parish, where the labourer market is only fairly supplied with hands, might be for the sake of "curing the place," considerably extended where there are many more labourers than the cultivation of the land in farms can find work for, but I am afraid that such a cure can only produce temporary relief, and that the disease which sleeps for a time may break out in a form more difficult to grapple with, when the allotment-bred children grow up to think that it is the business of their life to grow wheat crops by spade husbandry, as their fathers did.

81. The actual value of an allotment, such as 20 poles, to a farm labourer does not altogether depend on the money value of the produce, and the labourers themselves find it difficult to estimate the value, taking, however, the money value of the produce of good land, cultivated as an allotment should be, to be 1s 6d per pole, and the rent (including rates and taxes) 6d per pole there would be a payment in return for labour of 1s for every pole he could so cultivate; 6d per pole should secure the best land for spade culti-vation, and 1s 6d would about represent the money value of the produce. If then 20 poles is all that a farm labourer can cultivate by spade husbandry, without interfering with his regular employment, the allotment is worth to him, as an addition to his earnings, 20s a year; if, however, without injuring him as a hired servant he could be entrusted with 30 poles, as I am not pre-pared to deny that he could, the increase to his earnings would rise to 30s a year, and that paying a rent which would be sufficient to induce most land-owners to adopt an allotment system, putting aside all the moral and physical benefits which arise from the possession of a "bit of land" which provides him with a wholesome and educating employment for his leisure hours, keeps him out of the beershop, and opens his eyes to the advantage of keeping in his pocket the shilling which he would have spent there on Saturday night if he had not been too busy on that "bit of land".

82. The tabular statement of the allotment system in Woburn Union (see Beds evidence 87), shows that there are about 800 allotments such as I have described provided for 29,603 acres, or say 27,000 acres of cultivated land, employing about 945 adult labourers, and that there are (even if all the allot-ments were held by men employed on farms, which is not the case) 18 per cent. of the labourers for whom no such provision is made.

Benefit societies existed to provide for a labourer in need.

. . .

84. I would now call your attention to the evidence which I received, acting under your instructions, on the subject of benefit clubs, more especially such as are held at public-houses. It will be seen from Beds evidence, 120, that Mr. Charles Howard, who read an interesting paper upon this subject at the Cen-tral Farmers' Club in November 1867, then estimated the number of public-house benefit clubs in Bedfordshire to be 260, or nearly two to every parish; the number is now no doubt somewhat smaller, as the old public-house club is yearly dying out, and the inclination of young men is to join larger soci-

eties, such as the "Odd Fellows," "Foresters," or local societies, such as the "South Bucks Friendly Society," conducted on a much larger scale and safer basis than the old beerhouse club. The desire to make some provision for sickness and old age is a most laudable, and happily common one, and we cannot wonder that labouring men, finding it necessary to meet at a public-house for the purpose of forming a society, under rules which they thought would insure such a provision, should commit the grave error of combining business of so serious a nature with the pleasure of drinking beer. To the publican such a society was a little fortune, if only he could insure the adoption of such rules as those of the King's Arms, Hockliffe, Friendly Society. And accordingly the publican became the ruling spirit of the club. At first, when all the members were young, the annual Whitsuntide feast was what an old member of the Duncombe Arms Club called an "all joble;" but as time went on the original members became old, young members would not join, preferring to hold their "all joble" together, and the club funds were exhausted at the very time when most of the members were in need of their assistance. I have spoken in the past tense, but the process of exhaustion is going on now, and all the hardships that accompany it. That the public-house club should have its place taken by such societies as the "South Bucks Friendly Society", which I have already quoted, is a step in the right direction, and all praise to the promoters and honorary members. But I hope the day will come when the labouring man will have within his reach the power of investing his savings in such a manner that he will be certain in sickness or old age to reap the benefit of his thrift without the aid of honorary members.

LACE MAKING AND STRAW PLAIT. The importance of domestic industries including lace making and straw plait was considered.

85. A report on the condition of the agricultural labourers and their families in the counties of Bedford and Buckingham would be very incomplete if some account were not given of the manner in which their children are employed in making lace or plaiting straw. Speaking generally, in North Beds and North Bucks all the females are engaged in making lace, in south Beds and the centre of Bucks all the females, and not a few boys and men, are engaged in plaiting straw. In the lace district a farm labourer treats it as a matter of course that his daughters will be sent to a lace school at 4 or 5 years of age, and that from the time of their leaving the school to the time when they leave his house for good, it is his wife's business to see that they stick to their lace pillow, and work at least as many hours as he does himself. Lace making, from the fact that it entails sitting in a stooping position with the hands out in front of the body, and must generally be performed in the cottage room, causes fully as much physical injury to the frame of the worker as straw plaiting, though there are not such loud complaints of its effect on morals. Lace schools, in their arrangements, and the extent to which they injure children

by close confinement in badly ventilated rooms and interfere with their education, so much resemble plait schools that the description of the latter, which will be given presently, may be held to apply equally to them.

The earnings of girls engaged in lace making are very difficult to get at, but according to the evidence of the lace makers themselves and those who know them best, the earnings at the time I was in Bedfordshire, when the trade was very much depressed, as it has been for some time, were about as follows: — Working 11 or 12 hours a day girls of from 10 to 12 years of age could earn about 1s per week, and girls of from 16 years upwards from 2s 6d to 3s per week.

The place of plait and lace 'schools' was more apparent for its contribution to family income rather than to children's education.
86. As farm labourers in the lace district send their daughters to the lace school, so farm labourers in the plait district send their children, both male and female, to plait schools, where for a payment of from 2d to 3d (more commonly 2d) per week, a master or mistress (generally a mistress) teaches them to plait, and sees that they execute the task set them by their parents, the plait so made being the property of the parents, who buy the straw and sell the plait when made.

A return of the number of children attending such schools in the central and south-eastern divisions of Bucks was kindly given to me by the chief constable, from which it appears that there were 1,457 children, of whom 658 were under 8 years of age, in attendance at 102 plait schools in those districts, and there can be no doubt that if the straw plaiting trade had not been in an unusually depressed state at the time the return was made a very much larger number of children, especially of the younger ones, would have been found in attendance. I visited several plait schools about the time this return was being collected, and in three of these where I asked the question the teachers confessed to having from 30 to 40 per cent. more children when "plait was good." From these returns it will be seen that the hours of work most common in schools at the time the returns were made were six or seven hours, which, however, are lengthened to nine or ten when "plait is good", or the extra three or four hours considered necessary to make out a fair day's plaiting are worked out at home. Some of the schools I visited, even with the reduced number of learners, were very close and offensive, and the accounts I received of their state in times when plait "went well" were enough to justify the very strong feeling existing in the plait district that some legislative interference is necessary, if only to protect the children from the physical injury sustained by working in close heated rooms. Warmth appears to be so necessary to insure sufficient suppleness of the fingers, that in cold weather every breath of air is carefully excluded from the little cottage kitchen where 30 or 40 children are packed together as closely as they can sit.

Although there is a general pretence of teaching the children to read, the teachers themselves are often unable to do that which they profess to teach the children to do, and the reading is reduced to the repetition of a few verses of the Bible which they all know by heart. In some plait schools there is not even this pretence, and the result is that a great many children (girls especially) are growing up without any education. . . .

Evidence of George Culley, Royal Commission on the Employment of Children, Young Persons and Women in Agriculture (1867).   *BPP 1867-8 XVIII.*

Finally, a picture of Bedfordshire rural life at the end of the century is provided by William Bear who reported to the Royal Commission on Labour 1893. Between the report of Culley in 1867 and Bear in 1893 had occurred the most severe depression ever to hit British agriculture in modern times. The completion of the American railroads across the prairies and the development of the chilled meat trade from Argentina and Australia had led to British farming having to face international competition on an unprecedented scale. Since 1846 there had been no protection from import duties to shield a farmer from the full effect of overseas competition. Orthodox farming whether arable or pasture had been unable to cope with this double blow. For the labourer, already underpaid by international standards, employment offered even more bleak prospects. The flight from the land became a full scale retreat.

Bear examined conditions in Woburn P.L.U. where the farming was orthodox in nature although perhaps unusually well placed to receive investments from landowners like the Duke of Bedford on a scale which amounted to subsiding farming from the proceeds of urban rents and mining royalties. He went on to look at St. Neots, a P.L.U. shared between Bedfordshire and Huntingdonshire, which included market gardening parishes.

Bear 1893.

. . .

8. **Is the land labour-starved?** In spite of the charge made by a few of the labourers from whom I took evidence, to the effect that the land in the district is "labour-starved," I came to the conclusion, after driving through every parish in the union, that there was not generally much room for this complaint. At a small meeting of labourers which I held in the open air at Toddington, I was assured that a good deal of land was "laying itself down with twitch." In a few places I did see more twitch than there should be in the land, but generally the fields appeared to be kept fairly clean. Indeed, judging from the condition of the crops in the district, which are not nearly equal to those which I have seen in most other parts of the country this year, it ap-

peared to me that there was more reason to suppose that the land was manure-starved than that it was labour-starved, unless it is below average in natural fertility. In bad times farmers have good reason to economise in their expenditure for labour, as there is nothing less remunerative than unnecessary hand work on a farm.

10. **No considerable migration of labourers at particular seasons.** There is no considerable immigration of labourers from other parts of the kingdom at particular seasons. A few Irishmen come at harvest time to Toddington and two or three other parishes, but not so many as came in past times.

11. **Comparative efficiency of labourers.** The general testimony of employers, and other witnesses who may be regarded as more impartial, is to the effect that the labourers are less efficient, as a body, than they were formerly. "All the best of the young men go away, leaving only the old men and inferior young ones". This was the complaint of most of the employers who gave evidence. They also complained that few of the young men who stay on the land take the trouble to learn to thatch, or hedge, or do other work requiring special skill. In some cases, too, it is difficult to obtain a sufficient number of men skilled in the management of live stock.

12. **Migration and its causes.** It will be gathered from the preceding remarks that the migration of farm labourers from the district affects the quality of the labour supply more seriously than it affects the quantity. It is the strong, the intelligent, and the enterprising who fly from their native villages to seek their fortunes in the towns or on railways; and it is the weak, the dull, and the listless who stay. To this general rule there are, of course, exceptions; but in my travels through the district I saw very few capable-looking young men among the agricultural labourers. I made a point of asking nearly every labourer whom I met why the young men migrated, and the reply in every instance was "to earn more money." On being pressed as to other reasons for leaving the rural districts, my witnesses stated that the love of excitement influenced some of the young fellows; but this they evidently regarded as quite a secondary consideration. That they are right I have no doubt, for my experience of many years among farm labourers has led me to the same conclusion. Country life is not dull to those who are brought up to it. On the contrary, it is full of interest. Strange as it may appear to those who have not experienced it, there is an intense delight to the cultivator of luxuriant crops in a garden or allotment, or to the feeder of a prospering pig, in the contemplation of the results of his efforts and in the exhibition thereof to appreciative neighbours. Then, the village gossip, vacuous as it seems to an outsider, is interesting above all other things to the villagers. There is no lack of merriment in the gatherings of men and lads to be found in village streets on summer evenings and on Sunday, or in the meetings of familiar acquaintances in the public-houses, which are all too numerous in the Woburn Union. But

there is one cause of diminished interest in village life to young men which may probably be ranked as next in importance to the desire of earning high wages and rising in the world, when the reasons for this migration are under consideration. This is the migration of the young women, which has greatly increased from the Woburn district, in consequence of the decay of the straw-plaiting and lace-making industries. There is no doubt that the girls who go into service in the towns act as magnets to the lads they leave behind them. One statement made by several witnesses was to the effect that the boys, as the result of their improved education, acquired a contempt for farm work. Probably it is so in many instances, although there is nothing of a degrading character in agricultural labour, and not much that is unpleasant. Many classes of employment in towns are much less agreeable. Indeed, as a rule, the work of mere labourers in towns is far more repellent than anything they are called upon to do regularly in the country. The position of the bricklayer's "slab" or the dock labourer is certainly less dignified than that of the agricultural workman. When the urban immigrants come down to their native village for a holiday, decked out in gorgeous apparel, they excite the envy of their old associates. But the truth of the adage "Fine feathers do not make fine birds," is illustrated by the case of three young men who left farm work in disgust, and came down to their old parish on Sunday, dressed, as the people said, "like gentlemen;" for it turned out that their employment was that of scavengers.

13. **Do the men better themselves by migration?** The question whether the majority of the men who migrate from the rural districts improve their position permanently or not is one which cannot be answered positively. That those who obtain employment as railway porters, getting comparatively high wages and many tips, better themselves there cannot be any doubt, and the same may be said for those who enter into service as gentlemen's grooms, or coachmen, or join the police force. Others, too, obtain good positions, or posts from which they may work up to good positions, in warehouses or shops. Not a few men, however, have returned from towns to the country, because they found themselves worse off after their first shift of quarters than they were before it; and many who are still in the towns freely admit that they would be better off in the rural districts. Men from the Woburn district have admitted that the pound or the guinea a week which they earn as town labourers "does not go as far" as 14s or 15s in the country, for they have to pay 5s or 6s a week for two rooms, and to buy every bit of garden produce which they and their families consume. Bearing in mind also the great temptations of town life, and the numerous wrecks which are produced thereby, as well as the loss of health which many countrymen suffer from being housed in stifling courts or employed in injurious classes of work, the question proposed above cannot with confidence be affirmatively answered.

14. **Usual conditions of engagement.** Farm labourers in the Woburn district are engaged by the week. I did not hear of any instances of monthly or yearly hirings, or of men being lodged and boarded in farmhouses.

15. **Regularity of employment.** Employment on farms in the Woburn district appears to be exceptionally regular. Nearly every farmer whom I visited assured me that he employed as many regular hands in winter as in summer, and that the few extra men who do hoeing, hay-making, or harvesting in the latter season are, as a rule, men who prefer to work irregularly at comparatively high wages instead of regularly at the ordinary rates. They are mostly men of the loafing or poaching class, who go round with the thrashing machines in winter and take piecework in summer. At Toddington some of the men congregated at a street corner complained of lack of employment, not only in winter but in rainy weather at other seasons. The appearance of these men, however, bore out the statement just made. Mr. Matthews, the relieving officer, informed me that men were occasionally out of work at Toddington, but added that it was generally their own fault. Residents in the parish, too, who are not farmers, assured me that no steady and industrious man in it need lack regular employment. Moreover, the Duke of Bedford every winter opens relief works for any men out of work, paying 2s a week less than the current rate of farm wages, so as to afford a living to men who need it, without attracting any from farm work.

16. **Work in wet weather.** Another satisfactory assurance given to me by every employer whom I met was that he found work for his regular men, when working by the day, whatever the character of the weather might be, if they chose to come. When at piece-work the men make what time they please, and they occasionally lose time in rainy weather, which they possibly make good when it is fine. Some employers said they could usually find something for the men to do under cover on a wet day, however unprofitable it might be to themselves. In other cases it probably happens that the offer of work in wet weather is only made under the condition of its being done in the open, which may be almost impossible when rain falls heavily. But when inspecting labour books obligingly shown to me, I did not come across any evidence of loss of time from wet weather among men on the regular staffs of the farms.

17. **Daily hours of work.** The usual hours of work for ordinary labourers are from 6 a.m. till 6 p.m. in summer, and from 7 a.m. till dark in winter, with 1½ hours off for meals. But in Toddington, Harlington, and Holcut the men leave off work in summer at 5.30 p.m. It is not difficult to understand why there should be this difference in the case of Holcut, where there are only three cottages, two of which are occupied by servants of the resident landlord, as the men employed in the parish have to walk a mile and a half or more to and from the farms on which they are employed. In the case of Tod-

dington, too, many of the men have a long way to walk to farms in that or adjoining parishes. As to Harlington, the labour supply there is said to be insufficient, and it is to be presumed, therefore, that some of the men are from a distance. Where there are workmen on a farm who have good reason for expecting to leave off work before the usual time, it not easy to compel others to work till 6 p.m. In summer a rest of half an hour is taken for breakfast, and the only other time to which the labourers are entitled is an hour for dinner. But in several parishes it is complained that they have begun to take an intervening time, varying from ten minutes to half a hour, for lunch. A short pause for refreshment has never been uncommon, and has not been objected to; but in some cases 10 minutes have gradually been extended to 30, and this extension is regard by employers as an unwarrantable encroachment. The actual time spent in work in summer may be reckoned at 10 hours a day as the average for the district. In winter the men have breakfast before they go to work, but take half an hour for lunch. In the short days they cannot make much more than eight hours of work, and for three months of the year the average is not above 8½ hours. It is impossible to make any general statement as to the hours including the time taken in going to and returning from the farms, as it varies greatly, and is not precisely the same perhaps for two men on the same farm. Instances of men having to walk three miles night and morning were given to me. This is a great evil, and it arises partly from the fact that nearly all the cottages in the district are congregated in villages and hamlets, and partly from the insufficiency of cottages in some parishes. Horsekeepers and stockmen are expected to be with their animals at 5 a.m. in most parishes and at 5.30 in others. One farmer at Battlesden, informed me that he expected them at 4.30 a.m. which was formerly the regular time for beginning. On the other hand, a farmer at Holcut, whose men have fully two miles to walk, is satisfied if he sees them at 6 a.m. and they leave at 5.30 p.m. The usual time for men of this class to leave work is 6 p.m. Their hours are nominally the same all the year round, but in reality the days are shortened more or less at both ends in winter. Some men who drive milk carts to the station make much longer hours. One of them stated that he left home at a quarter to five in the morning, and got back at a quarter to eight. The time for meals is the same for horse keepers and stockmen as for ordinary labourers. Ploughmen or carters who are not horsekeepers make the same hours as ordinary labourers. In harvest the regular day is from 5 a.m. till 7 p.m. with 2½ hours off for meals – breakfast, lunch, dinner, and bever (at 4 p.m.). When corn is being carted overtime is often made, extra beer or money being given when the men are working by time.

18. **Sunday work**. The proportionate number of the men on a farm employed on Sunday generally varies from one-fourth to one-half, but seldom exceeds one-third. The time occupied is from four to six hours, varying with the

seasons of the year, as well as with the character of the work. Cowmen, who have to milk twice a day, are occupied longest on Sunday, taking all seasons of the year into account.

19. **Women and young children not employed on the land at all frequently.** In 1868 Mr. Culley reported that, except in hay time and harvest, female labour in agriculture was "hardly known in Bedfordshire," and this is still true, in the Woburn district at least. Indeed, very few women do anything in the hayfield, and none in the harvest, I believe, unless in assisting their husbands or fathers at piece-work. In answer to the question, "Do women work on the land?" the reply was, in all but two parishes, an unqualified negative, and in one of the two exceptions it was "No, except a little in hay time." At Toddington, the other exception, I was informed that a few women did a little work at pea and fruit picking, as well as in the hayfield; but it is so little as to be hardly worth mentioning. It struck me as very remarkable that I did not see a woman working in an allotment during my visit. I asked several people whether they did help the men on the allotments, and in every case was informed that they did not. When Mr. Culley wrote, the women had something better to do than to work on the land. They had straw-plaiting, which usually paid much better than farm work for women, although the industry was in a somewhat depressed condition when he visited the Woburn district. Lace-making, too, at one time paid sufficiently well to keep a number of women employed at it. It is easy to understand, therefore, why it has not been customary in the past for women to work on the land in South Bedfordshire; and now that the industries referred to are utterly unremunerative and nearly extinct the women still refrain from farm work. This is not to be regretted, as far as women who have families are concerned, as they have quite enough to do in attending to their house duties, but there are many who could well spare time to do occasional work on their husbands' or fathers' allotments. Women are not commonly employed even as dairymaids. Men do the milking, and usually turn the churn, while farmers' wives or daughters generally make the butter. As to young children, the school attendance regulations prevent their employment.

20. **The age at which boys go to work.** In reply to inquiries as to the age at which boys usually begin to work on the land, I was informed that it was 13 years, only one witness putting it at 10 years. Probably the latter statement applies to only a few specially clever boys, who are able to pass the requisite standard at so early an age.

21. **Farm labourers' wages.** Mr. Culley, in 1868, stated that the wages of ordinary farm labourers in the Woburn Union were 11s a week, and those of horsekeepers, shepherds, and others who have Sunday work 12s to 13s a week. In the Bedford Union wages were 1s higher. In 1881 Mr. Druce gave 12s to 13s for ordinary labourers, and 16s to 18s for carters, stockmen, and

shepherds, as the weekly wages current in Bedfordshire as a whole. At the present time wages are a shilling a week higher in North Beds than in the Woburn Union, as they were when Mr. Culley reported, and no doubt the same difference prevailed in 1881. The wages, therefore, in that year may be taken as having been 12s for ordinary labourers, and 16s for men having Sunday work in the Woburn district. Since Mr. Druce reported there has been a fall in wages, followed last spring by a recovery as far as ordinary labourers are concerned. But the Sunday workers are not at all commonly getting the minimum given by Mr. Druce for that class of men. Last year, and up to March, in most of the parishes of the union, ordinary labourers were getting a shilling a week less than the current rate of wages, which is 12s a week in all the parishes of the union excepting Harlington and Holcut, where it is 13s. In the former of these two parishes there is a scarcity of labour, the cottage accommodation being bad and insufficient, while the migration of able-bodied men to work on the railways or in towns has been considerable; and in the latter parish there are no cottages for farm labourers. In Aspley Guise and Toddington the rate given to me was 12s to 13s, but the lower one is the prevailing rate. Ploughmen or carters who are not horsekeepers get the same wages as ordinary labourers. Horsekeepers and stockmen, including shepherds, receive 14s to 15s as a rule, but there is a good deal of variation, partly attributable to the differing hours of Sunday or evening work, as with a milk-cart, and partly to the fact that some men have a cottage rent free. The extreme rates given to me were 13s to 16s. The lower of these two sums is paid to those stockmen who are not required on Sunday, while the higher rate is given generally only in Harlington, to some men in Holcut, and to men who are employed in driving a milk-cart to the railway station in a few other places. Details for the several parishes are summarised in Table C. in the Appendix. The Duke of Bedford's ordinary labourers have 15s a week all the year round, and his stockmen 2s to 3s more.

22. **Piece-work.** As a rule there is comparatively little piece-work, as might be expected in a district in which permanent pasture prevails. Except where harvesting is done by the piece, hoeing and hedging, with a very little mowing in some places, were the only kinds of piece-work by farmers. Several employers informed me that the men did not care to take piece-work, or to exert themselves to earn much at it if they did take it; also that after doing enough to come to 2s a day a man would often leave off to work on his allotment. Others stated that their men earned 2s 6d to 3s a day at hoeing (the former sum being most common), and 2s 6d at hedging. The price paid for hoeing ranges from 3s 6d to 5s an acre, according to the character of the work and the nature of the soil. For hedging, 2s 2d a chain appears to be an ordinary price. Nearly all mowing is done by machine. The prices named when it is done by hand were 4s 6d to 5s an acre with beer, or 6s without, good hands earning 4s or more a day.

23. **Hay time. Modes of payment and earnings**. The most common mode of payment in hay time is that of paying extra for overtime only, and giving beer. For overtime it is usual to pay 3d an hour, and the quantity of beer given varies from four to six pints. When no beer is given 6d a day is sometimes paid instead, while in others 6d a day extra with beer is paid, to include overtime. In Harlington, according to Mr. Foll, who was very obliging in affording me information and in showing me the cottages in his parish, the payment is 3d to 4d an hour for overtime, with four to six pints of beer, the men commonly earning 10s beyond their ordinary wages, and getting beer valued at 7s 6d in 12 days. In Tingrith, Mr. Cooper stated, the men earn 3s to 4s a week each extra, with five pints of beer, for four or five weeks. But hay time does not commonly last so long. The receipts of the men must vary a good deal at this season, and it is difficult to estimate the average with approach to confidence, but Mr. Foll's reckoning of 17s, to include beer, is probably a modest one, as more than a fortnight is occupied with haymaking on some farms. Judging from all the evidence taken upon the point, I should say that the extra earnings of the men in hay time, including the value of the beer at 1½d a pint, commonly range from 15s to 20s. Where there is any hand mowing to do the amount is considerably higher. For machine mowing it is usual to pay 2d an acre to the horsekeeper.

24. **Harvest earnings**. Where harvest is let by the month it is usual to pay double the ordinary labourer's usual wages for four weeks, and to give beer. But in three or four parishes the sum of 20s to 21s or 22s a week; in one it is 20s to 25s; in others 24s, 25s, and 24s to 26s respectively, in all cases with beer, while in one it is 25s without beer. As this evidence must have been based on last harvest's payments, when ordinary wages were a shilling a week less than they are now, it is probable that the rates of the current year (1892) will be higher. There is no payment for overtime in harvest, except extra beer. Where beer is not taken by a man he gets 4s to 5s a week instead in most cases, but in Husborne Crawley, Chalgrave, and Toddington the beer appears to be valued at only 3s if money be paid instead. If the beer be valued at 1½d a pint, 4s a week seems a fair allowance for it, as with the extra beer given for overtime the average must be nearly or quite six pints a day, which, at 1½d a pint, would come to 4s 6d a week. Allowing 16s for the month's beer, then, the extreme range of harvest earnings in the union, when the letting is a time one, would be £4 16s to £6. When harvesting is done by the piece at prices which vary with the crops, the men appear to earn £5 to £7 without beer. Several farmers informed me that their own men earned £6 to £7 each last harvest, and one said that his men received £6 for piece-work in four weeks, and 16s instead of beer. When the work is done by the piece, however, it is not usual to give beer. Some of the labourers whom I questioned said that they earned over £6 last harvest.

25. **Perquisites, allowances, and payments in kind**. Excepting beer, alluded to already in references to haytime and harvest, there are no allowances or payments in kind worth consideration as additions to the earnings of ordinary labourers generally. The horsekeeper commonly gets 1d an acre for drilling, as well as the 2d an acre for mowing with a machine, already alluded to, in addition to his regular wages. Cowmen have 6d for each calf reared, and shepherds 2d per lamb. In many cases, if not all, too, the cowmen have milk for their breakfast free of charge. This milk would cost at least 1s a week if purchased, but whether its receivers would value it at so much is doubtful. As to the money allowances above mentioned, they vary so greatly with the number of acres or animals that it is impossible to give a general statement of what they amount to in a year. In the case of a shepherd with a large flock the lamb money comes up to a considerable sum, as may be imagined when it is stated that one employer informed me that he paid his shepherd £50 a year altogether.

As a rule, however, flocks are not large in the Woburn Union. As to the few cases in which horse-keepers or stockmen have cottages rent free, these are already allowed for in the statement of the range of weekly wages.

26. **Earnings apart from those derived from farm work**. The only work done by agricultural labourers apart from farm work mentioned to me, was a little digging of coprolites and a little wood-cutting; but the number of men affected seemed to be so small that I did not make detailed inquiry into the subject. At coproliting, I was told, men could earn £1 a week; but I heard of it in only one parish, and the same may be said of wood-cutting. The Duke of Bedford has his own staff of woodmen, and does not need the help of agricultural labourers.

27. **Annual earnings**. In order to ascertain beyond all question the annual earnings of typical agricultural labourers, I requested a few employers to let me take out the weekly receipts of one or two men from their labour books, and my wish was readily gratified. Mr. Millard, of Aspley Guise, was good enough to assist me to take out the earnings of a skilled day labourer and a teetotaller, who earns regularly a shilling a week more than his fellow day labourers who are not horse-keepers or stockmen. He also gets more by piece-work than others, because of his skill and industry, and a further advantage is obtained by his taking money instead of beer. His earnings were set down from May 1st, 1891 to April 30th, 1892. In May he was paid 12s a week and afterwards 13s. He lost one week's wages, 12s, through illness, in May, 6¾ days on his allotment, or otherwise on his own account, and five days on a visit to a relative. Altogether he lost £1 17s 3½d through his unusually long absence from the farm during the year, which goes some way in bringing down his extra earnings as compared with what his fellow day labourers on the farm receive. His total receipts were £39 3s 3½d in the 12 months. Of this

the sum of £6 8s 7d was for harvesting done by the piece, 16s paid instead of beer being included. All other extras above ordinary wages came to £2 19s 6d, including 6s earned in hay time, half of which was instead of beer. Obviously there is but little haymaking done on the farm. Harvest lasted 4½ weeks, during which period the man earned 15s for day labour when harvesting was impracticable. His average weekly earnings were 15s, or 2s more than his ordinary wages, in spite of the fact that he received only 12s for the first four weeks, and that he lost a good deal of time. I have given these details to show that the case was thoroughly investigated; but it would be tedious to do likewise with other cases. Mr. Robert Mossman, of Battlesden, is another farmer who kindly allowed me to see his labour book. I selected a day labourer who appeared to be an average one, and put down his earnings week by week from May 1st, 1891, to April 30th, 1892. Ten months out of the 12, it is to be borne in mind, wages at Battlesden, as in nearly all other parishes of the union, were 1s. a week less than they are now. His total money earnings amounted to £36 7s 8d, and his beer is valued at 10s for hay time (six pints a day) and £1 for harvest, making £37 17s 8d in all, equal to an average of 14s 7d a week. It would be nearly a shilling more at the current rate of wages, if continued for winter as well as summer. The harvest money (exclusive of beer) was £5 for 24 fine days, and as harvest was spread over five weeks the extra over ordinary wages during the period came to £2. Other extras, including those of money (excluding the value of beer) earned in hay time came to £2 11s 8d. Mr. Mossman informed me that his cattleman and shepherd earned fully 1s 6d a week on the average more than this day labourer, and his horsekeeper 2s more. Mr. Stopp, of Woburn, to whom I am indebted for much valuable information, allowed me to take the yearly earnings of his horse-keeper and cattleman out of his labour book. The former was unfortunately ill for 16 days, through which his earnings were seriously diminished. His total came to £38 10s, or barely 15s a week for the whole year. If he had not lost any time the average would have been 15s 9d a week. In this case it is to be remembered that, during 10½ months out of the 12, wages were 1s a week less than they are now. The stockman's total was £40 6s, as he lost no time worth mentioning. His average was 15s 6d a week. Beer is not included in either of these two cases. It was given in hay time, but not in harvest. Mr. J. Cooper, of Tingrith, another farmer to whom I am indebted for a great deal of assistance, estimates a cowman's annual earnings at £38 15s, and an ordinary labourer's at £34 10s. Mr. Adams and Mr. Pickering, who obligingly visited me together for Chalgrave and Hockliffe, put the annual receipts of farm labourers of the several classes at £35 to £40. On the other hand, at a small meeting of labourers held at Hockliffe, the men said they earned barely £30 a year. None of them could give exact receipts for a year, and I may here remark that I have not yet met with a farm labourer who could so so. The amount cannot be as little as £30, unless a man has lost a good deal of time; for the ordinary and harvest wages, without any extras for hay time and piece-work, would amount to more than the sum named. Other farmers than those named estimate the average weekly earnings for the whole year at 1s 6d to 2s more than the ordinary weekly wages. This, I think, would be the usual range of extra earnings, while 1s to 2s 6d would be more accurate as a comprehensive range. The comparatively few horsekeepers and stockmen who have 16s a week as their ordinary wages, must earn £48 to £50 a year, including all extras and the value of beer allowed. The Duke of Bedford's men, as already stated, receive 15s to 18s a week all the year round. The Duke has no arable farms in hand, and there is therefore no harvesting for his men to do.

28. **General correspondence of farmers' and labourers' evidence.** Except for the discrepancy as to annual earnings noticed in the evidence of farmers and labourers in respect of Chalgrave and Hockliffe, mentioned in the last paragraph, I have been gratified in finding that whenever I have tested the statements of employers as to wages by the evidence of the men, as I have done in most parishes, they have been confirmed.

29. **Earnings of boys.** Boys beginning regular work at the age of 13, or in some cases earlier, get 3s 6d to 4s a week at first, gradually receiving more until they have men's wages at 18 to 20 years of age. In hay time boys get 1s to 1s 6d a week extra, and in harvest their wages are doubled.

30. **Family earnings.** When a labourer has two or three boys at work the family earnings are often double those of the man alone. In the case of Mr. Millard's man, whose earnings are given in paragraph 27, the ordinary takings of the family are 26s 6d a week without extras. This man has three boys at work, the oldest, who is 15 years of age, getting 5s 6d, and the other two boys 4s each. Including the harvest, hay time, and other extra earnings of this family, the yearly income can hardly fall short of £75. Mr. George Humphreys, of Ridgemount, informs me that last winter he paid a man and two boys 26s 6d a week, a rise of 1s a week having taken place last spring. Presumably, therefore, this family will now be getting fully 29s 6d a week, as boys' wages rise at least a 1s each year independently of any advance in the rate of men's wages. The average per week for the year would be 2s to 3s more. Mr. Foxon, of Toddington, who kindly gave up a good deal of time to me, pays 23s a week to a man and two boys, extras not included. Mr. Bailey, of Milton Bryant, says a man with two boys, 13 to 15, would earn 24s a week, not including any extras.

31. **Cottage accommodation.** The cottage accommodation varies greatly in the several parishes. The evidence taken on this point from residents is that the accommodation is sufficient in Chalgrave, Eversholt, Hockliffe, Husborne Crawley, Milton Bryant, Ridgemount, Tilsworth, Tingrith, Toddington, and Woburn, and insufficient in Aspley Guise (because of the immigration of the large staff of a printing establishment), Battlesden, Harlington, Holcut, Pots-

grove, and Salford. The chief cause of the shortness of supply is the demolition of old and bad cottages without a corresponding erection of new ones. As the population of the district has fallen off, and the new cottages as a rule are much more commodious than the old ones were, it is not necessary to erect as many as have been demolished. But the late Duke of Bedford, who had a wholesome fancy for the destruction of bad dwellings, is generally credited with having pulled down three cottages for every one that he has built. In Battlesden, I was informed, there are only five cottages, where twenty-four once stood. In Holcut, where the Rev. B. C. Smith is lord of the manor and the principal landowner, there are only three cottages, two of which are occupied by Mr. Smith's servants. In Harlington, where Major Cooper and the Rev. B. C. Smith are the chief landowners, the former owning very few of the cottages, it is probable that the shortness of the supply arises from the lack of rebuilding as old dwellings became uninhabitable. Potsgrove, I believe, has always depended for its cottage accommodation on Sheep Lane, a hamlet of Woburn, and there the Duke of Bedford effected a great clearance of wretched hovels, erecting several, but not an equal number, of excellent cottages instead. The deficiency in Salford is partly attributable to that of Holcut, and partly to the fact of the parish being the property of a Corporation (All Souls, Oxford), and let on a long lease (recently expired) to the Rev. B. C. Smith. Now that the college authorites have resumed the management, they are slowly building excellent new cottages to replace some of those which have been pulled down.

32. **Distance of cottages from work**. The great fault of the cottage accommodation in the district lies in the lack of cottages on farms. Even on the Duke of Bedford's estate there are rarely more than two cottages to a farm, however large it may be, and on many farms belonging to other landowners there are no cottages at all. The case of Holcut, where there is no cottage on a farm, has already been referred to; and at Toddington, where Major Cooper is lord of the manor and the principal landowner, the case is similar, as there are eight farms with one cottage for the lot. Throughout the union the cottages are nearly all in villages or hamlets, and the consequence is that most of the agricultural labourers have a long way to walk to their work. I heard of many cases of two miles, and some of longer distances.

33. **Construction of cottages**. The great majority of the cottages are of brick and tile, and the new or comparatively new ones built by the Duke of Bedford, All Souls College, and a few other landowners, are substantial buildings. In most parishes there are more or less of the old plaster (or mud) and thatch cottages, which are not always the worst, often being much more roomy and comfortable inside than the new ones put up by persons seeking a profitable investment.

34. **Condition of cottages**. With regard to the condition of cottages, I had the

advantage of the evidence of the two medical officers of the union, Mr. King, M.B., of Aspley Guise, and Dr. Waugh of Toddington, who, between them, have charge of all the parishes. In all cases my own observations confirmed their evidence, and I visited every village in the union. Taking the union as a whole, the cottages may be described as exceptionally good, and in good condition. But there are more or less discreditable cottages in several of the villages. The proportion is greater in Harlington than in any other parish, I think, for there are very few good cottages in that village, and some are more like inferior stables and lofts than human dwellings. Some that I inspected had roofs out of repair, and out-door closets quite exposed to the rain, and thus unfit for use. One bad one, occupied by a widow at 5s 10d a month, with no garden, was in a wretched state of repair. The dwelling-room is 11 ft. 9 ins. square, and there is one bedroom over it of the same size. Several large families in Harlington are dwelling in cottages of this description. A neighbouring cottage is much worse, the dwelling-room being a long, narrow place, more like a passage than a room, the bedroom being like it, while a loft, reached by a ladder above, is used as a lumber room. In another case there is one large bedroom for a man, his wife, and five children. There is only one pole of garden, and the rent is 1s 6d a week. At Aspley Guise, the most charming village in the district, the cottages are for the most part good or fair; but there are nests of dilapidated plaster-and-thatch cottages at Mount Pleasant, in that parish, most of which, however, are not uncomfortable inside. Several brick cottages at Mount Pleasant have dwelling-rooms 12 ft. square, and two to three bedrooms, and are in good condition. At Battlesden, the few cottages are those of the Duke of Bedford, and they are models, with large dwelling-rooms, three bedrooms, and large gardens. At Eversholt and Husbourne Crawley, too, the Duke owns most of the cottages, and consequently they are in excellent condition. At Chalgrave and Hockliffe there are several cottage owners, not including the Duke. Generally the cottages are in good condition in these parishes. Some of the worst in Chalgrave are now empty. In Hockliffe, however, there is a set of cottages, standing a little way back from the street, which are utterly unfit for habitation. The people who live in them look as wretched as the houses, which few of them attempt to keep in decent order. In short, the place reminded me of some of the worst of the congested districts of Ireland, with their wretched cabins and miserable inhabitants. Even worse, if possible, are some hovels in Pond Head and Fireball Alley, Toddington, as these have no back way, and the so-called privies are literally in the street. It is strange that they are of such little value that the person who owns one group of four offered to sell the lot for £50. There are all kinds of cottages in Toddington, but the great majority may be described as in fair or good condition. At Ridgmount, where the Duke owns about one-third of the cottages, and most of those belonging to him and to others in the

main street are good, there is a higgledy-piggledy congregation of small hovels
at a place called Lydd's Hill. They are stuck about in all directions, as if their
builders had squatted down on any piece of land they could find unoccupied.
Most of them are of brick, and tiled or slated; a few of plaster and thatched.
The size of the dwelling-room in some of the smallest, which are not those in
the worst condition, is 10 ft. square. Nearly all have gardens. They belong to
different owners, and the rents are 1s to 1s 6d a week. At Salford the worst
cottages have been pulled down, but there are still a few bad ones left. Tilsworth, too, has some poor cottages, without gardens, but not discreditable in
outward appearance. One that I inspected has no garden or backway, and the
rent is 1s 6d a week, or as much as a tenant of the Duke of Bedford would
pay for a cottage with much better accommodation and a large garden.
Milton Bryant, under Miss Synott as the chief landowner, and Tingrith, formerly the property of the late Miss Trevor, but recently sold by her execu-
tors, may be described as model villages. As to Woburn, the Duke of Bedford
owns nearly all the labourers' cottages, and they are generally excellent. But
there are a few very bad cottages belonging to private owners, small and
cramped, and not in good repair.

35. **Number and size of rooms in cottages.** Reference has already been made
to the small number and size of rooms in some of the worst cottages, but the
great majority of cottages in this district have two bedrooms, and many
three. The Duke of Bedford's cottages are of all sizes from those with one
bedroom for single persons or couples without children, to houses with three
or four bedrooms. The sizes of the rooms vary a good deal also. In some
which I inspected at Birchmoor Common, Woburn, the living room is about
12 ft. square, and the back room is a little smaller. There are two bedrooms,
covering the same space as the living room and the back room with its cupboard or pantry. The height of the down-stair rooms is about 8 ft. There are
20 poles of garden allotment attached to such cottages, and the inclusive rent
is 1s 4d a week. The only fault I noticed in these cottages is the very inconvenient placing of the stoves, the one for cooking and baking purposes being
in the front or living room instead of the back room, which should be the
kitchen. Thus a good deal of dirty work has to be done in the room which a
good housewife likes to keep in spick and span condition. The walls inside are
whitewashed or colour-washed and the conditions under which the cottages
are let require the tenants to rewash them every year, and to do a few other
things to keep the interior in good condition. The roofs are troughed, the
water going through a drain to a small brook. Cottages with three bedrooms
have larger living rooms.

36. **Paternal arrangements.** Regulations which the cottagers do not like, but
which are for their good as a class, are imposed upon the Duke's tenants. An
occupier is required to move into another cottage, not only if it is too small

for his family, but also if it is too large or larger than he needs. One man complained that he had to leave the commodious cottage he occupied at 1s 9d a week, although he was quite willing to pay that rent as he wished to remain where he had lived for many years; but, as his family had grown up and left him, he and his wife were obliged to move into a small cottage at a lower rent. This was felt as a grievance, and yet it is obvious that large cottages cannot be found for large families if couples without families are allowed to occupy them.

37. **Ventilation**. One of the points upon which the Assistant Commissioners are directed to make inquiry is the ventilation of cottages. There are no arrangements for ventilation, so far as I observed, except windows, chimneys, and doors; but this may be said of the vast majority of houses occupied by the middle class, and of many mansions also. There are means of ventilation if the people will open their windows, as they will not generally. In many of the cottage bedrooms there is no fireplace, and therefore no opening into a chimney. In such cases, when several people sleep in them with the window shut, the air must become shockingly vitiated.

38. **Drainage**. In most of the larger villages there is a drain for surface water and kitchen slops; but water-closets are not common, I believe, except in Woburn, a fact which is not to be regretted.

39. **The earth-closet system**. The Duke's tenants in many, if not all, cases are required to carry out the earth-closet system, and I am glad to learn that they attend to it properly. All having gardens or garden allotments, there is no difficulty as to the disposal of the refuse or as to the supply of earth. Under such circumstances the system is the best that could be adopted. It is followed in some cottages not owned by the Duke, but the old privy system is usual in villages where the Duke is not owner of most of the cottages.

40. **Water supply**. As a rule, the water supply is excellent throughout the union. The only complaints I heard were those of cottagers having to go to the town pump for water in a few cases, as at Toddington. Upon this point I accepted the evidence of the medical officers and residents in the several parishes.

41. **Out-houses**. Almost invariably the cottages have little out-houses, called "barns", which are very useful, not only for coals and firewood, but also for tools and the produce of allotments.

42. **Tenure of cottages**. Nearly all the cottages are held direct from the owners, farm tenants in some instances having the privilege of nomination when a cottage is vacant. Except where farmers own land and cottages, I did not hear of any instances in which they had the power of turning out the occupiers. They would not be likely to have such a power with regard to cottages in villages, and there are very few on farms.

43. **Cottages owned by labourers**. Very few cottages are owned by labourers in any of the villages of the union, so far as I could ascertain.

44. **Periods of tenure and notice to quit.** Cottages are let by the week, the month, or the year, and the periods of notice to quit vary accordingly. I was informed that the Duke's cottage tenants held subject to a week's notice to quit on either side.

45. **Rents of cottages with or without gardens.** The rents of cottages range from 6d to 2s 6d a week. There are some at 3s, but not commonly occupied by agricultural labourers. From 1s to 1s 6d a week is the usual range of rents paid by farm labourers, and a good garden commonly goes with a cottage at the higher sum. This point, in relation to the Duke of Bedford's cottages, is further referred to in the Appendix. The garden is always included, where there is one, but one of the great evils of having cottages congregated in villages is that space for gardens cannot always be found. Garden allotments are frequently rented separately from the cottages. Such evidence as "1s 6d with 40 poles of garden", or "1s to 2s with 20 poles of garden," was frequently noted in the course of my travels through the district. On the other hand, I have previously mentioned cases of villages containing many cottages with gardens, and others with very small gardens. These are often let at rents quite as high as those of cottages with 20 to 40 poles of garden or garden allotment.

46. **Rates on cottages.** Rates on cottages are almost universally paid by the owners. The only exception that I heard of was that of one owner of land and cottages in Chalgrave and Hockliffe, who requires his cottage tenants to pay rates. The amount of the rates on cottages varies greatly. The overseer at Woburn obliged me with the amounts for a few parishes. In Woburn parish the Duke's cottages are assessed at £1 10s, the rates being 3s 6d in the pound. In Milton Bryant the Duke's cottages are valued at £3 10s to £4 10s, and others at £2 to £3 10s. In Potsgrove the assessment is £2 5s to £4, rates being 2s 3d in the pound. In Chalgrave the amounts are £1 5s, to £2 10s, and the rates are 3s in the pound.

47. **Gardens, their sizes and cultivation.** As already stated, gardens are common, but by no means universal. About half the cottages in Toddington, I was informed, have none, and several in other villages. Where there are gardens the size ranges from one pole up to 40 poles. They are nearly always well cultivated. The great lack in the gardens of the Duke's tenants is that of fruit trees. There are fruit bushes, but very few trees. The reason given for this is the liability of the owners to be shifted, under the regulations noticed in paragraph 36.

48. **Supply of allotments.** It would be impossible to find a district better supplied with allotments than the Woburn Union. Bedfordshire, as a whole, is well supplied, but the Woburn Union better. The Return of Allotments and Small Holdings issued for 1890 by the Board of Agriculture shows that there were 15,194 detached allotments (garden allotments not being returned) in a

cultivated areas of 295,509 acres. The number is exceeded only in Bucks, Leicester, Lincoln, Nottingham, Northampton, Oxford, Somerset, Warwick, and Wilts, all much larger counties. There was in 1890 one detached allotment in Beds to every 19 acres of cultivated area (crops, bare fallow, and grass), a ratio greater than that of any other county in Great Britain. I have no means of ascertaining the cultivated area of the Woburn Union exactly, but if it bears the same proportion to the total area as that of the whole of the county does, it is about 25,500 acres. The number of detached allotments returned in 1890 for the union is 1,424, or one to every 18 acres; but this is not all, for there is an extraordinary number of garden allotments in the Woburn Union, nearly all the Duke of Bedford's cottages being provided with them. Therefore it may be regarded as probable that the Woburn Union is better supplied with allotments than any other union in the country. This is partly owing to the liberality of the Dukes of Bedford, but not by any means entirely, for they were not the first to start the allotment system in the county.

49. **Ratio of allotments to population**. At present the Census Returns of 1891 are not sufficiently complete to enable me to ascertain the number of agricultural labourers in the Woburn Union, but in every parish I was assured that every man who desired an allotment could have one, and in most parishes that many men had more than one. In all Bedfordshire, including the people living in towns, there is one detached allotment to 10.58 people. In the Woburn Union the ratio is one to 6.37. If garden allotments were included, there would probably be found to be nearly one to every head of a family, townsmen included.

50. Table C. in the Appendix shows the number of detached allotments, as returned in 1890, under a quarter of an acre and from a quarter to an acre respectively, for each parish in the Woburn Union, and for the whole. The evidence which I collected gives either from 20 or 40 poles to an acre as the range in most parishes, 40 poles to three or four acres (those above an acre being over the limit of allotments as defined in the Allotments Act) in two parishes, 10 to 40 poles in Hockliffe, and eight to 40 poles in Woburn. A summary of evidence on this point will be found in Table D in the Appendix.

51. **Cultivation of allotments**. The only regulation as to the cultivation of allotments that appears to be at all common is the insistence on spade husbandry. In a few cases, however, corn growing is prohibited. Most of the allotments are excellently cultivated, but there are marked differences in this respect, and instances of plots being thrown up in very bad condition were mentioned to me.

52. **Crops grown on allotments**. Garden crops and corn are grown on allotments as a rule, the former in all cases and the latter to some extent in many. Fruit is not grown on allotments, partly because those who planted trees or

bushes would have no security for their value on giving up the land, partly because there would be no safety against pilfering, and also because of the difficulty of disposing of fruit in rural districts. Fruit is grown to some extent in gardens.

53. **Rents of allotments.** The rents of allotments in the Woburn Union as shown in Table D. of the Appendix, are usually at the rate of £2 an acre. Some charity allotments at Aspley Guise are let at 3s 6d for 20 poles, the rent being returned in bread. At Holcut and Salford the Rev. B. C. Smith lets some at 32s to 40s an acre, and at Eversholt there are some charity allotments at 35s an acre. On the other hand, at Hockcliffe, according to the labourers, the glebe allotments are let at £2 10s an acre; at Harlington the charge is £4 an acre, of which the men bitterly complain; at Ridgemount the men say they pay 12s 9d per 38 rods for some land, or at the rate of £2 13s an acre; and at Toddington, the usual range is £2 to £2 10s, while some land is let at £3, and one little field close to the main street, belonging to a small owner, is let at £5 an acre. As a rule, these rents are inclusive of rates, which are paid by the landlord. The only exceptions I heard of were those of one owner's allotments at Chalgrave (let at only 30s an acre), and of those of another owner at Toddington, whose tenants have to pay rates. The former also requires his rents half-yearly in advance, but this is quite exceptional, as they are usually paid at the end of 12 months. Generally the rents are well paid, but in Toddington, the Rev. F. A. Adams says a good deal of rent is lost at times, which accounts, he thinks, for the comparatively high rents charged in the parish. He lets 96 acres of his glebe in allotments at £240, but the actual income does not average more then £200. Some of the tenants throw up their allotments after a bad season, leaving the land in such a bad state that only half the usual rent can be charged for the next year. Still, he says that the allotments are generally well cultivated.

54. **Disposal of produce of allotments.** In most of the parishes the holders of allotments have a difficulty in disposing of any surplus produce at paying rates. They can usually get rid of potatoes satisfactorily, but not of some other vegetables. At Toddington, however, the allotment holders either retail their surplus produce or more commonly sell it to occupiers of small holdings, who retail it with their vegetables.

55. **Benefit of allotments, but not sufficient to prevent migration.** The Rev. F. A. Adams, the Rev. James Andrews, and others strongly expressed their appreciation of the benefit of allotments to the labourers. Indeed, there is no doubt that those of them who get the lowest rate of wages in the district, and have families to support would be very badly off without the food produced on their allotments. It is obvious, however, that allotments do not prevent migration from the Woburn Union.

56. **Do allotments lower wages?** It is said by some persons that allotments

lower wages, and this is obviously true up to a certain point where their possession prevents labour from becoming scarce in a district. But if the limit which farmers can afford to pay for such labour as they can obtain is reached, the lack of allotments would not make them pay more. They would throw their land down to grass, and do with hardly any labour. The question of rent comes in here, of course, but land all in grass would command as much rent as land partly arable. Besides, even if allotments tend to lower wages, it is because they make men too comfortable to migrate excessively. There is every reason to believe too, that the value of allotments to labourers is a great deal more than any increase in wages which they would obtain by the painful method of making themselves scarce, if they gave up their plots of land.

57. **Farmers' opinion about allotments.** The general opinion of farmers appears to be that a garden of 20 poles is better than a quarter of an acre of allotment ground away from a cottage. Many of them complain that the men spend their strength on their allotments which should be spent in earning their wages on farms. Still, those who said this to me admitted that a man who spends his evening on his plot of land is better fitted for work the next day than he would be if he spent it in the public-house. As to the question of how far the men accommodate themselves to their employers' conveniences when they have work on their allotments which they wish to finish there is some conflict of evidence. Some employers say that there is very little to complain of, while others assert that there is a good deal. It is said by witnesses who are apparently unprejudiced that a man who has half an acre of land seldom works regularly on a farm, and that he is apt to become a mere jobbing worker, to his own hurt. This seems probable in a district where the women appear to disdain work on an allotment. If they are as badly off as some of them say they are, they might, with the help of their children, do all the work on half an acre that the man cannot get through in the evenings, except for a day or two when potatoes have to be dug or other crops gathered.

58. **Allotments Act not needed in the Woburn Union.** It is scarcely necessary to say that the Allotments Act was not needed for the Woburn Union, either to supply land or to render allotment rents generally moderate or low. I was informed that a little land was obtained under the Act, or under the threat of putting it into action, at Hockliffe and Chalgrave, but nowhere else in the union.

59. **Small holdings.** Table C in the Appendix gives the number of small holdings up to 50 acres in each parish of the Woburn Union, as returned by the Board of Agriculture for 1890. Why all up to an acre were not included with allotments it is difficult to imagine. However, the total is only 232, which is not a great number, and only 46 were owned by the occupiers. Nearly half are in the three parishes of Aspley Guise, Toddington, and Woburn. In Aspley Guise and Toddington there are some market gardeners, while in Woburn

most of the small holdings are used as accommodation ground by shop-keepers and others in town. The total number of detached allotments and small holdings in the Woburn Union according to the return, was 1,656 in 1890, or at the rate of one to 5.6 persons of all ages.

60. **Condition of small holders.** Many of the small holders have done well in the past. One whom I met told me how he began as a farm labourer, acquired first an allotment, then two or three plots, and afterwards several acres, saving a nice little sum before he became old. Mr. Horley, too, landlord of the principal inn, did well years ago in sending market garden produce to London or the manufacturing towns of the midlands and the north. But now he says this business does not pay, as rail freights eat up all the profit, and the only small holders who do any good as a rule are those who retail their produce. Some of them go as far as Luton, and at least one goes to Harrow to sell vegetables from house to house. They act, too, as dealers, buying up the surplus produce of small holders. Thus they make a decent living; but there are apparently as many of them as are required.

61. **No considerable demand for small holdings.** I asked a number of labourers whether there would be any demand among their class for small holdings under the new Act. Not one said that there would be any demand for the purchase of holdings, the opinion appearing to be that hardly any farm labourers were "men enough" to buy even 10 acres of land, paying the instalment required, and finding capital to cultivate it for a year. Some, however, could hire 10 acres, they thought, and would be glad to do so.

62. **Live stock kept by labourers.** Many of the labourers keep a pig or two, and some keep poultry, but hardly any keep bees. I did not hear of any case of an agricultural labourer keeping a cow in the district.

63. **Men in benefit societies.** Most of the young men are in a benefit club of some kind, but many of the old men are not in any, the small local clubs to which they formerly belonged being broken up. A few of these wretched traps for poor men's savings still exist, but not many. Most of the young men belong to the Odd Fellows, the Foresters, or the parish clubs established at Tingrith, Aspley Guise, and Eversholt. The Tingrith club has a high reputation in several parishes, and is registered.

64. **Industries competing with or subsidiary to agriculture.** There are no industries in the district which seriously compete with agriculture for labour, unless the railways which traverse it be included. There are lime works near Toddington, and fuller's earth works near Woburn Sands, but these do not employ many men.

65. **Decay of plaiting.** The plaiting industry once hardly inferior to that of agriculture as the mainstay of the working class in the district, is all but extinct. I conversed with some of the few women who still do a little plaiting, and they assured me that they could not earn more than 2d if they worked at

it all day, while some said that they actually did not earn more than 1d. For 20 yards of plait, once worth 9d only 3d is now paid, and straw costing 1d to 1½d has to be bought by the worker. Yet a few women, chiefly at Toddington, still work at this wretchedly-paid trade when they are not occupied in household duties. Some make hats, and they probably do better than the mere plaiters. In the prosperous times of plaiting the men, as well as the women, could earn 1s a day or more. Some good hands earned 10s a week, and then the men were indifferent as to being out of farm work in winter. Indeed, many of them preferred to sit over the fire plaiting to working in the open. Children also did plaiting, and families earned high wages.

66. **Lace-making.** Another local industry still more nearly extinct than plaiting is lace-making. One woman whom I saw doing this work informed me that she could earn only 1d a day at it. But there are very few now who injure their health by stooping over this monotonous and tiresome work.

67. **Wood-carving.** At Ridgemount Miss Crouch has a class of labourers and boys in which wood-carving is taught. Some of their work, which she kindly showed me, is excellent. A good hand, I was told, could earn 3s if he worked at carving all day.

68. **No trade unions among the labourers.** The Agricultural Labourers' Union got a little hold in parts of the district many years ago, but appears to have no members in it now. There was a strike or threatened strike at Toddington some 15 years ago which led to a rise of wages, quickly followed by a fall. During the last 10 years, however, no disturbance has occurred.

69. **Relations between employers and employed.** Employers and employed appear to be under fairly friendly conditions. There is some grumbling on both sides, as there usually is everywhere, but not to any uncommon extent, I think. It is not surprising that neither should be perfectly satisfied, for, while the wages are not high, the quality of the labour, so far as can be judged by the general appearance of the men whom I saw, is not the highest. If it may be said that good pay makes good workmen, it may with equal truth be said that the converse is the case.

70. **The sanitary condition of the districts.** I was assured by the medical officers that the sanitary condition of the district was generally good. No overcrowding is allowed in cottages, unless it be where large families have only one bedroom, which is not a common state of affairs. Lodgers are not allowed in the Duke's cottages without the consent of the agent, and this rule I believe is in force in respect of cottages belonging to some other owners. The sanitary authorities, too, as a rule, prevent flagrant abuses, either in overcrowding or in other arrangements. Dr. Prior, of Bedford, the medical officer of health for the union, is said to look after them well. But the cases of bad cottages in Toddington, Hockliffe, and Harlington, are not creditable to the authorities.

71. **Morality.** The evidence of clergymen and others is to the effect that the morality of the district is generally good, so far as it is tested by results which come into public notice. It is vastly improved since the days of prosperous plaiting and lace-making, industries which, as shown in Mr. Culley's report, before alluded to, were fruitful sources of immorality. Mr. Matthews, the registrar of births, says that he does not now register five illegitimate children in a year. He also says that there is not much drunkenness "except at Toddington," which seems to be the "black sheep" of the parishes in the Woburn Union.

72. **General condition of the labouring class.** Of the general condition of the labourers in the district I may say that it might be better and it might be worse. If it were not for the generally good cottages and the allotments, I should pronounce it rather bad, as the weekly wages are low, and the opportunities of earning extra payments are few. But those who have lived long in the district say that the condition of the people has improved greatly. That they should give this evidence in spite of the decay of plaiting seems strange, but plaiting was depressed for a long time before it became entirely unremunerative, and possibly the comparison is drawn from comparatively recent years. Mr. Matthews, who speaks from 30 years' experience, however, says that whereas from about 1865 to 1873 he used to expend £70 to £80 a week in poor relief in the union, he now spends £30 or less, in spite of the fact that the guardians are liberal in giving out-door relief where help is needed. Out-door relief is given permanently a good deal. A man and his wife get 5s and two loaves; a woman has 2s 6d and a loaf if she can plait or go out charing, or up to 3s 6d if she has rent to pay. There is a good deal of private benevolence, too, in most of the parishes, and the clergy, the relieving officers, and the medical officers say that there is very little actual distress. Toddington is the chief sufferer. This parish, as a large open one, has long been a refuge for the destitute, receiving men turned out of other parishes in which the owners of the cottages require good character in their tenants. But even there, the witnesses say, distress, when it occurs, is usually through the fault of its victims. It is obvious that men with large families, not earning anything, must have a very hard struggle to supply themselves and their wives and children with food if their average earnings are only 13s 6d a week — to mention the lowest average. But the prices of bread, meat, and provisions generally are much lower than they were. I endeavoured to obtain some labourers' budgets, but was not successful except in one instance, which is given, with the prices of provisions, in the Appendix. Not one of the men whom I asked for a balance sheet of receipts and expenditure could give one. They appeared to deem the request inquisitorial. All the labourers' budgets that I have seen resemble farmers' accounts of crops, in so far as the expenditure exceeds the receipts. Most farmers live, in spite of growing crops apparently at a loss, and labourers

and their families flourish on wages less than their supposed minimum expenditure amounts to. Stranger still, the women and children are well dressed. How it is done is a mystery, when there are children earning nothing. When the boys begin to add to the family income, the mystery exists no longer. The help in maintaining a family derived from an allotment, and from the pig that often goes with it, is a very important consideration. Farmers say that, while their own outlook was never more gloomy than it is now, labourers were never as well off as they are at the present time. Apart from the plaiting this would probably be true, and it is a question whether allotments, slightly advanced wages, and low prices for food not produced on allotments, do not counterbalance the plaiting earnings of the old times. The total money earnings of the labourers and their families are certainly much less than they were in the times when plaiting and lace-making were fairly remunerative, and when every member of a family not a mere infant contributed to the total takings. But money is not everything, and the best friends of the agricultural labourers of Bedfordshire would hesitate before recalling, if they had the power, the old times, with their drunkenness, immorality, premature marriage, and unhealthy child-work. It is better for young women to be in service than wandering about the lanes and fields with a piece of plait in their hands, and it is better for children to be at school than to be slaving at lace-making or plaiting. The extraordinary number of little public-houses in the villages of the Woburn Union may in great measure be regarded as a legacy from the days of prosperous plaiting. If four out of five of them were abolished there would still be more than enough for any reasonable requirements. Evidence shows that there is less pauperism, less distress, less disease, and less immorality now than existed in the times referred to; and, therefore, taking all things into consideration, there appears to be good reason to say that the general condition of the agricultural population of the Woburn Union is better now than it ever was before. If agricultural prosperity should return, a further improvement might be confidently expected.

I am, Sir, Your obedient servant,
(Signed) William E. Bear
Assistant Commissioner.

Report of William E. Bear, Royal Commission on Labour (1893-4)   B PP 1893-4 XXXV.

2. THE POOR LAW

2.1 Administration of the Old Poor Law

*2.1.1 The rising cost of the poor rates combined with the occasional out-
break of unrest in the years after Waterloo led to a series of Parliamentary enquiries into the workings of the Poor Law. In 1817 evidence concerning Bedfordshire was provided for a Select Committee
of the House of Lords by two county magistrates: the Rev. Hugh
Wade-Gery of Eaton Socon, and William Wilshere, the Hitchin attor-
ney and from Michaelmas 1817 Chairman of Bedfordshire Quarter
Sessions.*

Minutes of Evidence taken before the Lords Committees on the Poor Laws
*14 May 1817 . . . The Reverend Hugh Wade Gery is called in; and having been sworn, is
Examined, as follows:*
You reside in the parish of Eaton Socon in Bedfordshire ? – I do.
Are you rector of the parish? – No, I am not.
You are an acting magistrate for that county? – I am; and also for the county of
Huntingdon.
Can you speak to the effect of the poor laws in the northern part of the county of
Bedford? – I can, in some measure . . .
How long have you resided in Bedfordshire? – Ever since the year 1797; I did not act as
a magistrate for the first three or four years; I believe not till the year 1804 . . .
In applications that have been made to you as a magistrate, have not the poor applied for
relief for their children? – Very frequently . . . We have generally allowed half a
crown a head per week where the family consisted of five or six persons.
In calculating that half a crown per head, were the wages of the labourer and the earnings of each of the family taken into consideration? – Yes; the whole earnings of
the family were included in the half crown; when the family has been small, not more
than two or three, there a greater allowance is usually made than half a crown per
head.
From your knowledge of the manner in which the labouring poor in Bedfordshire live,
do not you know that the females particularly, and even the male young children in
each family, are employed in lace-making? – Yes; a great many of them.
Does not the effect of that domestic manufacture add to the general earnings of the
family? – Certainly.
In the calculation that has been made by you as a magistrate, do not you consider the
earnings of the family in the lace trade as making part of the half crown which is allowed? – Yes.
Has not that domestic manufacture of the lace trade been less profitable within these
two years than it used formerly to be? – I believe considerably less; so it is stated by
them; there is a great difficulty in selling the lace at all without taking it out in goods
in return; they cannot get ready money for their lace; they are obliged to take shop
goods in return.

You have stated, that the custom of sending labourers who have applied for parish relief, round to the different farmers for employment, had within these few years considerably increased? − It has very much increased within these last two or three years.

From your observation, what effect, if any, has that practice had upon the general conduct of the labourers with regard to their industrious habits? − A very bad effect it has had upon them, in very much diminishing their industry; those persons who are sent round go late and return early, and do not exert themselves in working.

From the parishes you are best acquainted with, can you form any opinion with regard to the proportion of the labouring poor who are in that situation of going the rounds? − I should think, in some parishes, as much as one-half nearly; but they vary considerably; sometimes there are a great many, and sometimes fewer in the same parish.

From your knowledge of your neighbourhood, do you know whether the farmers who employ roundsmen employ in the shape of roundsmen a greater number of labourers than they would employ if they employed labourers only? − I doubt whether they do; I rather think they do not; that the work is not so well done, but that they trust to the roundsmen instead of having other labourers.

Do you happen to know any farmers who employ no labourers whatever but roundsmen? − I think I have heard of several that employ no labourers, but trust to roundsmen and to their own family, their sons and so on, and that in consequence of that they have not half so many servants as they would have had; those who have one or two have depended upon roundsmen . . .

Has the burthen of the poor rates been of late years more a subject of complaint in your neighbourhood than you recollect it when you first knew that part of the country? − It has; not merely the rate, but the burthen of having the roundsmen has been a subject of complaint. . .

In point of fact, are rates levied on any persons in your parish who are in the actual situation of labouring for others? − I do not know of such an instance; the small occupiers to which I referred [of property valued at £5, the lowest property rated] are principally shopkeepers; but I apprehend that it is the case in several instances, that persons pay rates who are in the situation of labourers.

You have stated, that there has been a calculation formed, which has been acted upon, of giving an allowance of half a crown a head per week to persons having large families; was that so before you acted as a magistrate in the county? − It was not so high before the late rise in corn; but, ever since I have acted, there has been a plan of that kind, but not so thoroughly carried into effect as it is now . . .

Do you mean that the roundsmen are employed at all times, or only at the present time, when there is a great want of employment for labour? − Only when they are in want of employment; when a pauper is in want of employment he goes to the overseer, and the overseer send him to the different farmers in turn, till he can find employment for himself.

You mean, that the superfluous population are now employed as roundsmen? − Yes; the superfluous part of the population, and perhaps the worst workmen.

You say that, during the time the roundsmen are employed, the farmers do not employ more labourers than at another time? − The farmer who used to have a servant, finding there are likely to be a number of people sent round, dismisses his servant, and takes his chance of having those persons sent.

That is, if the labourer belongs to another parish? − They make an agreement amongst themselves, thinking they shall have less poor rates to pay to employ those in rotation who have no other employ; and some of the farmers dismiss their regular labourers who belong to another parish perhaps, and take them on in their turn.

He does not gain unless the labourer belongs to another parish, does he? — If he belongs to the same parish, he throws him generally upon the parish, not upon himself individually.

Is it the fact, that since the system of roundsmen has been introduced, every farmer has employed a smaller number of constant labourers? — That is generally the case.

Can you state when the system of roundsmen was first introduced? — I think it has been introduced for these dozen years, but not to so great a degree as it is at present.

Had it begun about the year 1804, when you became a magistrate? — It began to prevail about that time.

Has the rent of cottages increased or diminished, within your knowledge of Bedfordshire and Huntingdonshire? — I think the rent of cottages has increased, but is now diminishing.

Has the population increased? — Yes, I think it has; there is a great want of houses for the poor.

What may be the general rate of cottage rents? — About forty and fifty shillings.

Including a garden? — With sometimes a very small garden; hardly any garden in the parish of Eaton; in the town itself it is considerably higher; I speak particularly of the villages. . .

Do the cottagers generally hold their tenements of the proprietor of the land, or of a farmer who is the occupier? — I think there are instances of both; in several cases of the farmer, but more, I think, of the proprietor.

Is there any difference between the wages of an ordinary labourer and the wages of a roundsman? — The common price of labour is from ten to twelve shillings weekly for good workmen, but when those persons are out of work and are sent round, they very frequently, if they are single men, do not get more than half that.

Are they allowed their victuals? — No.

That rate of wages is exclusive of harvest wages? — Yes, it is.

What is the addition to the wages of the labourers in harvest? — In harvest-time they have about three pounds or four pounds for the month (it varies very much) together with their maintenance and lodging.

Does that make an addition equal to ten shillings a week? — Yes. . .

State the district to which your evidence immediately applies? — The hundred of Barford and Stodden in Bedfordshire, and the hundred of Leightonstone in Huntingdonshire.

Are there many gentry residing in the parishes to which you allude? — Not a great many. . .

Is it the custom of that part of the country in which you act as a magistrate, to apprentice the children of the poorer class of labourers to the farmers, when they exceed the age of nine years? — I think they are never apprenticed to the farmers; they are sometimes apprenticed to trades.

Is there any poor house within your parish? — Yes, there is.

What description of poor are relieved within the poorhouse? — Not only the old and the young, but other persons who go there, merely because they cannot meet with cottages to reside in.

How many will your poorhouse contain? — I should think about fifty.

Is any kind of work supplied to them or required of them in the poorhouse? — Not a sufficient degree of work; there is sometimes; but they are frequently sent out of the poorhouse to work either upon the road, or with a farmer who has jobs to do, or as roundsmen. . .

In the parish of Eaton or St. Neots is there any school upon the principle of Bell and Lancaster? — There is none in the parish of Eaton; in the parish of St. Neots I believe there is; but in the parish of Eynesbury, which immediately adjoins, there is a considerable school, under the management of the rector of the parish, and several of the Eaton children go to that school.

Is there a saving bank or friendly society in any of those parishes? – There is a saving bank at Bedford; in some of the parishes there are friendly societies, but few; there is no saving bank in the parishes.

You have stated, that you disapprove of the plan of sending roundsmen; has any other plan occurred to you for employing those men, though not the best of labourers? – I think it would be best to employ those men upon the roads, which are in a bad state in general, and it would have two good effects; in the first place it would employ those persons who are not wanted by the farmers, and it would make those persons endeavour to look out for work, which they are not desirous of doing, and therefore they throw the burden entirely upon the farmer.

Do not you conceive, that the having only half wages is a sufficient stimulus to a man to induce him to look out for work? – But he gets the remainder made up by the parish; they make up the half-crown per week for each individual in the family.

Then, in point of fact, the roundsman is as well paid as the man who finds work for himself? – If he has a large family he is, but if he has a small family he is not.

Then the fact of the allowance of half-a-crown a week to each individual makes it a complete matter of indifference to the workman himself, whether he earns ten shillings or five shillings, or what it may be? – It makes no difference to him if his family is large; if his family is small, he has so much less than he could fairly earn, that it is an object for a single man to find work for himself.

In the case of a single man, it would be from four shillings to ten or twelve shillings? – It would.

Are many of the roundsmen put out by the authority of the parish or the justices? – By agreement of the farmers among themselves.

Is any difference made with respect to the proportion of persons the farmers respectively employ? – They take them, in proportion to their rents, a certain number of days . . .

It appears by the former part of your evidence, that the population upon the whole has increased in the parishes with which you are conversant? – I think it has.

Can you attribute that increase of population to any circumstance independent of the demand for labour? – I think it depends in some measure upon the persons marrying earlier now, without having provided for a family, which they were in the habit of doing formerly, now depending upon parochial relief.

Is the use of machinery prevalent among the farmers in the parishes with which you are acquainted? – I think not quite so much as it was.

Then it is not from the increase of machinery in those parishes that the supply of labour is grown beyond the demand? – No, I think not; I think there is quite sufficient employ for every labourer, if the farmers could afford to pay them.

Have you the means of judging from your own observation, whether the state of the agriculture within those parishes has deteriorated in consequence of this state of things? – I think it has in some instances, but I think the state of agriculture in general is at a low ebb in that part of Bedfordshire.

Have the agricultural cottagers any land with their cottages? – A great many of them have pieces of waste by the side of the road for potatoe gardens, but not further than that.

To what extent? – From a rood to half a rood.

Are they in the habit of keeping a cow? – Very seldom. . .

From your experience as a magistrate, has any remedy occurred to you for the improvement of the poor laws? – I have thought, that if the magistrates had a power of ordering the poor to be employed on the roads, or any public work which would take the pressure from the farmer, it would be beneficial; and I have also thought, that if the younger children of the poor were taken and put into the poorhouse, or any place of safety, it would set the mother of the family at liberty to do some lace-making or other work, weeding or stone-gathering, which she is prevented from doing now by the care of her children of three or four years old.

Have you formed an opinion, whether the introduction of lace-making into those parishes has been upon the whole beneficial or otherwise? – I think it is beneficial; they have been lace-makers beyond my remembrance.

Do you mean that the poor set upon the road should be paid out of the poor rates, or out of some other fund? – Out of the poor rates; they are now paid out of the surveyor's rate; and the surveyor keeping a separate rate from the overseers, they do not act so much in concert as always to employ that rate to the best advantage. At the time when there is very little employment, it would be desirable to have the poor then employed upon the roads, and at the time when there is employment, then it would be desirable to take them from that work; but there being two distinct officers, they frequently do not concur.

Are you aware, that there is now a power in the magistrates to direct the employment of the poor upon the roads, if necessary? – A magistrate may certainly direct the roads to be amended, but I am not aware whether he has a control over the surveyor; that which I refer to is repairing the sides of the roads, filling up the hollows, and taking away the banks, which is seldom attended to by the surveyor, though the road may be passable, but in many things it is inconvenient and narrow; the plan I propose would make the road more commodious and employ the supernumerary labourers; I do not refer to necessary repairs of the road strictly.

15th May 1817 . . . William Wilshere, Esquire, is called in, and having been sworn, is Examined, as follows:

You reside at Hitchin in Hertfordshire, and act as magistrate for the counties of Hertford and Bedford? – I do.

And you have so done for some years? – I have.

Can you give the Committee any information with respect to cases of parishes within your knowledge, either where the poor rates have been particularly burdensome, or in the case of parishes, where the administration of the poor laws has been particularly good, where the fund raised by the rates has been well administered? – The districts in which I act, which are principally the north part of Hertfordshire and the south part of Bedfordshire, are agricultural wholly; the amount of the rates is not very high; we have no manufactories but the ordinary trades; the rates have always been moderate; I think they may be said to be under the average of the kingdom; they have increased, but I believe much less than in most other places; I should, I think, say, that the increase of last year has not added more than one-third to the rates of the preceding three or four years; not one-half has been added; I do not mean to say, that there may not be particular parishes in which one-half has been added, but the average is certainly under that.

Has it occurred to you, in your experience as a magistrate, that any alteration might be beneficially made in the poor laws, without infringing on the spirit of the 43rd of Elizabeth, which would be an improvement in the general system, as well with a view to the management of the poor as to a diminution in the charge on the occupiers of land and houses; the question referring to the mode of acquiring a settlement, as well as the appointment of a permanent officer to assist the overseers? – I think the law of settlement might be very considerably improved; the way in which settlements are obtained is scarcely a system; inconveniences have been found from the original settlement by a residence of forty days, and remedies have been applied as the occasion arose. I have always supposed, that a residence of a certain and considerable length, without being chargeable, was a fair settlement; it might be two, three, four, or five years, but I should think, that a residence of some years, without being chargeable, would be the best settlement. I have known many instances of removals after very long residence: I will state one, in which I was called upon to sign an order of removal: A man, in the early part of his life, as a servant boy or groom, spent the last part of his year's service with his master in Yorkshire, and gained a settlement there; he came back into Hertfordshire; lived there more than fifty years, without being chargeable; brought up a family, and, at the age of seventy was brought to me and another magistrate, to be removed into Yorkshire. I thought that a case of extreme hardship. I never met with any other that went all that length, but I have very often found men who have spent the best years of their lives, ten or even twenty years or more, removed, in the decline of life, to a parish, where they had no connection, and where their settlement was perhaps accidental; it has appeared to me upon that ground, as well as upon a general consideration of the subject, that the settlement by birth should only be changed for a settlement by residence for a certain number of years, without being chargeable.

You conceive that the residence of a person in a parish, without being chargeable, would be a sufficient security to the parish that such a person is a person of industrious habits? − I do not know that it is a security, but I think it places him where he ought to be placed.

In the taxation under the 43rd of Elizabeth, do you tax any person who is not the occupier of land or houses? − There is no such taxation; personal property is not taxed in the neighbourhood in which I live.

You do not tax a man because he is an inhabitant in the parish? − We do not.

Except for the house in which he resides? − Except for occupation; occupation is the rule of taxation. . .

Have you had any opportunities of seeing, from the increase of rates, persons who were rated not able to pay? − Many.

What do you do in such cases? Whenever I can (and it may now be done in some cases under a late act) I direct the charge to be struck out; where it cannot be struck out, I recommend to the parish officer not to insist upon it.

But in many instances there are distresses upon their goods? − I have signed many, when, if it was not a legal duty, it would have been an act of cruelty.

You know, independently of your own immediate practice, that it is extremely common, when persons cannot really pay the rates, for them to be enforced by distress? − Very common.

Which of the two classes of pauper do you think, in many instances, the most distressful, those who pay the rates, or those who receive them? − I think many persons paying the rates are more distressed than those who are supported by them. I think there are a great many instances, in which the persons supported at the expense of the parish are much better provided for than those who contribute to the rates.

In the parishes within your knowledge, has it been the practice to rate those who occupy from three, four or five, to ten acres? − Yes, it has been almost universal to rate those who occupy land to that extent.

However small the quantity? − Yes, of land; I distinguish that from their cottages.

Has it been the practice to assess persons for any portion of land under an acre, for gardens attached to small tenements? − I think that 20s rent of land has been the more general rule. . .

Do you know any instances, where men perfectly able to work, nevertheless, from not having employment, or from having children, who are a burden upon them, are relieved? − Very many; particularly within the last year.

In the case of a strong man, as strong as any man can be by the constitution of human nature, if it is found difficult to get employment, or he has the pressure of children upon him, you relieve him? − When it has appeared to me that the applicant had no other means of support, I have felt it my duty to order relief; I have found, on many occasions, that I have been compelled to order relief for those whose distress has arisen from their own gross improvidence; but I nevertheless felt that I was bound to order it; that they could not perish.

In cases, where a man, though an able-bodied man, cannot find employment, and you are satisfied that he cannot, or that he has such a number of children, that he cannot support them by the labour of his body, you relieve him? − I have always recommended the parish officers to find some work, and to pay them lower wages than were usually paid to other men.

You do not, in such cases, compel the poor man to sell his furniture before you relieve him? − No, certainly not. . .

But if a man has to contribute to the relief of the poor, and from loss of trade, or from the pressure of children, he is not able to pay his rates, you sell his furniture and effects? − I have been compelled to sign a warrant of distress.

So that when a man, from the want of employment, which he used to have before, or from the pressure of children, is not able to pay his rate, you sell his property to relieve the man who keeps his furniture and effects? − It is so.

Then is not the pauper that is relieved in a much better condition than the pauper who contributes? − He is so far in a better condition, that what he possesses is more secure to him.

In consequence of many, who are put upon the rates, not being able to pay, the rates are increased for those who are able to pay? − That would follow, but the bulk of the rates in the districts in which I act, are upon farms, and it is not often that the rates on farms have been lost.

You know that there are various instances of the rates being raised very high from arrears uncollected? − Yes, I do know instances, in which the farmer has run away, and left the rate to be paid by those who remained.

Then those who continue to be able to pay, though perhaps with great distress, are obliged to pay, not only for those paupers who are relieved, but for those paupers who cannot pay? − They are; in some parts of Cambridgeshire, I believe the pressure has been very great, in consequence of the failure of tenants, and their farms remaining unoccupied.

Is not this, which you have been describing, an evil which must be constantly and rapidly increasing? − I think it must go on to increase, as long as there are any means of payment; the demand will exhaust the means . . . the period at which that will happen may be accelerated or retarded, but I think it will not be very distant upon the present system.

Do you consider that, as a justice, you have the absolute power to order relief to a pauper, as long as that pauper is possessed of property? − I do conceive, that a magistrate has a power to order relief, without divesting the pauper wholly of property. I think there is no decision, nor, I believe, any dictum that precludes a magistrate from ordering relief before all the property is exhausted; I think, if a magistrate were to say, you must sell your bed (putting it in the extreme), that he would go beyond his duty; when he shall begin to order relief must be a matter of discretion; if I am right in supposing that the pauper is not to be completely exhausted, I should say, that which was necessary for his continuing in the occupation of his cottage is not required, and ought not, as the law stands, to be disposed of . . .

Are you of opinion, that the surplus population of an agricultural parish must, from time to time, go off to find employment in towns, and in the army, and other situations? – I think, in all cases, the population is likely to increase beyond the employment, and perhaps more in agricultural parishes, than in most others. . .

Is your order for relief for a fixed sum of money? – Unless in cases of permanent disability, I have made the order very short, and applicable to the occasion, for a sum of money, or sometimes for provisions, to be renewed from time to time, if the necessity continues; I have seldom ordered it for any number of weeks to come, unless in cases of permanent inability.

You think that the alteration as to the time [of residence as qualification for legal settlement] will not add to the burthen of agricultural parishes? – I think it would to the burthen, but I think it will distribute it better than any other plan I can suggest at present. A settlement may be gained much too easily; a lodging for a few weeks will enable a man to charge himself upon the parish; but, perhaps, if I am not going beyond what I ought to say, I should state that any system, under which a man is to be entitled to claim relief, because he has not the means of supporting himself, must occasion an intolerable burthen, and cannot very long go on.

What is your reason for thinking that it cannot very long go on? – Because I think that the claims upon the public will be greater than can be answered; I think the population will increase, till there will not be the means of support.

You think that the population will increase faster than the means of support? – Yes, I think that population will increase more rapidly than the means of support can be increased.

When you say, you apprehend that the population will increase beyond the means of support, do you mean beyond the means of support according to the present system of taxation upon lands and occupiers only? – Beyond the means of support upon the present system sooner, but beyond any means of support ultimately. . .

Has any considerable increase of the rates arisen of late, from the passage of persons discharged from the army or navy, through any of the parishes in the neighbourhood? – I think not considerable with us; more has been obtained by fraudulent passes than by those entitled to subsistence.

Have the farmers been great sufferers in the district for which you act? – From all the information I have obtained, they have suffered less than in almost any other part of the kingdom.

Have the rents been considerably lowered? – They have been lowered, but I should say not more than ten percent.

Compared with that period? – Compared with the highest period; a period of six or seven years since.

Do you conceive the rents are as high now, or higher than they were ten years ago? – I think there is little variation about the part of Hertfordshire or Bedfordshire, which I best know, between this time and ten years ago; they had not then attained the highest . . .

One of the causes of the increased number of poor is a want of labour? – With us, labour is lessened by the farmer being less able to pay for it. I think there are now pretty nearly the same number of labourers employed; but the labourers have increased with the increase of population, and by the return of a considerable number from the army . . .

Do you conceive it would give facility, in finding labour in a parish, if the application of the statute labour for the repair of the roads, and the amount of the composition rates levied for that purpose, were put under the management of the same officer, for the employment of the poor, and the better management of such rates? — I think there are many cases in which it would be beneficial, as the overseer would then have some labour, to which he could set those who apply to him upon the pretence of not having work; the overseer, as overseer, has seldom any work; the surveyor of the highways could set him about something. . .

What should you think of an allotment of ground for a spade cultivation? — I think, if it goes to the length of furnishing individuals with gardens for their own subsistence, it would be useful; but beyond that, and if it be to be managed as a general concern, I think that very little could be expected. . .

When you order relief, do you direct that relief to be paid by the overseers in money? — It depends upon the circumstances; where a pauper is of such a description in intelligence and character, as to lay it out for himself, he will always make more of it than can be made by the overseer; but where there is reason to suppose that it would be applied improperly, I have often directed relief in potatoes or flour, bread or fuel. . .

It is occasionally your practice to order relief in clothing and fuel? — I have ordered it in every thing that the pauper could want; and, where I could not trust the pauper, have directed the particular articles to be furnished. . .

Do you conceive that the establishment of friendly societies and provident banks would be generally beneficial with a view to the comfort of the poor, and to render them less dependent upon the rates? — Whatever creates another fund for the relief of the pauper is, no doubt, beneficial to the parish; if he appropriate a fund at his own expense, he secures the parish to that extent against a claim upon them.

Does it not frequently happen, that young able-bodied men, without families, apply to you and to the other magistrates for employment? — It has happened at all times; but more within the last year than at any former period.

Do you consider, that, as a justice, you have a power of ordering the overseers to find employment for such able-bodied young men without families? — I think that I have not the power to order the overseers to find them work; but if it appear to me that the man cannot obtain work, or, in other words, that he has no other means of subsistence, I can order the overseer to pay him money; it brings itself round to that I should certainly say to the overseer, and have often said, "Can you find this man employment?". If he could not find him employment, and it appeared to me that the man had no means of subsistence, I should order him relief.

There is a clause in the act, directing the magistrate to find employment for those who cannot procure it? — Yes, and as far as it has been practicable it has been done with us, principally on the roads; I have never made an order in writing simply to find work; but overseers, where they could find work, have usually done so.

Has it been the custom within your parish for the superfluous labourers to go the rounds among the farmers? — Not in the parish in which I live; but in many villages it is the custom . . . It has produced dissatisfaction on both sides.

You were understood to say, you had recommended that the surplus labourers should be employed occasionally, at low wages, among the farmers; have those low wages been paid by the farmers, or charged upon the rates? — The wages, when they were employed by the overseer, have been charged upon the rates; the way in which the poor that I have directed to be employed have usually been employed, has been in the repair of the highways; and the surveyor of the highways in that case has paid their wages, or a proportion of them.

Has the effect of this been, that in any instances a farmer has had his necessary labour done for lower than the average rate? — I believe that has been the effect in many parishes; I think more in Bedfordshire than in Hertfordshire; I think there are many parishes in which so great a proportion of the labourers have been made roundsmen, that the employer has paid less wages, and the parish paid what ought to have been paid by him. . .

Do you think the building cottages in country parishes an advantageous system for the labourers in general? — It is better for the labourer that he should live alone in a comfortable cottage, better for his morals, and better in every view. The objection I should have to cottages arises from what I have before stated on the poor laws, that whatever invites an increase of population increases the evil.

Do not you consider, that making the simple fact of residence a settlement for a person, will operate as a great discouragement to build in parishes; and that the poor will in that case be driven more into towns? — I think it might have that effect. . .

What is the rate of labour in your parish? — The lowest rate of labour is nine shillings per week.

Is that sufficient for the support of a man and his family? — It will keep them, I think, in health; it is extremely low, but I think it will support them.

If a man has a large family, will it support them? — No; I have computed that three-pence per day for an individual, is the lowest rate at which they can be subsisted in health.

Are you in the habit of ordering relief, in addition to the wages, to a person with a large family? — I do it very cautiously and very sparingly, and not till I am convinced that they have not the means of subsistence without.

Do you do it merely with reference to the size of their family, or with reference to their character and habits ? — I have not thought myself at liberty to consider their character and habits.

In the quarter sessions of the counties in which you act, has there been any statement made of what the magistrates conceive to be sufficient for the subsistence of an individual? — None in Bedfordshire or Hertfordshire.

In the part of Bedfordshire and Hertfordshire you know best, is there the domestic manufacture of straw platting? — Considerable in Hertfordshire, and now it is becoming general in Bedfordshire.

Is not the produce of that a considerable assistance in the maintenance of a family? — Very considerable; the wife and the children can often earn more than the husband.

Then the labourer, his wife and his children, have other means of subsistence besides the wages of labour that he earns? — Very considerable in some instances.

Do you speak of the present moment? — I speak of the present moment, and it has been extending for ten years; a great deal has been earned by straw platting.

Has any inconvenience arisen from the straw platting, in consequence of the parents being disinclined to let their children go into service, as earning more in straw platting than at service? — The girls have been brought up ignorant of every thing but of straw platting.

Has there been a want of servants? — Yes, there has been a difficulty, particularly when straw plat was sold at the highest rates.

Have you national schools established in your neighbourhood? — There is a general school established in the town of Hitchin, and there are very extensive Sunday schools, as well as a free school; there is an opportunity for education to every one.

Do the manufactures tend to keep the children from the school? — The straw platting does tend to keep girls from the schools.

Are the poor labourers in your district supplied with cottages? — There is a want of cottages.

Do those who have them pay the rent for them? — Generally they do.

You do not reckon them to be able to do that upon the three-pence a day? — No: I take that as the lowest rate of subsistence, applying to food only, and I mention it rather as a rule, which I have laid down in considering relief. . .

Is there any number of parishes within your knowledge, to which there are charitable donations or estates to any considerable extent? – Yes; there are charitable donations in the parish in which I reside, to the amount, I think, of from four to five hundred pounds a year.

Has it been the practice to employ the income of those estates in aid of the rates generally, or in the apprenticing children, or in what way? – The application of the greater part is regulated according to the donation; very little indeed is applied to the poor generally; there are two or three small old donations for the support of the poor; donations made before there were poor laws; those with us, however, are not applied in reduction of the rates, but are given to those who are supposed to be the most deserving poor . . .

You have said, that three-pence a day was sufficient for the support of an individual; in what manner would you lay it out? – I think they would lay it out much better than I can; I meant to speak of three-pence per day as a minimum. With your Lordships permission, I will explain myself on that head; thinking it improper that a parish should be ordered to pay more for the support of paupers, than the lowest rate at which a labourer can provide for himself and his family, I ascertained, by inquiry and personal examination, that in many instances a man, his wife, and from three to five children, were supported upon his earnings of ten, eleven, or twelve shillings per week, without assistance from the parish; and I laid it down as a rule to myself, not to order for a family in health more than would make up 1s 9d weekly for every one of the family. I am speaking of families in which there are young children, and of a temporary allowance; if the necessity for relief should continue, something must be added for clothing and rent. An individual could not be supported at the same rate.

In that three-pence you do not include either lodging, fuel, or clothes? – No, subsistence only, feeling it my duty to keep the relief ordered within as narrow a compass as I could. . .

Select Committee of the House of Lords on the Poor Laws, 1818   *BPP 1818 V*

2.1.2   In 1824 a second and more comprehensive investigation was carried out by another Parliamentary committee. Bedfordshire evidence was provided in considerable quantity not only by magistrates and overseers of the poor but also by a village labourer from Eversholt near Woburn.

Among the more sophisticated arrangements for administering the Poor Law before 1834 was that of the "Labour Rate", by which ratepayers could opt for payment of a poor rate or to employ labour at agreed wages. Thomas Bowyer, a Bedfordshire overseer, explained to the Select Committee how the system operated at Wilden. It involved each Labourer being assessed at a standard minimum wage.

. . . Here is a Statement of the manner in which it is acted upon in the parish of Wilden; it is put in practice in that parish, and many other parishes.

"At a Vestry Meeting, in the Parish of Wilden, in the County of Bedford, held pursuant to public Notice, on Wednesday the 7th Day of November, 1821.

William Day, Esq. in the Chair.

It was unanimously Resolved:

That a levy of one shilling and four-pence in the pound, should be paid by every occupier of land in the said parish of Wilden, as a rate, for the relief of the poor; or, to meet the amount required, to employ the labouring poor of the said parish for six weeks, from Monday, the 17th instant.

Sir,

I Have to inform you, that the amount assessed on you, agreeable to the above resolution, is £73; £4 13s 6d of which you have the opportunity of discharging, by employing at any time during the six weeks, men or boys named in the list annexed, at a rate not less than stated opposite their respective names, (as much more as you please or can agree on). I inclose for your government, papers to make your weekly returns on, which I shall be obliged by your filling up regularly, and returning at your convenience to the overseer of this parish. The amount calculated to be required for labourers for six weeks, is £109 13s; amount of assessment, £110 16s.

I am, Sir, your most obedient servant,
Thomas Davis, Observer.

List of Labourers, and Pay per Week

Watts, James.	6s	Franks, James.	9s
Peete, Woodham	8s	Ball, James.	6s
Lovell, John	7s	Pantelow, John	6s
Fensome, James	7s	Gadsden, William, sen.	9s
Simpson, William.	9s	Dawson, William	9s
Fuller, James	7s	Favell, William	9s
Fairey, William	9s	Swales, William, sen.	6s
Dunham, Richard	8s	Swales, William, jun.	6s
King, John	8s	Clayton, William	8s
Gadsden, William, jun.	7s	Pell, Edward.	6s
Fensom, John.	9s	Pell, Thomas.	8s
Worley, Edward	8s	Townes, William	6s
Bull, Samuel.	6s	Bell, Robert	6s
Masters, William	6s	Ambridge, Edward.	6s
Cope, William	6s	Mayes, John	8s
Fuller, John	9s	Ambridge, John	6s
Pope, Thomas.	8s	Rust, William	8s

Fuller, William	8s	**Boys — Large**	
Bull, George	8s	Fuller, John	3s
Draper, Thomas	9s	Fuller, William	3s
Lovell, Samuel	8s	Lovell, William	3s
Johnson, William	6s	Lovell, James	3s
		James, William	3s
		Gadsden, Joseph	3s
		Rust, John	3s
Boys — Less		Law, William	3s
Fensom, George	2s	Franks, William	3s
Fensom, James	2s 6d	Ambridge, Benjamin	3s
Lovell, Robert	2s	Mayes, Joseph	3s
Gadsden, Samuel	2s	Favell, Elijah	3s
Dawson, John	2s 6d	Johnson, John	3s
Dawson, William	2s 6d	Pell, Edward	3s
Rust, James	2s 6d	Clapham, William	3s
Pell, Eli	2s 6d	Ball, Samuel	3s
Mayes, Reuben	2s 6d	Peete, John	3s
Fuller, John	1s 6d"	Peete, William	3s

Does the list of labourers contained in this paper contain all the labourers in the parish? — Certainly.

It includes those with families, as well as single men? — Yes.

Did any of those labourers receive allowances from the parish, in addition to what the farmers have paid them? — Very large families would receive something in addition.

It appears that some of the labourers are marked 6s 7s 8s and 9s; is that according to the size of their families? — No, according to the value of their labour.

Those that are called large boys are young men, single men? — Yes, single men; the farmer was obliged to pay those prices; he might give them what he thought proper more, but he was obliged to give them those prices.

Did some of them receive no more than 3s a week? — Not according to the labour rate.

What age were those boys? — That is mentioned in the particulars in the book; that plan is not acted upon in the parish in which I live; but that has been acted upon very generally in the county. . . .

Select Committee on Labourers' Wages, 1824,   *BPP 1824 VI*

Under the Old Poor Law one commonly used system of applying poor relief was the Roundsman system. Thomas Todd a poor law overseer from Woburn

*told the 1824 Select Committee on Labourers' Wages how it worked in his
district.*

. . . Can you state any thing, with respect to the neighbouring parishes with
which you are acquainted, as to the practice of paying the wages of labour
out of the poor rate? — I can give some account of it, because I have made it
my business to look into it. In the parish of Crawley, they have been in the
practice, and are in the practice now, of sending the men out upon the round;
and the employer pays the men one-half, and the other half is paid from the
parish books at this present time; and there have been some instances where a
man has been paid almost entirely out of the parish book without receiving
any thing from the employer at all.

Do you or do you not believe that the employer, in those cases, gets
labour which he must necessarily have, cheaper than he ought to get it? — He
certainly does. In the parish of Eversholt they are more particularly young
men, that are not married; they send them out on the round, and they allow
them only half a crown a week.

The labour you speak of is labour done on farms? — Yes, they give them
tickets, and by so doing their spirit of independence is entirely broken, and
the men do not care whether they are employed or not; the farmer pays the
men fourpence a day for their work.

Do you know this of your own knowledge? — I took it from the overseer's
book.

In what way were the entries made in that book? — Such a person so much
per week for labour; every man's name is mentioned in the book regularly.

Is there an entry of the farm upon which the man is employed? — No, but
the overseer gives a ticket, and he knows who they send them out to.

They do not enter that in the books? — No; young men they allow to have
half-a-crown a week; men that are married they allow to have 6s a week; men
that have six or seven children have 8s a week; and if they have more than
that, they have 10s a week, and the farmer pays four-pence a day for their
labour.

Do you believe that the farmer gets the necessary labour on his farm for
four-pence a day? — He gets all the labour of the men that are sent him.

They are not employed in superfluous work, but in the necessary work of
his farm? The necessary work of his farm; boys that are sent out are wholly
paid by the parish; they allow them to have from eighteen-pence to two
shillings and half-a-crown a week.

In Eversholt parish, are there many persons paying that rate who are not
farmers? — There are not a great many, but there are a few individuals; in the
parish of Crawley the farmer pays one-half, and the other half is paid out of
the book, except in a few instances.

How long has this been going on? — More or less for a number of years. . .

But Philip Hunt a Bedford Magistrate explained to the same committee that the roundsman system had been open to abuse and in 1819 the Bedford Quarter Sessions had issued a resolution to suppress the practice of using roundsmen – but with only limited success.

. . . may I here be allowed to put in some resolutions that the magistrates of Bedfordshire came to on this subject, at the general quarter sessions held at Bedford, on Wednesday the 13th of January 1819:—

(It was delivered in, and read, as follows:)

"*Resolved,*

"1st. That the system of roundsmen, or paying labourers a certain portion of their labour out of the parish poor rates, which has too long prevailed in this county, is destructive of the moral energies of the labourer, and equally injurious to the interests of the farmer, who has a right to expect a fair and adequate portion of labour from the hands employed on his farm.

"2d. That, in order to discourage this pernicious practice, we recommend to the several magistrates in this county, within their respective divisions, not to allow in future any sums which shall, after the first day of February next, be so paid out of the poor rates, in the overseer's accounts.

"3d. That a sufficient number of these resolutions be printed and circulated forthwith, and advertised in the Northampton Mercury and Bedford Gazette.

(signed) "William Wilshere, Chairman".

Has the practice continued, notwithstanding that resolution? – In some parishes it continues to this day, but it has produced this good effect, that much fewer men in each parish are considered as roundsmen than were employed formerly.

Why is it, do you suppose, that the practice has been continued in other parishes? – From the supposed profit gained by the farmers in obtaining labourers at the low rate fixed by the parish.

Is it expensive, to those who wish to appeal against the rate, to apply at the petty sessions to get it quashed? – I conceive it to be by no means an expensive proceeding.

Is it so troublesome as to prevent persons from taking that method? – I have only known one instance, in the county of Bedford, in which an appeal has been made to the quarter sessions against the expenditure of a rate, part of which had been paid to labourers for work done on farms of individuals, when the overseer was ordered to repay the money out of his own pocket that had been so expended.

That was an appeal against the order, was not it? – No; I think it was an appeal against the overseer's accounts of the expenditure of the year.

What is the use of appealing to the quarter sessions, if the petty sessions can disallow them? – The petty sessions generally allow the overseers to verify their annual accounts of expenditure, if the parishioners have met in vestry, and have overlooked their books; but if an individual parishioner comes forward, and says, "I can show that sums have been entered in that book for labour done on the farms of A.B. and C. and not for the support of the poor and impotent," then an appeal may be made to the quarter sessions, and the quarter sessions determine whether the money has been properly or improperly expended, and make the requisite order.

Then, in fact, persons who wish for redress are obliged to apply at the quarter sessions? — Yes; I think that is the course that a person dissatisfied with the expenditure of the poor rates must pursue.

Do not you believe, that either the expense or the trouble deter many people from appealing? — Perhaps there may be a want of knowledge of the means of redress in those who are, or think themselves aggrieved, and there must, I conceive, be some expense in the proceeding, as a brief must be prepared, and the court moved by counsel, and other expenses connected with an appeal may be incurred by a complainant.

You know that it is a most unjust proceeding, that an individual, already aggrieved, should be saddled with a further expense? — Yes.

Can you state any other plan which has been adopted? — I have already mentioned two plans, one of which was, sending a certain number of labourers round to the farmers; the other is, employing men entirely on the roads, or in digging gravel. . .

Hunt explained that few Bedfordshire farm workers could live on their wages: —
. . . What is the course which a labourer takes to increase his income or wages, when he marries and has a family? — He applies to the overseer of the parish for assistance; and that assistance in general is doled out in so limited a way, that very few labourers marry voluntarily.

Select Committee on Labourers' Wages, 1824,   *BPP 1824 VI pp.33-53*

A Bedfordshire farm labourer, Thomas Smart, was called to give evidence on 12 April 1824.

Thomas Smart, called in; and Examined.
Where do you live? — At Eversholt, in Bedfordshire.
Have you been employed there as a labourer for many years? — Yes, twenty years; I was seven years a labourer at Sir Gregory Page's before that.
Have you been married? — I have been married 28 years.
How old are you? — Forty-six.
How many children have you had? — Thirteen.

Have you ever received any relief from the parish for the support of any of those children? — For funerals, when any of them died, but not otherwise.

How many children have you alive now? — Seven; I buried six.

During the sickness of your children, have you had no assistance? — No, only for burying them.

What have been your wages for the last five years? — Ten shillings and eight shillings.

Is that summer and winter? — In harvest we have more; the last two years I have had 8s and the three years before that we had 10s and they have sunk us down to 8s.

What had you in harvest time? — Forty shillings and our food for the month of harvest.

Have you had that every year? — Yes.

Then the food was the only addition to your wages in harvest time? — Nothing else.

Do you belong to any benefit society? — I belong to a club; I have been in it 24 years.

Has your wife been able to earn any thing besides those wages? — She always did as far as she could.

Had you or your wife any thing when you married? — Nothing at all.

Have your children obtained any thing by their labour for you? — We kept them at work as soon as they were able.

What have they been able to obtain? — Platting and lace making.

How much have they been earning in a week? — I do not know; the platting and lace making is gone, and they cannot earn anything hardly.

How much in the last year? — The oldest would earn about 3s a week, and the youngest would come in; I have only one boy.

How many of them can assist you with their labour? — Three.

At what age do they begin to earn any thing? — About nine.

From that age up to the oldest, how much have they got you per week, the average, for the last year? — About 2s a week each.

Have you had pretty constant employment summer and winter? — Always pretty constant employment.

Have you been employed upon the same farm? — Yes.

What master have you worked for? — For Sir Gregory Page seven years, and then he died; then I had a fresh master to seek.

Have you had the same master for some years after that? — Yes.

Has the employment been pretty constant for your children in the lace-making? — Pretty constant, only very low.

What have you paid for your rent? — Fifty shillings a year.

What have you paid for your coals every year? — I have generally paid as much for wood or firing as I have for rent, or rather more.

How much have you paid a year to this club to which you belong? — It costs me about one pound a year, it is fifteen pence a month.

Have you ever had assistance in sickness from the benefit club? — I have never had but a month's pay out of the benefit club since I have been in it.

What is the food on which you have supported yourself and your family? — Bread and cheese, and what we could get; sometimes we were short, and sometimes we got enough for them.

Did you get meat on Sundays? — I have not had a bit of meat for a month together sometimes.

What do you drink? — Water.

Have you no bacon? — We get a little bacon; that is the chief meat we get when we get any.

You do not keep a pig? — No.

Have you a garden? — Yes.

Is that of much use to you? — A great deal of use to me.

Do you get potatoes? — Yes, I get plenty of potatoes.

Do you ever get any milk? — Now and then we get a halfpenny-worth of milk, but the farmers are very shy of letting us have it.

What wages had you by week in 1813? — I have never had more than 2s a day.

You had then 12s a week? — Yes, when I was under Mr. Potts, about eight years ago.

Were you much better able to live then than you are now? — No, I could not get so much as I can now, particularly because my children are grown up, and they help me.

Have you had no kind friends to assist you in any way occasionally? — None.

Have you potatoes every day? — Yes, I get potatoes every day.

What is the extent of your garden? — I do not know; it is a good bit of ground, it is a good bit under a rood.

Does that grow potatoes sufficient for your family? — We make it serve us.

How many bushels of potatoes do you suppose it grows in a year? — On an average about 18 bushels.

Do you use tea in your family? — Yes.

And sugar? — No, sometimes we do not.

Do you have tea for breakfast? — The children do, and sometimes water gruel, and what we can get; we cannot get tea always.

Do you find tea do better for them than other things? — Not so well as water gruel.

Do not you find it answer to keep a pig, having a garden? — I could not afford to buy one.

If you had been able to afford to buy one, you think it would have answered? – Yes, it would have answered if I could have bought one and kept it.

Have the poor felt any benefit from getting salt cheaper? – That is a great easement to us, we cannot do without it.

Do you find you get it cheaper than you used? – Yes.

Does it make much difference in your expense? – It makes a trifle.

A man is able to salt a pig now that could not salt one before? – If he has got one it would come a good deal easier with the salt.

Have you any idea what your clothes for yourself and your family have cost you in a year? – My shoes cost about 15s a year, for a pair of strong shoes to go to work in, and the rest of my family makes it another pound. I dare say it stands me in 2 £ for shoe bills.

Did you ever know of a practice in your parish of paying a part of the wages of labour out of the poor rate? – They do at this time.

Do they do it as much as they used to do, or did they do it more a few years ago? – They did not use to do it as they do now.

They do it now more than ever? – Yes.

The men to whom they pay this money have families of children? – Yes; they take it out of the parish; they have an allowance from the parish.

Have you ever applied to them for any addition to your wages? – No, I never did; I always try to do without.

How low have you known labour to be had by the farmer that was paid in that way? – As low as 7s.

At a time when the general rate of labour was 8s? – Yes.

Have not you sometimes known a farmer get his labour cheaper than he ought? – They give them fourpence a day when it is paid out of the round.

Then the farmer gets a benefit by that? – Yes; the tradespeople help to pay it.

Do you know any labourers with so large a family as you have, who have brought them up without assistance from the parish? – Never one but me.

Do you not find tea much dearer than gruel for your children? – A good deal; but they are sickly sometimes, and they cannot have gruel always.

Do not you think, that tea is less wholesome for them than gruel? – Gruel is wholesomer than tea, a good deal.

Is your cottage kept in good repair? – Very good.

Have you ever worked by the piece? – Sometimes.

What do you earn then? – Then I can earn 2s a day, when I work by piece.

Without distressing yourself? – Yes.

What would be the daily wages when you can earn 2s a day by piece work? Sixteen-pence.

Can you always get work by piece? – No, not always; now and then I get a job by piece.

You prefer it, of course? — Yes.

You would like always to be working by piece? — I should like always to work by piece, if I could get it.

Are any of your children capable of working with you? — They are all girls, except the youngest; he is a boy; he is five years old.

Is it much the practice in your parish to give work by piece? — Sometimes there is a job, but not very often.

Where do you reckon your settlement to be? — In Eversholt.

So that if you had any thing to claim from the parish, that would be the parish from which you would receive it? — Yes.

What is the greatest number of children you have had alive at one time? — Eleven.

Do you cut down much timber? — I do sometimes.

Upon those occasions, you have a right always to as large a faggot as you can carry home? — No; they will not allow us any now.

Then you have it in pay, do not you? — No.

Select Committee on Labourers' Wages, 1824,   *BPP 1824 VI pp. 53-6*

2.1.3.   *About the year 1830, the parish of Bletsoe worked out a table to show what income the Industrious Poor should have, depending on the size of the family, and the price of bread, Beds. C.R.O. P 36/12. See Plate I.*

2.1.4   *It was always difficult to estimate a labourer's budget. In January 1830 the Bedford Estate Chief Steward in London, W. G. Adam, estimated weekly payments as: rent 1s; bread 1½ quartern loaves @ 10d, 1s 3d; 3½ lbs bacon @ 8d, 2s 4d; 1 pint of beer a day @ 3d, 1s 9d; tobacco, 6d; tea or coffee and sugar 6d. This came to 7s 4d, and he did not estimate for potatoes, butter, firing, coal and clothes. In reply Edward Crocker, the Steward at Woburn, wrote on 2 January 1830:*

I believe the following to be an exaggerated account. I fear there will always be this difficulty in ascertaining the details of a Labourer's expenditure — that when asked for the information, they will be inclined to suspect the purpose for which it is required, and make the most of it. A man, his wife and 4 young children:

Bread — 8 quartern, or 4 lb loaves @ 10d	6s	8d
Meat or bacon — 3½ lb @ 7d	2s	0½d
Potatoes		8d
Coffee and Sugar, Milk and butter		10½d
Candles and Firing	1s	2d
	11s	5d
Rent	1s	
	12s	5d

In this case the house belonged to him, and he paid no rent. It is built upon the waste land at Ridgmount. He could not tell the cost of clothing, and stated he very seldom drank any beer. He is an industrious, steady man (one of the Carters) and earns exactly upon the average 12s 3d per week, that is, 11s 8d in the winter and 12s 10d in the summer. He could not explain to me how he paid for his clothing, for himself and family, but said he was a little in debt . . . The amount for each article (except perhaps for bread and potatoes, and I forgot to ask him if he did not grow the latter) does not appear too much for a family six in number, yet I suspect it is overrated. I believe he is behind hand, as he some time back, asked for an advance of wages stating his inability to support his family upon his earnings, being as I thought, quite enough for his labour . . . I believe his eldest child is only 4 years of age, and his wife has been very ill, and I do think it hard in his case, that he cannot obtain relief from the parish for the reason his house belongs to him . . . I have likewise spoken to a Labourer who is single — he is certainly one of the better order of his class, honest, sober and industrious. He tells me that he can keep himself well and comfortably for 7s per week. He cannot give me the details as he did not board himself . . . I have been told by as many as 12 or 14 men in His Grace's employ that they can do very well, when the family altogether including himself and wife, does not exceed six, with 12s per week, and find their own tools, without parish aid, if it happens that they have a good Hay and Harvest Season. If otherwise, they would require assistance to make up their loss. The tools of the woodmen . . . are very expensive, they state as much as 1s a week . . . I am satisfied from all I have learnt . . . that 10s per week is the lowest wages that should be given to an efficient labourer, whether single or married, according to the present cost of bread, meat etc.

I feel it necessary to press upon your consideration the Rents exacted from the Labourers round here. In every instance where they are not His Grace's tenants, the lowest price at which they can obtain two rooms, is 2s per week, miserable places, and no gardens.

Beds. C.R.O. R 3/2855,3574. See also B.H.R.S. 57 pp. 86-8.

Scale to show at one view, what should be the Weekly Income of the Industrious Poor [circa 1830].

The Earnings are to be considered in the calculations, or including all earnings.

When the price of Bread per ½ peck loaf is	For a Man	A Single Woman	Man and Wife	with 1 child	with 2 children	with 3 children	with 4 children	with 5 children	with 6 children	with 7 children
s. d.	s. d.	s. d.	s. d.	s. d.	s. d.	s. d.	s. d.	s. d.	s. d.	s. d.
1. 0.	3. 0.	2. 0.	4. 6.	6. 0.	7. 6.	9. 0.	10. 6.	12. 0.	13. 6.	15. 0.
1. 1.	3. 3.	2. 1.	4. 10.	6. 5.	8. 0.	9. 7.	11. 2.	12. 9.	14. 4.	15. 11.
1. 2.	3. 6.	2. 2.	5. 2.	6. 10.	8. 6.	10. 2.	11. 10.	13. 6.	15. 2.	16. 10.
1. 3.	3. 9.	2. 3.	5. 6.	7. 3.	9. 0.	10. 9.	12. 6.	14. 3.	16. 0.	17. 9.
1. 4.	4. 0.	2. 4.	5. 10.	7. 8.	9. 6.	11. 4.	13. 2.	15. 0.	16. 10.	18. 8.
1. 5.	4. 3.	2. 5.	6. 2.	8. 1.	10. 0.	11. 11.	13. 10.	15. 9.	17. 8.	19. 7.
1. 6.	4. 6.	2. 6.	6. 6.	8. 6.	10. 6.	12. 6.	14. 6.	16. 6.	18. 6.	1. 0. 6.
1. 7.	4. 9.	2. 7.	6. 10.	8. 11.	11. 0.	13. 1.	15. 2.	17. 3.	19. 4.	1. 1. 5.
1. 8.	5. 0.	2. 8.	7. 2.	9. 4.	11. 6.	13. 8.	15. 10.	18. 0.	1. 0. 2.	1. 2. 4.
1. 9.	5. 3.	2. 9.	7. 6.	9. 9.	12. 0.	14. 3.	16. 6.	18. 9.	1. 1. 0.	1. 3. 3.
1. 10.	5. 6.	2. 10.	7. 10.	10. 2.	12. 6.	14. 10.	17. 2.	19. 6.	1. 1. 10.	1. 4. 2.
1. 11.	5. 9.	2. 11.	8. 2.	10. 7.	13. 0.	15. 5.	17. 10.	1. 0. 3.	1. 2. 8.	1. 5. 1.
2. 0.	6. 0.	3. 0.	8. 6.	11. 0.	13. 6.	16. 0.	18. 6.	1. 1. 0.	1. 3. 6.	1. 6. 0.
2. 1.	6. 3.	3. 1.	8. 10.	11. 5.	14. 0.	16. 7.	19. 2.	1. 1. 9.	1. 4. 4.	1. 6. 11.
2. 2.	6. 6.	3. 2.	9. 2.	11. 10.	14. 6.	17. 2.	19. 10.	1. 2. 6.	1. 5. 2.	1. 7. 10.
2. 3.	6. 9.	3. 3.	9. 6.	12. 3.	15. 0.	17. 9.	1. 0. 6.	1. 3. 3.	1. 6. 0.	1. 8. 9.
2. 4.	7. 0.	3. 4.	9. 10.	12. 8.	15. 6.	18. 4.	1. 1. 2.	1. 4. 0.	1. 6. 10.	1. 9. 8.
2. 5.	7. 3.	3. 5.	10. 2.	13. 1.	16. 0.	18. 11.	1. 1. 10.	1. 4. 9.	1. 7. 8.	1. 10. 7

Bletsoe Overseer's account book.   Beds. C.R.O.   P 36/12

PLATE I

2.1.3

2.2   Reform of the Poor Laws

In 1834 a Royal Commission was appointed to enquire into the administration and operation of the Poor Laws. It included a rural questionnaire that was published as an appendix containing evidence from a number of counties that happened to come first on a list of English counties in alphabetical order, and included Bedfordshire, Berkshire, Buckinghamshire, Cambridgeshire, Cheshire, Cornwall and Cumberland. The Bedfordshire parishes of Blunham, Bromham, Caddington, Cople, Kempston, Lidlington, Maulden, Meppershall, Northill, Podington, Sharnbrook, Southill cum Warden, Turvey, Westoning and Willington provided evidence.

Report from His Majesty's Commissioners for inquiring into the Administration and Practical Operation of the Poor Laws. London 1834.

Extracts from the Questions and (A) (C) Parliamentary Documents:

(A) Population in 1831.

(C) Expense per head on the whole Population in 1831.

4. Number of Labourers sufficient for the proper cultivation of the Land?
5. Number of Agricultural Labourers in your Parish?
7. How many Non-Parishioners have you in general, distinguishing Irish and Scotch?
24. Have you any, and how many, able-bodied Labourers in the Employment of Individuals receiving Allowance or regular Relief from your Parish on their own Account, or on that of their Families; and if on account of their Families, at what Number of Children does it begin?
25. Is Relief or Allowance given according to any and what Scale?
29. Is there any and what Difference between the Wages paid by the Employer to the Married and Unmarried, when employed by Individuals?
37. Is the Industry of the Labourers in your Neighbourhood supposed to be increasing or diminishing; that is, are your Labourers supposed to be better or worse Workmen than they formerly were?
38. Do the Labourers in your Neighbourhood change their Services more frequently than formerly? and how do you account for that circumstance?
53. Can you give the Commissioners any information respecting the causes and consequences of the Agricultural Riots and Burnings of 1830 and 1831?

[In the following returns, questions to which no reply was given are omitted.]

BLUNHAM-CUM-MUGGERHANGER
J. H. B. Mountain, Rector and J.P.; *Robert Judd*, Overseer

A   580.
C   14s 7d.
5.   120.   *R.J.*
7.   Forty. No Irish or Scotch.   *R.J.*
24.   During the Winter and Spring a large proportion of them.   *J.H.B.M.*
      Generally no allowance on account of large families. No wages paid directly out
      of the Poor Rates.   *R.J.*
25.   The Magistrates prescribe no scale, but decide on individual cases.   *J.H.B.M.*
29.   Generally none.   *J.H.B.M.*
      None.   *R.J.*
37.   They are much degenerated; and being generally disaffected to their employers,
      they work unwillingly and wastefully. The disaffection is in a great measure to
      be attributed to continual disputes respecting the Parish Relief, and it has
      doubtless been aggravated by agitators.   *J.M.*
38.   They are addicted to change their service, from a restless and dissatisfied temper
      which prevails among them.   *J.M.*
53.   In this neighbourhood the object has been, by keeping the Farmers in awe, to
      extort higher wages, and a greater parochial allowance: when this is refused,
      policy and revenge produce incendiarism. It has been threatened in Vestry
      where relief has been refused, and the relief has, in consequence, been granted.

BROMHAM
J. J. Goodall, Vicar of Bromham and Oakley

A.   324.
C.   £1 0s 5d.
4.   53.
5.   53.
7.   Five; neither Irish nor Scotch.
24.   None in the employment of individuals. The allowance begins at three children,
      1s per week, and increases 1s for each child under 10 years of age.
25.   Relief is afforded at the rate of 1s per week for every child above two, and less
      than 10 years of age.
29.   1s difference occasionally.
37.   Much the same as usual.
38.   No difference perceptible.
53.   Private enmity; perhaps excited by the very general diffusion of inflammatory
      Journals.

CADDINGTON
H. B. Morris, Woodside Farm

A.   386.
C.   13s 10d.
4.   I do not know.
5.   I do not know; there are not enough labourers in harvest, although there is a
      surplus of them in winter; partly real; partly artificial.
7.   There are as many non-parishioners resident as parishioners. There are no Irish
      or Scotch.

24. No allowance is given to able-bodied labourers in the employment of individuals, on account of themselves or families, with the exception of cases of illness in families. I think the Overseer in this parish did once take some work of a gentleman, who paid him a sum of money. The Overseer agreed to do the work for that sum, and paid the labourers by the grate: of course the Overseer was out of pocket by the job. In the adjoining parish a brick-kiln has just been erected by a Quaker, who actually calculates on a profit by giving his work to the adjoining Overseers at a low price, rather than employ men himself to dig his clay.

25. No scale of allowance; all permanent relief is considered and fixed by a vestry.

29. No distinction is made.

37. No difference.

38. No.

53. No riotings have taken place. Several large fires took place in Dunstable parish, which were attributed to two individuals, who wanted to create a revolution; they have now enlisted as soldiers. The Duke of Bedford's farm at Lewsey, in Luton parish, was totally burnt: this was the work of some individual who owed a spite against the tenant. Another fire destroyed a farm in Flamstead parish; it was attributed to an individual who owed the tenant a grudge for preventing him committing petty thefts on his hedges and turnips; the man was tried and acquitted.

COPLE

J. Clayton, Churchwarden

A. 643.

C. £1 1s 4d.

4. Above 50 men and 20 boys.

5. About 83 men; from 30 to 40 boys.

7. Very few. No Irish nor Scotch.

24. For able-bodied labourers, receiving an allowance on account of their families. Allowance is made to large families exceeding four children. Work done for individuals is not partly paid for by the parish.

25. The scale of allowance, where required, is from 1s 6d to 1s 9d per head, including families. Infirm men and widows at from 3s to 4s weekly.

29. Not much difference when by the day-work; but the married men with families are mostly preferred in giving them work by the piece. Single men, if by the day, have from 6s to 9s per week.

37. Labourers considered not such good workmen as formerly: accounted for by the surplus number of men and boys unemployed, except on the round system.

38. Less change of service than formerly, there being less hiring by the year, on account of gaining settlements.

53. Generally supposed to originate from the dissatisfaction of able-bodied young labourers, being out of regular employment, (excepting the gravelpit or round system) associating together, and not getting such wages as they demanded.

KEMPSTON

G. O. Fenwicke, Vicar and J.P.

A. 1,571.

C. £1 7s 7d.

4. The men actually employed. The poor laws, as at present administered, act as a bounty upon marriage; nor can they be materially altered, until by some means or another the number of labourers be made proportionable to the work our parish can afford them, which can only be done by an extensive emigration. In

this case relief might be restricted to the aged, infirm, and sick, as it was formerly done.

5.   350.

7.   All the persons residing at Kempston belong to it. No Irish or Scotch.

24. No work done for individuals is paid for by the parish. We have 53 agricultural labourers receiving weekly allowance from the parish on account of their families. When a man has a wife and 3 children, which children are under 10 years old, he has 1s 6d per week in addition to his earnings; if 4 children, 3s; and if 5 children, 4s.

25. There is no particular scale, but relief is given according to circumstances.

29. No distinction is made between the married and single when employed by individuals.

37. The industry of the labourers is confessedly diminishing. Those who are out of work are employed by the parish on the roads. Any one passing by will see them loitering about, and trifling away their time in idleness, and may think himself fortunate if he escapes being insulted by them.

53. In this neighbourhood there have been more than twenty fires, and some insubordination. I was engaged, with my brother magistrates, in examining into the causes of three of them. I questioned an unhappy young man who was executed for setting fire to another farm-yard near to this place, and I am of opinion that they all originated in private pique taken against the farmer, for refusing some demand for relief.

LIDLINGTON
Thomas Batchelor

A.   814.

C.   £1 15s 8d.

4.   At one man for 25 acres arable, or 50 of pasture, about 64 men; but the indolence acquired by loitering on the roads, etc. makes a larger number now necessary.

5.   About 113 above 20 years of age in 1831, and 78 boys under 20 (the boys and young men are not included in the return of the population).

7.   Scarcely any non-parishioners.

24. No work done for individuals is at the present time paid for by the parish; but in the neighbouring parish of Ridgmount, the overseer pays four-fifths of the wages of surplus men, who are employed in ditching, digging or forking land, or digging clay or drains: 1s additional is allowed by the overseers for 3 children; 2s for 4; 3s for 5, etc.

25. Of late, relief is given only if there be 4 children; formerly money was often allowed for the third child, and in dearer times I believe for the second child.

29. Unmarried men sometimes work for 6s or 7s a week, while the married men have 9s. If we say 7s for an unmarried man, who would have only 3s 6d if employed (as it is called) by the overseer, he gains by working for a master 3s 6d a week, and the master 2s; an inducement to both.

37. Diminishing very much, in consequence of the evil example of paying many persons on the roads for doing scarcely any thing; and the reason why they are permitted to have wages almost without work is, because the farmers have no interest in the permanent improvements of the roads, or even the lands, while the laws permit the public, or the landowners, to receive nearly all the profits of work, which they refuse to pay for, or encourage by allowances.

38. Change of service is more frequent, in consequence of the indolence and ill-

conduct resulting from superfluous labourers.

53. I believe the riots and fires, and almost every other evil which has been charged on what are termed *perversions of the Poor Laws*, are chargeable solely to the unjust and impolitic, if not unlawful, system of sending all who can get no other work to be employed by the overseer, and at the same time, leaving the profits of such employment to be enjoyed by the public etc. who pay nothing towards it.

MAULDEN

T. M. Overman, Churchwarden

A. 1,231.

C. 8s 7d.

24. No. I have always objected to that system, considering there was no law to compel me to adopt it. The magistrates began it to court a little popularity from it. To that measure I trace the reduction of wages. The labourer, when he found that the parish was to make up his money, became indifferent about the quantity he did; and the ordination that 'man was to live by the sweat of his brow' was broken down.

25. Not in this parish. We give it as the occasion may require.

29. There is a difference when the quantity of labour in the market is greater than is wanted; but when the demand is equal to the quantity, the single man gets as much as the married, if he can do as much work.

37. Decreasing; 12 men now only do the work that 9 did when I commenced business, 18 years since; and as long as the magistrates keep up that system of ordering the overseers to make up men's money, the evil will keep increasing; it takes away that nice feeling that the family is maintained by himself, which must be restored, or property will be of little value soon.

38. The farmers are afraid of making settlements, which deters some from hiring; and from the great increase of population, there are more labourers than are wanted.

53. Restore that feeling amongst the labourers that their well doing depends upon their good conduct, which can only be done by enabling the farmers to employ them.

MEPPERSHALL

James Webster, B.D. Rector

A. 444.

C. 13s 5d.

4. More than sufficient.

5. Know not; but more than are wanted.

7. Several non-parishioners, but no Irish or Scotch.

24. Able-bodied labourers never receive relief from the parish, except when sick, and not in a benefit club. Cases of allowance, on account of large families, so various, no specific answer can be given.

26. No general rule can be given in regard to relief, for every case differs from another.

29. Wages generally the same to the married and unmarried, if they are equally able-bodied.

37. The industry of the labourer is the same in general as it always has been when they can obtain proper labour and proper wages; but population has of late so much increased, that proper employment for them cannot always be found, and then they are put under the direction of the surveyor of roads at and under

price, and must be assisted by parochial relief.
38. Farmers for the most part refuse to hire servants by the year, to avoid giving a legal settlement.
53. I think they have frequently been caused by the distress of the times, and for want of proper employ by the labouring classes.

NORTHILL
John Taddy, Minister
A. 1,106.
C. 12s 3d.
5. The proportion between the quantity of acres in the parish and the number of labourers, is 3 men to each 100 acres.
24. None.
29. None.
37. I cannot say.
38. They do not.

PUDDINGTON
Richard L. Orlebar
A. 563.
C. £1 0s 9d.
4. 80.
5. 70.
7. Only one labourer's family, belonging to a neighbouring parish.
24. 15. To men of large families an allowance is generally made, according to the price of bread, usually commencing at 3 children.
25. According to a scale founded on the price of bread, allowing about 3 gallon loaves to a man, 2 to a woman, and 1 to a child.
29. Single men generally have 3s less wages, except they are very superior workmen. There are very few *unmarried* men, as they generally marry very young in order .to get higher wages; in some cases, to spite the parish. The few single men there are, can, if very good workmen, get wages nearly equal to married men, but are always the first to be turned off by the employer; if indifferent workmen, they are employed at very low wages.
37. The workmen are generally not equal to their fathers, more especially the very young men. This may be attributed to the fact, that farmers seldom employ any but married men with families in works requiring skill; such as draining, thatching, felling wood, ditching, etc.
38. Much more frequently, on account of their idleness, carelessness, and insolence, which spring from, and are encouraged by, the notion, here acted upon, that they must at all events be supported by the parish.
53. No.

SHARNBROOK
George Church, Churchwarden; *J. Gibbard*, J.P.
A. 754.
C. 13s 8d.
4. 85.   *G.C.*
5. 95.   *G.C.*
7. 11 heads of families, exclusive of their children. No Irish or Scotch.   *G.C.*
24. Perhaps there may be 10.   *J.G.*
Allowance often made out of the poor-book when the number of children ex-

ceeds three. Sometimes idle able-bodied men are let at a low rate of wages to the
farmers, and the deficiency paid out of the poor book.   *G.C.*
25. It is given according to scale.   *J.G.*
29. Married men have more wages than single, when employed by individuals.   *J.G.*
    Married men generally receive more wages than single men. There are many ex-
    ceptions.   *G.C.*
37. Diminishing.   *J.G.*
38. I am not aware that they do.   *J.G.*
53. The excitement leading to these crimes has been produced by the antipathy of
    the pauper to the overseer, by the game-preservers, and by the prejudice enter-
    tained against threshing machines.   *J.G.*

SOUTHILL-CUM-WARDEN
Fred. H. Neve, Vicar
A. 1,267.
C. 12s 7d.
5. Southill 250; Warden 130.
7. Scarcely any non-parishioners.
24. None. Work done for individuals not partly paid for by the parish.
29. Not any difference usually, though it does occur occasionally. Sometimes single
    perhaps 2s less.
37. Not diminishing.
38. No.
53. There was one agricultural riot at Stotfold, in this neighbourhood; a parish
    where there was no gentleman, nor, at the time, any clergyman residing; and I
    believe that the parish system pursued there was such as would not improbably
    lead to very great discontent.

TURVEY
C. Longuet Higgins, Turvey Abbey; *W. Finch*, Churchwarden
A. 988.
C. 17s 11d.
4. About 120.   *W.F.*
5. About 120.   *W.F.*
7. About 4 families.   *W.F.*
24. Where the family is large, relief is given.   *C.L.H.*
    No part of work is paid for out of the rates; but relief given if the earnings are
    not sufficient.   *W.F.*
25. The scale is about sufficient to obtain 2 half-peck loaves for the labourer, and
    one for every other member of his family. Where families are small, the scale is
    rather higher.   *C.L.H.*
29. No.   *C.L.H.*
    No.   *W.F.*
37. On the whole increasing, owing to the late arrangements of letting out land for
    gardens.   *C.L.H.*
38. Yes; owing to the ill working of the settlement laws.   *C.L.H.*

WESTONING
Thomas Pearse, Vicar
A. 627.
C. £1. 13s 3d.

4. 70 men and boys might be sufficient, according to the open field system of farming, which at present prevails. If the parish were inclosed, or the lands allotted and exonerated from tithe, it is generally supposed that a better system would prevail, and all the labourers of the parish be well employed on the land. Notwithstanding the present demoralization of the labourers, owing to their having been generally maintained in idleness during a great part of the year, for some years past, I am of opinion, that the greater part of them would be very thankful for regular employment at fair wages; and that such employment would be, in a great measure, effectual to recover them from their present degraded state.

5. 90 men and boys, able bodied.

7. 10 to 12 English families; the labourers in general belong to parishes in the neighbourhood, whither they generally go daily for work.

24. There is scarcely 1 able-bodied labourer in the employment of individuals but what receives regular relief on account of his family. A married man and his wife, without any child, receive 5s per week, if he be out of employment; for 1 child, he is allowed 1s, whether in or out of employment; for 2 children, 2s, and so on in proportion to the number of children under 10 years; above ten years, each boy out of employment is allowed from 1s 6d to 3s 6d.

25. A married man and his wife (the former being out of employment) are allowed 5s per week without a child; with 1 child 6s; and on an increasing scale, according to the number of children under 10 years.

29. Yes; before the labour rate was agreed upon, the wages of a married man varied from 9s to 12s; the highest wages of a single man 9s, commonly not more than 6s. According to a plan lately agreed upon by the farmers, they propose paying to a single man of 21 years, and upwards, 9s; between 18 years and 21, 7s; between 15 and 18, 5s; and so on.

37. The industry of the labourers in this parish is supposed to be greatly diminishing. For many years they have, unfortunately, not been able to obtain regular employment, but have been thrown on the parish during a great part of the year, during which they were required to do very little or no work for the parish; persons out of employ were all sent to the gravel-pit, (commonly), men and boys, of various ages and characters; the evil consequence of which is obvious. *Poaching* and *drunkenness* have increased very much during the last few years; and these habits have greatly tended to make the labourers worse workmen, and to lead them to the commission of other offences.

38. Yes. The farmers in general are not able (they say) to employ more than one or two labourers for a continuance; the discharged labourer is thrown on the parish, and engages with any farmer afterwards who happens to want another hand, and is willing to hire him. It is also true that too many of the labourers do not take much pains to give satisfaction to their employers, and cause themselves to be discharged and thrown on the parish.

53. During the latter part of the year 1830, only 20 able-bodied labouring men, and about as many boys, were in regular employ: the rest of the labouring poor were left to themselves, day after day, in idleness; in the evening, many of the worst regularly adjourned to the new beer shops, and their weekly pay being unequal to their consumption of beer, they agreed together to demand of the principal inhabitants a higher allowance. In this parish some of the farmers accompanied the labourers, when they surrounded me in the village, and demanded higher pay: on their making this demand, the farmers exclaimed against the pressure of rent and *tithe*. Neither the landlords nor the lay rector resided in the parish;

therefore the labouring poor surrounded me, instigated (as I am credibly informed) *by the farmers*. At my recommendation the people quietly dispersed, and no mischief was done then or since by the people of this parish, as a body, to any person or property.

WILLINGTON

Philip Hunt, LL.D. Vicar; *Thomas Twitchell*, Churchwarden

A. 332.

C. 19s 11d.

4. About 40 men and 16 boys.

5. About 45 men and 20 boys.

24. Scarcely any. There is, indeed, now only one able-bodied labourer having a very large family, and he receives 1s 6d a week, in addition to his 11s wages.

25. Whenever by casualty or disease a family becomes chargeable, the scale of relief is about 2s a head weekly. Single or infirm men, and widows, 3s to 4s a week, exclusive of what little they can earn.

29. A little difference if employed by the day, but none at task work; but both task or piece work is given in preference to married family men. At day work, married men have 10s a week; single, from 8s to 9s.

37. In this parish, owing to the labourers being continually employed by the farmers, we find them as industrious as formerly, and as good workmen. But in other parishes, where young able-bodied men are much employed at the gravel-pits, or on the roads, or as roundsmen, they have become considerably worse labourers than formerly; for in such employment they receive the minimum of wages, or rather mere support, and they become lazy, dissatisfied, and mischievous.

38. The practice of hiring yearly servants has decreased, but servants hired for a year like to attend the Michaelmas statute hirings, to try to better themselves.

53. Dissatisfaction with parish employment made them hostile to overseers and members of vestries. The game laws appear also to have been very odious to the unemployed labourers; and the frequent commitments to crowded prisons, led to evil communications and rancorous feelings, and the agricultural riots and fires of 1830 and 1831. As the peasant has lost his attachment to the farmer, through the poor laws, so he has lost his respect for the landlords and the aristocracy through the administration of the game laws.

The Poor Laws. Report from H.M. Commissioners. London 1834.

2.3   The Working of the New Poor Law

2.3.1   The application of the new poor law to Bedfordshire sparked off a riot in Ampthill in May 1835, which gave rise to an urgent report to the Home Office.

endorsed To The Earl De Grey, St. James' Square [Lord Lieutenant]

Magistrates Bench, Ampthill May 14th 1835

My Lord,

In the close of our letter to your Lordship yesterday, we promised to give your Lordship the earliest information of the necessity of farther aid, should such aid unfortunately be found indispensable to repress the hostile spirit which has manifested itself against the operation of the Poor Law Amendment Act. We greatly regret that we are now compelled to acquaint your Lordship that a very serious riot has this day occurred at Ampthill, which renders it necessary for us, as Magistrates, to seek for some farther power beyond the means of enforcing the execution of the law now at our disposal. A Body of about five hundred people assembled before the Ampthill Workhouse while the Board of Guardians for the Union were in deliberation. They were in a state of great excitement, and behaved with great violence. They used very violent language, broke the windows of the Workhouse, and assaulted the Guardians. Their conduct became so violent and formidable as to render it necessary to read the riot Act. This was done, and great numbers of the Mob still remain undispersed.

Warrants were issued yesterday against some persons who had been guilty of rioting at Lidlington, which it was found impossible to execute. The Parties were rescued out of the hands of the Constables. We have sworn into Office about ninety Special Constables, but many of these, we are sorry to say, instead of coming forward in aid of the Magistrates, left the Town and deserted their duty. We are preparing to swear in a greater number of Special Constables, to enable us to execute our warrants. Mr. Adey, the Assistant Commissioner for this Union, has just left us, to report to the Board of Commissioners what has occurred, and to take their advice. The Labourers conceive that the new Law will place them in a worse condition than they were before, and they are especially hostile and clamorous against receiving relief in bread or kind. Mr. Adey was requested to desire the Poor Law Commissioners to send down a body of Police to our assistance.

> We have the honour to be, My Lord, your Lordships obedient Humble Servants Thomas Barbor, George Cardale, George Musgrave, Henry M. Musgrave, James Beard.

> Magistrates' Bench, Ampthill, ½ past 7 o'Clock P.M.
> May 14th 1835

My Lord,

A body of twenty Policemen arrived at Ampthill about 10 O'Clock this Morning, by the aid of whom, in conjunction with the Special Constables we have sworn into office, we have been able to execute warrants against such of the rioters as could be found, and some of them have been examined, and are about to be committed to Gaol.

There has been no farther rioting today, and we trust we shall be able to preserve the public peace with the force now at our command. We are happy thus to be able to relieve your Lordship from the necessity of coming among us.

> We have the honour to be, My Lord, your Lordship's Obedient Servants, Thomas Barbor, George Cardale, George Musgrave, Henry M. Musgrave, James Beard.

Beds. C.R.O. L.C.G. 12

2.3.2 A Select Committee on Agricultural Distress took evidence from the Duke of Bedford's Steward on 23 March 1836. In his opinion the new measures had eased the condition of the farmers, and there were fewer unemployed labourers.

Mr. Thomas Bennett, called in; and Examined.

Where do you reside? — At Woburn.

Are you a practical farmer? — I am not at present farming; I am steward to the Duke of Bedford . . .

Comparing the condition of the farmers at the present time with their condition in 1833, should you say it was better or worse? — I think so far as we are concerned in Bedfordshire, we are decidedly better now than we were in 1833, that is our prospects are better . . . entirely from the decreased amount of poor's rates . . .

What should you state to be the condition of the poor at present? — Better than it was three years ago.

Have you many labourers out of employ? — Very few.

Had you many labourers out of employ in 1833? — A great number.

Can you state what number were out of employ in 1833? — Not exactly. I should think in several of the parishes there were as many as twenty and sometimes thirty out of employment, at that time we were working not exactly on the labour rate, but on measures similar to that, and in some parishes at the time our farmers employed as much as one labourer to 20 acres of land, which was almost double the quantity that can be wanted.

Where can those labourers find employment in their own neighbourhood, or do they go into manufacturing districts? — I think at present we have been very much benefited by the Birmingham Railway going on; a good many have been employed there, and some have gone into the manufacturing districts, and some who have gone are very much pleased with the result of their going.

Have the wages risen in consequence of the removal of those labourers? — No; I think we have only cured the glut in the market; the people are now well employed.

Are the wages sufficient to find the labourers the comforts of life? — The necessaries, I cannot say the comforts; I think that wages must necessarily rise as wheat has risen; in making our contract for the union for the next three months, there is an advance of three halfpence on the four pound loaf; we have had excellent household bread at a penny a pound.

What has been the moral effect of the new poor laws, do you find the labourers make better workmen? The masters generally say that their servants are much better satisfied than they were formerly, and that they now come and ask them for a job, instead of refusing it when it was offered.

There is a better understanding between the master and his servant in consequence? — I think there is.

Select Committee on Agricultural Distress, 1836. BPP 1836 VIII pt. 1

2.3.3   *The Select Committee on the working of the Poor Law (Amendment) Act were anxious to discover whether the withdrawal of outdoor relief had resulted in labourers being forced to work for starvation wages. James Turner and Mark Crabtree were investigators sent from the Anti Poor Law movement after the Ampthill riots in order to look into cases of extreme hardship, and they claimed that employers, some of whom were also poor law guardians, had found in the new act greater leverage to exploit the farm workers. Employers of labour gave evidence against Turner and Crabtree, and they were supported in his evidence by Daniel Goodson Adey, an assistant poor law commissioner who lived at Markyate Cell on the Beds and Herts border near Luton. Adey had done most to organise the Bedfordshire parishes into unions for the administration of the new poor law.*

MINUTES OF EVIDENCE BEFORE SELECT COMMITTEE ON THE POOR LAW AMENDMENT ACT (1838)

23rd March 1838 . . . **Daniel Goodson Adey**, Esq., called in, and Examined. . .

Have you the means of telling the Committee what number of persons were receiving parochial assistance at the time of the formation of the union? — Not at the date of the union, but at the date of my examination I can; I have gone through every parish book myself, and have taken out every name myself, and have not, in the slightest degree, depended upon the parish officers . . . I made it in 1834; it applies to the Christmas preceding . . . At Christmas 1833 the whole number receiving relief within the month was 554 aged and infirm, and 1,021 able-bodied . . . in the Ampthill Union, making together 1,575 . . .

With regard to the able-bodied, in what shape did they receive relief? — In every way that, I believe, was possible, almost; they received it in making up the wages of labour for every day that they were out of employment, and they received it on account of children, and there were many parishes in that union where at least half the labourers were receiving part of their income from the parish. . .

Was there any general scale upon which relief was given to the able-bodied? — No, there were scales in particular parishes, and perhaps there was a scale as to the age of children, but it varied in many parishes. . .

Were there any workhouses within the union? At Ampthill there was a small one.

In the other parishes of the union were there any workhouses or parish houses . . .? Not in the shape of workhouses; . . . there were two or three . . . cottages in which paupers were permitted to reside rent-free, or where they were boarded, instead of boarding themselves. . .

Were they in the habit of using the workhouse in the parish of Ampthill as a test, applying it to the able-bodied applicants for relief? — . . . they did not apply it as a test, except to some few people; there was no space. . .

Can you state the number now receiving relief? — In Christmas 1836 the numbers were 558 aged and infirm, and 25 able-bodied; of those aged and infirm 36 were in the workhouse.

Then the number of aged and infirm receiving relief appears to be pretty stationary? — It is, and that is pretty nearly the same throughout the county . . .

Was the reduction [of the numbers of able-bodied receiving relief] made at once, or was it made gradually? — As far as regards the able-bodied, the guardians, having the example of the parish of Ampthill before them . . . almost immediately adopted the plan of refusing relief to the able-bodied, except in the workhouse; as far as they could carry out the principle, it was carried out at the moment . . .

At present, up to this moment, the board of guardians at Ampthill are acting upon their own conviction of the propriety of refusing relief to the able-bodied out of the workhouse, and not under any orders of the Commissioners? — Certainly.

What has been the effect of withdrawing this out-door relief from the able-bodied labourers. . .? — . . . Men now obtain employment who did not before obtain it; you now never see them idling about, whereas formerly they were constantly idling about for months together; . . . When I first went into the union there was hardly a place into which I was not afraid of entering, lest I might be mobbed, but there is no such thing now.

Were there, when the union was first formed, a great number of able-bodied who found a difficulty in obtaining employment? — . . . A great number were out of employment, and I believe the reason why I was sent into that county was, because there were so many that the magistrates were in a state of alarm respecting them.

Confining yourself to the Ampthill Union, have you understood that the amount of employment has very much increased? — That is the general information . . . that has been given to me, that the employment [upon the land] has greatly increased.

Is this exclusively an agricultural district? — It is . . . I believe there is a little lace, and perhaps there is some little straw-plait, but it is a domestic manufactory entirely; it is carried on in the cottages of the poor.

What was, at the time of the formation of the union, the general rate of the wages in that district? — I think they were then about 8s; but the amount of wages must depend entirely upon the class of people that are employed . . .

Take the best labourers at weekly wages? — I should say that the able-bodied men of that class, the best class of common husbandry labourers, in 1833 received 9s a week.

From 9s, have you any statement of any gradation of diminution in the amount of wages? — No; I should say the wages were from 6s to 7s and 9s a week . . . The great body of agricultural labourers will be divided into about three classes, namely, the day-labourers. . .; the day-labourers who come on a Sunday . . . to attend to the horses and the cattle . . . who would receive an additional shilling; and . . . the task-men; those are the three great classes of labourers . . . Probably a fifth or a fourth will get Sunday wages, or if they do not get it in money they get it in milk, or something of that sort.

What could a labourer employed in task-work earn, do you think? — I should doubt very much whether they exceeded 11s.; you may say 11s to 12s . . .

How many hours a day were they in the habit of working? — From six to six are the common hours in Bedfordshire. . .

Do you understand that the amount of task-work has increased very much? — I understand very much indeed. . .

Has the amount of employment for the wife and the children increased much? —

I believe it has, with respect to some of the boys; it is a common observation that the boys were never taken out by their parents when they went to their work, and I now see those boys at work, hedging and ditching, with their parents. . .

Do you believe the number of labourers employed upon the farms has increased? — I understand, very considerably; not only increased in point of number, but in point of the periods for which they are engaged. . . They are not thrown out of work in the way that they were formerly.

How were they thrown out of work formerly? — If there was a little bad weather, or a little jealousy in the parish, or any other circumstance arose to make the farmers think that they would lose rather than gain by keeping their labourers on, then they threw them out of work. . .

With regard to the aged and infirm, the number relieved appears to be much the same as it was before? — I believe it is.

Have their allowances been diminished generally or not? — I should think that very little alteration has taken place, with the exception of giving a small portion of relief in bread. . .

The allowances to the able-bodied having been either very materially reduced or altogether withdrawn, what has been the effect . . . upon the condition of that class of persons? — I do not perceive any material difference outwardly; all I can say is, that I see more people in the fields, and more people employed generally, and I hear no complaint; I have frequently stopped, when travelling in my carriage, and walked into the fields and asked labourers respecting their condition, and I may mention, that in the riot that took place in Ampthill, the only cry was, "We want nothing but work."

When was the riot? — . . . At the beginning of the formation of the union, in the year 1835.

What was the origin of the riot? — The origin was the change of the allowance system from money to bread, but the general feeling against the introduction of the law was another cause, the men being apprehensive of being shut up in the workhouse, and they stated to me most distinctly (I was in the crowd for three hours, in the middle of them, talking to them), that all they wanted was work; that was their constant cry; one of the observations was this, "that the land was in such a state that you might plough a furrow, and drag it from Ampthill to Bedford", meaning that the land was so extremely foul. . .

Have you heard . . . that there is any improvement in the cultivation of the soil, arising from greater employment of the labourers? — I believe there is no doubt at all of that. . .

You say you see no difference in their appearance; do you perceive any difference in their disposition, in the feeling that exists, as between the employer and the employed? — I should say there can be no doubt whatever upon that subject, judging from the single circumstance, that those people now touch their hats to you as they pass; before they were always sulky; four years back, if you passed them, they were generally sulky looking people, and now they are civil and polite; I can perceive that difference. . .

You have spoken of the wages of labouring men as being 9s and 10s and 11s a week previously to the alteration of the law, and to the introduction of the Union system; have those wages increased since that time, or has there been any alteration at all? — I find that, in 1834, the wages went down from 9s to 8s a week; that they continued at that in 1835; that in 1836 they rose to 8s and 9s a week, and that now, in 1837, they run from 9s to 10s a week; that is the return which I have got from the books of an extensive farmer. . . There is a great deal more piece-work given. . .

What was the practice that prevailed in the parish of Ampthill with regard to the relief of the poor before the union was declared; how was relief administered? — I believe in the parish of Ampthill they had in a great measure stopped making up the wages of labour; I am not prepared to say to what extent. . .

Do you know what the rates were in the parish of Ampthill before the Union was formed? — The rates were £1,003 in 1832; £1,036 in 1833; and £1,067 in 1834.

What have they been since? — In 1834-5 they are £968; in 1835-6 they are £603; and in 1836-7 they are £442. . .

In the parish of Ampthill the rate was 12s 3d per head upon the population, before the union was formed? — Not the rate, but the expenditure.

And the expenditure per head for the whole of the parishes in the Union, when the Union was formed, you have stated to be 20s 4d per head? — Yes.

How had the reduced expenditure per head been effected in the parish of Ampthill before the formation of the union? I understand by getting rid, in a great measure, of able-bodied pauperism. . .

With regard to the condition of the labourers themselves, if they should be unable to obtain private employment, and be deprived of parochial assistance, except through the workhouse, is it your impression that they come into the workhouse and receive that relief, or that they remain out of the workhouse and suffer severely from the privation of relief? — I have no doubt that individuals have suffered; I cannot entertain any doubt about that; but my general impression is, that they have obtained sufficient employment to support them during the short period that they do now from time to time get thrown out of work; I cannot suppose that they can bear beyond a certain quantity of suffering. I have no doubt that there must be suffering, and that they would not go into the workhouse till the last moment; but I have never heard of extreme suffering.

Have you ever understood that persons have been under the necessity of selling their furniture and stripping their cottage of its effects before going into the workhouse? — I have heard from pawnbrokers that a vast number of petty articles, particularly during the last winter, upon the cessation of labour, were brought to the pawn-shops.

Do you understand from the pawnbrokers that those articles were brought from the agricultural labourers? — Yes.

[In this case, what course do you recommend to the union to follow?] — The way in which I have recommended to unions to act is, to take the men in and leave the families out, in order that we may be fully satisfied that the men were not employed at lower wages, and that we might obtain what little return we could in the workhouse; that has been the plan I have recommended. . . I think it has this further advantage, that it enables the wife to make inquiries for labour for her husband, and that she gets him work. . .

How do the family subsist? — They are supplied by the relieving officer with bread, as a matter of course; they are all relieved. . .

Can you state for what space of time these men are generally taken from their families and shut up in the workhouse? — It is a limited period; I am not aware that any able-bodied man has been separated from his family for more than a fortnight, and there are very few cases of even that; in general they decline even that relief; it is not a new plan; it is a plan that I acted upon before the Poor Law Amendment Act took place, and in one union . . . it was carried out . . . before we had the workhouses; it would have been impossible to have taken the families into the workhouses.

Would not the necessary effect of this system be, that a man, in order to return to his family, would accept a job of work at inferior wages, rather than be shut up in the workhouse and be under restraint? — I have found this to be the case, that the labourers will not generally accept of wages which will not support them and their families.

What do they do if they do not meet with those wages? — I infer they do obtain some means to support their families, or come in. . .

Has any permission been given to the parents of the children who may die in the workhouse that they may attend the funerals; or, on the other hand, has permission been given to the children that they may attend the funerals of their parents who may have died in the workhouse? — I have not the least idea that permission would be refused; I cannot say that it has been given, but I have seen the hearse going from the workhouse, and persons attending it.

Relatives of the deceased? — Very likely; I cannot say. . .

In the case of a child dying in the workhouse, in what mode is the funeral conducted? — I cannot give the details; it is left to the chaplain; I have directed them to be conducted with proper decency; in the Ampthill Union I met the funeral of a person in a cart, which is not certainly conducting it with the same decency that we should conduct it.

Mr. James Turner, called in; and Examined [23 March 1838]

What is your profession or business in life? — I used to be a dresser of cotton-yarn in a factory.

Have you lately been in the Ampthill Union? — Yes.

Have you been there for the purpose of making inquiries into the condition of the poor there? — I have.

In what state did you find them? — I have found them not in a good state; I found a good deal of distress existing amongst the cottages of the poor people.

Among what class of people particularly? — Almost all of them; those more especially who had not constant work.

With regard to old people, in what state did you find them? — I found some of them worse than they used to be, and some of them better than they used to be.

When you say worse than they used to be, had you been in the Ampthill Union before? — No; when I say worse than they used to be, I mean that the relief given to the aged and infirm, in some instances, is not so much as it used to be, and in some instances more than it used to be. . .

Among the able-bodied, what state of things did you find amongst them? — That class of labourers, as I before stated, who are in constant work, that is, work regularly for their masters, we did not find them so much worse than they used to be; that class that are the worst off are those that have not constant work.

Take the case of those who have constant work, what did they describe to you their condition to be? — Their wages are generally 9s a week, with one exception, where they had been having 12s with one master.

Are you speaking of the parish of Ampthill, or of the parishes about Ampthill contained within the union? — I am now alluding to Ampthill parish. . .

Had they any advantage besides that 9s a week? — Not any, with one or two exceptions; some farmers will give them some milk in the morning, but that is not very common, and nothing else but their 9s; I am speaking of those that work by the day.

Did you find many working by task-work? — A good many.

Did they say that there were more or fewer employed in task-work than formerly? — There is a greater inclination among the farmers to employ men at task-work.

More are employed in task-work than formerly? — Yes.

What did you find them earning at task-work? — Generally about the same wages that were earned by the day, or in some instances it would be an increase of 1s a week, but not very common.

At task-work, then, they earn 9s a week? — It is so contrived, when the farmer gives the work to his men, he contrives so that he shall earn a shilling a week more, but they do a shilling more work for it.

Do they, or do they not, earn generally more at task-work than they do by day wages? — They may, in many instances, earn a shilling more, but not beyond a shilling.

Generally, do they earn a shilling more? — Not always; but sometimes they do.

What sort of task-work are they employed at? — Threshing, ditching, draining, hedging; that is generally done by piece.

Are the children very much employed? — No; not to such an extent as I should have imagined.

Did you ask the farmers, or the labourers, whom you saw, whether there was more employment for the children since the law was introduced, or not? — I did . . . They could not state that there was any difference.

You do not think the number of children employed was increased? — As far as Ampthill was concerned I think not; there is plaiting done, and they put boys to the plaiting as well as girls. . .

Were there a great many people out of employment? — A great many.

In Ampthill, or the parishes around it? — In both.

What number of people did you find out of employment? — In the winter, during the very severe weather, there were from 30 to 40, in the parish of Ampthill alone, totally unemployed; on the 18th of February there were 50.

What became of those people? — They were about in the streets, standing in corners, and I saw some sitting at home.

How long were they out of employment? — I am speaking now, when I say that number, of the severe weather — from three to six weeks.

How did they live during that period? — That is a question that they could not themselves answer; I often asked that.

What explanation did they give you? — When I have asked them generally how they were situated, what they had coming in, and what they had to pay out, I used to ask them often how did they live; the answer is, "We cannot tell, but chiefly on bread and potatoes."

How did they, being out of employment, describe to you that they obtained the bread and potatoes? — In most instances some part of the family are making a trifle with plaiting; those families that plait are rather better off than those families that make lace. . .

Take the case first of a young man without a family, he being out of employment, how did he describe to you that he lived? — He would not hesitate for a moment to say that he went stealing, and was driven to it. . .

Did you collect that the amount of employment in the neighbourhood was greater than it had been in former years? — Very little, not much; but they did seem, as far as I could get information, to think that there was rather more work than there used to be; but a great many have been driven off to various parts, such as the railroad; a great many have gone from the part to the railroad. . .

At pretty good wages? — Some of them at 15s a week, 2s 6d a day; but if a man's family was in that part, and he went to work on the railroad himself, he hardly gets so much money to bring home as if he had 9s a week on the spot.

But you describe 30 or 40 in the parish of Ampthill, that were entirely out of employment for a period of from three to six weeks; did those people apply for relief to the board of guardians? — Not to a very great extent.

Why did they not? — Because it was of no use whether to apply.

Why was it not? — The impression on their minds was, "We have no parish now, it is of no use to apply for relief now, though we are out of work;" so that, though they were suffering the distress which I have now named, they did not choose to go to the board at all, because they did not like to go to the workhouse, and it was a well understood thing that it was either the workhouse, or no relief at all.

Was their distress very great? — In some instances it was very great, worse than I ever saw in my life. . .

Did you hear those statements of a determination not to go into the workhouse, and being willing to suffer death or any extremity rather than go there, made by persons who had not been in the workhouse, or by persons who had been there? — By both.

You found, from the general answer of the people, an impression that their condition was altered for the worse by the introduction of the law? — That was their impression.

Before the introduction of the law, they were in the habit of receiving an allowance from the parish? — Yes; whether they worked or not, they used to assemble on the roads in large numbers.

They used to apply to the parish officers, and if they did not succeed in their application to them, they went to the magistrates and were ordered a certain allowance from the parish rates? — As far as I could get to understand it, every man that there was no work for was put on the roads, or in the gravel-pits to get gravel, with a certain allowance according to his family.

What was that allowance when they were entirely supported by the parish? — Young men about 2s 6d a week; a man and his wife, without a family, 5s, and in proportion, according to his children upwards. . .

Mr. Mark Crabtree, called in; and Examined. [8 May 1838]

Did you accompany Mr. Turner down to Ampthill . . . ? — I did . . .

Have you, during your visit to Ampthill, gone into the cottages of many of those poor people? — We have, a great many.

Have you had an opportunity of seeing how they were living at the time you were there; what their furniture was, what their bedding was, and had an opportunity of ascertaining that they were, as has been said by the Commissioner, steeped in deep poverty? — Yes, they are.

Was there any particular cottage which you visited of which you could give a description of the furniture, of the number of the family, and of the means they had of living? — Yes. "Description of a cottage occupied by John Cooper, who worked for Mr. Overman, at Maulden, and has done for 20 years. The outside of the cottage, that is the outer wall, if it may be so called, is nearly down; the floor is a mud floor, with no tiles upon it; the window — there should be 32 diamond squares of glass, but there is only half that number. Furniture — there is a table of two boards and a piece, put together on four hedge-stakes; one chair, three stools and a coffer, which is an old chest; the bed is a fair one, laid upon straw, without a blanket, without a pillow, without a bolster; that is in the first bed-room: the second bed is a straw bed, part of it covered and part of it not; no blanket, no pillow, no bolster, no covering;" this is a description of one of the labourer's cottages.

How many were there in the family of that labourer? — Nine.

Were two beds the only beds that those nine had to sleep upon? — They were.

Have you described the beds? — I have.

What was one of them? — One of them was a hurdle, or something imitating a hurdle, as it is called in that country; it was a rail put upon two posts driven into the ground, and the ends are fastened to the wall, and the other ends nailed to this framing.

And on this was laid straw for the inmates of this cottage to sleep upon? — Yes.

Without any blankets? — Yes.

Have you been a blanket maker? — Yes, I have

If the poor people of Bedfordshire could all obtain blankets that have not them, would it give a great impetus to the business you have been engaged in, and an increased demand? — It would . . .

Have you heard, while you have been down there, labourers state to you repeatedly, a great number of them, that their circumstances have been gradually growing worse since the Poor Law Amendment Act has passed? They have.

Their means of purchasing blankets, and their means of purchasing the necessaries of life, have been abridged in the same proportion? — They have; there is a general falling off in all their circumstances. . .

You have mentioned the furniture in the cottage of one poor man; have you found a great many other cases during your peregrinations there, similar, or nearly so, to the other you have described? — I have.

Is there any which you wish to refer to? — Yes; in the parish of Lidlington, John Robinson has no work; in this house there is no tiled floor, it is part pebbled; the furniture consists of two chairs, a table, consisting of two boards put together on hedge-stakes, two saucepans, one tea-kettle, three plates, and two broken ones; two basins, two broken knives, one fork. In the bed-room upstairs there are two bedsteads, two beds filled with straw, one blanket, two coverlets, two bolsters; in the bed-room downstairs there are two beds on the ground floor filled with straw, no blankets, two coverlets; they have sold their furniture to buy bread with; they have pawned their clothes while they have scarcely any thing left; there are 14 individuals live in this cottage, six of them are grown-up persons; there are two families live in the cottage.

[From the evidence of **Mr. Thomas William Overman**, farmer of Maulden, 22 May 1838]

Have you any other letter to read, of any farmer? — Yes, from the parish of Marston; Mr. Thomas Bennett: ". . . I very much question whether one out of four keep such accounts as to be able to give the information required; I can only say, as regards myself, that I have employed more labour and given increased wages; instead of 9s I have given them 10s per week, which, with the additional labour, has increased my yearly expenditure £40 upon 160 acres arable and 100 acres of pasture; I believe every farmer has employed more labour and generally paid better wages; there are exceptions, but the thing is self-evident; instead of having 30 or 40, and sometimes, I might say 60, men out of employ, I could not this day get a man or boy without going out of the parish for one; all have employment." This is the parish in which they used to pay £2,100 a year for poor-rates; they have saved £1,500; they are paying under £700 now. I have another letter, from Mr. Francis, of Houghton-Conquest; that used to be one of our worst parishes in the county, where every crime, almost, has been committed: "In answer to yours of the 23d . . . I assure you that I have employed more labour, and see it to be an every-day practice. My expense of labour, from 1834 to 1837, has increased £50 or £60 a year, and my poor-rate decreased £25, and that upon a farm of 200 acres of land, being one-third grass land. Before the passing of the Poor Law Amendment Act, I recollect the vast quantities of labourers lying on the road-side in idleness, paid by the overseer, used to frequent the alehouses and beer-shops in the evening, and from thence to night-poaching, setting fire, cutting and maiming of cattle and such like depredations. All that appears to be abated; the farmer and labourer having more confidence in each other than ever known by the present generation, and I hear of no one complaining but ale-house and beer-shop keepers; I recollect in 1834 hearing an agent complaining of the difficulty in getting cottage-rents; I am well-informed in 1837 he has no difficulty."

James Turner produced a number of pauper case histories. The question was put by James Fjelden, M.P., himself a campaigner against the New Poor Law.
. . .

You have now stated the sufferings and distress of many able-bodied persons; I wish now to draw your attention to the case of aged persons, widows, and children; you published a second letter; you have already given evidence on the first; will you take the newspaper containing your letter, copied from the "Northern Star," and read it? — The cases in the letter are, "James Somer-ville, aged 68, has no wife; this old man used to have 2s 6d weekly relief, before the new law was passed; but since, he has had 1s taken off, and now he receives 1s 6d; this old man is very kindly dealt with; he may work, and earn a shilling if he can; then if he does not like it, he can go to prison, that is, to the great house; so you see how much this poor man is benefited by the new law. Thomas Bunker, aged 70, an old man who used to have 2s a week from the parish, but since the new law was passed, has had nothing; the reason assigned is, that he is an able-bodied man; but if so, many young men cannot get work; how then is an old man to get work? But how is such a man to live? He is not an able-bodied man, but he is told that he may go to the workhouse, that is, he may go to prison; to this he objects, and would sooner die. Susan Deacon, a widow, aged 49, has five children, the eldest 18, the youngest 8; when the new law was passed, this widow had 7s per week; it was reduced afterwards to 5s 6d; she applied to the board of guardians to have the 1s 6d put on again; the chairman told her she ought to be ashamed of herself, and she was ordered to withdraw; she did so, and they reduced her pay again to 4s 3d, and that she was to have in bread; not content with this, they had another go, and took all off; she must not have any; what was she to do then? Why, she might go down to Derby, into the silk factories, where there was plenty of work for her and her children; it was not far, about 100 miles; to this she objected, and must therefore have no more relief, and no more has she had; one of her sons is out of work, the rest are plaiters of straw, and earn about 6s per week; she pays no rent, for the hut she lives in stands on some waste ground; how she lives is quite unaccountable even to herself; but she may go to prison if she likes. This she objects to, and while she and her children can get one bit of bread and potato once a day she will not go there. Sarah Jellis is aunt to four orphan children, whom she has brought up. When she took these children, the oldest was 13, the youngest was a few days old, the mother having died of childbirth. She had with these children 9s per week, up to the building of the 'great house', after which the board of guardians took off 1s, and then took off two more. Very soon after they took the other two, and this reduced the allowance to 4s; they afterwards took all off. This was all done in less than 12 months; and she was ordered to the board. I suppose they felt ashamed at what they had done, for they gave her 2s a week afterwards, one in money and one in bread. This she continues to receive. In this state she applied to her brother to take one of her children; he did so. One went to see her grandmother at Christmas, and has stopped there. The oldest of these is a poor helpless creature, who will never be able to get his own victuals. On asking this woman how they lived, she burst into tears, and said, 'God only knows, for I cannot tell you.' Sarah Cox, a widow, aged 43 years, has been a widow five years; has six children, the oldest 22, the youngest 5; the two oldest have fits. This widow had, when the new law was passed, 5s per week from the parish; it was afterwards reduced to 4s, and soon afterwards again to 3s. They then called her before the board of guardians, and told her she must go to the factory in Lancashire. To this she objected; and they told her they had nothing more to do with her, and she has never had anything from them since. The children plait straw; but on account of the oldest having fits, they cannot do much in that line. She has 1s per week to pay for rent; whether she has any bread or not, it will cost her at least 1s 6d for firing; their earnings will not exceed 8s. This is a very distressed family; but because she refused to go to the factories she was not to have any thing. Charlotte Palmer, a widow, aged 55, has five children; the oldest 16, the youngest 10. This woman has been a widow 10 years. At the time of her husband's death she was possessed of property in the parish where she now resides; but, owing to circumstances over which she had no control, she was deprived of it, and became chargeable to the parish; and before the passing of the new law she received 5s per week. After the passing of the new law it was very soon reduced to 1s; and by and by that also was taken off, and she was ordered to the board, a distance of 3 miles, and 3 miles back." There is an error here, I said 13, but it is three miles. "When she got there, they told her she and her family must go to Leeds, to the factories. To this she objected, and they told her they had nothing more to do with her. So much for the widows being better off than they used to be. I will now state another case to you, which will make your blood run cold, if such a thing is possible. John Huckleby, aged 24, has a wife and two children. Now mind, this man is a man of very respectable character; this man has had very little work since harvest. About three weeks ago his wife was confined; and owing to his having no work, she was ill provided for such an occasion. When she was confined she had only a small portion of bread. After having been confined about a week, she had no fire, no food; in fact, she had not anything. In this distressing situation her husband applied to the relieving officer. This was on Thursday, and the answer he received was, he could not do any thing for them unless the husband would go to the workhouse, to which he consented; and on the Monday evening following she was relieved with 4s 6d, 1s 6d of which she had to pay for rent, leaving her with 3s. Now this woman was left in a house by herself (having been confined a few days) with two children, no one to lift a hand for her, and the husband sent to prison, that is to the workhouse, for being poor. Now, sirs, what do you, and what do the people of the north think of a law which can inflict such unheard-of cruelty on a poor woman at this inclement season, when in 'nature's sorrow'. I will not say any thing more about it, for I fear I should be thought violent."

The first case you have read is the case of James Somerville, aged 68, does he reside in the parish of Westoning? — He does.

Have you seen the returns made by the parish officers of the relief which this man was receiving? — I have, I have examined them this morning.

Have you seen that this man is put down in those parish returns as being infirm? — I have; he is so reported.

Did you find that till the union was established he had 3s a week? — I did.

And 2s 6d afterwards until the second week in the year 1836-7?. — Yes.

And 1s 6d since? — Yes, that is according to the returns which have been ordered by this Committee.

Is that the statement that you received from this poor man, or those who know what he had before you saw the returns at all? — It is; I had published the statement, and I found this morning, on looking over the returns, that they had given me a correct statement, and he is now receiving 1s 6d a week.

Will you state what are the circumstances of that man, and anything you wish to observe upon the case? — I found him an old man, 68 years of age; he lives in a house belonging to the parish, and he has 1s 6d to live upon; and how he lives I cannot describe.

His relief from the parish has been reduced from 3s to 1s 6d since the passing of the new law? — It has.

This man is entered as 65; on the 7th of April 1836, in the list of pauper applications I find the name of Somerville receiving 2s 6d a week; I find that he lives rent-free, and that he suffers with pain in his feet; and that his application was to retain the allowance, and that the order is that he should be allowed 1s 6d a week; do you know whether this man was in employment at the time? — I do not consider him capable of doing much work.

Will you go to the case of George Cox, which you have mentioned? — "George Cox is 44 years of age; he has a wife and six children; he lives in Ampthill, but I believe he belongs to Flitwick; that is in the union; the eldest of his children is 19 and the youngest 12; but the eldest, 19, has been, since this note was taken, married, so that the brings him down to five children; he had not very good health; last summer, about July, this man had sold his furniture, and he had sold his wheelbarrow, his potatoe fork, and his iron rake and other things, and his bed stocks had burnt for fire-wood; this man was under the necessity of going into the workhouse; he went into the workhouse in Easter week of 1837, and took five of the children in with him; remained in 11 weeks; during the time they were in, the rent accumulated to 16s 2d, and the landlord seized what furniture remained, they having left the two eldest children in the house; when this family came out, they had nowhere to go, but the first night they slept in Abbot's rick-yard in Flitwick; they then afterwards lived in Mr. Osborn's barn nine weeks, and then Osborn wanted his barn, and they removed into John Chapman's, and there remained nine weeks; this barn was wanted, and they were turned out, but found an empty house in Ampthill; in a few weeks after the husband had no work and was unwell, and they again went into the workhouse and remained there 14 weeks, and came out yesterday; and now they are with their son in a house, a very small one, not nine feet square, and one room up-stairs, this family together with the son and his wife and child; when they came out of the workhouse at that time, the youngest child had no clothes, and was brought out as naked as when it was born;" that is my information.

How old was the child? — Two years and four months.

Have you anything further to state; what has become of this family since? — I went to see them the morning I came up; I found them living in a house without windows; without any floor only the earth; all the tiles taken up and no windows to the house, and the husband not well; and since that they are gone into the workhouse again, and they are now in again.

He with his five children has returned into the workhouse? — Either four or five; I think one of them is left out.

What was the employment of this man before he went into the house? — He is a labourer; he has lived in barns and in this house without windows; and such weather as it has been, it has not been pleasant; and now his health is such that he cannot work, and he is in the workhouse again.

What character did this man bear; did you make any inquiry upon that point? — I did make some inquiry; when I made inquiry into circumstances, and found them such as they were, I wanted to know what character he bore, and I sent him over to get his character from the last employer, and I will read what they say of him: "This is to certify, that George Cox, the elder, has worked with me, and do not consider him either a drunkard or a spendthrift, and have not heard that he is considered so by his neighbours. (Signed) W. P. Squires; A. Brown, vicar of Flitwick; Frederick Henry Sharp, churchwarden."

Do you know the wages that he received when he was in the employment of that farmer? — I do not; I should think 9s a week, but I have no account of that.

Were his family able to earn anything? — Two girls could plait, but I think they are not very expert at it; it did not appear to me as if they were very active at it.

Do you think that they could, by any labour that they could perform, obtain a livelihood such as a labouring man and his family ought to have? — Certainly not; those two that plait would earn about 1s 6d a week each; this man, on account of living in this sort of way, his health is not such that he can do a day's work for a farmer.

This man has been compelled, from the pressure of poverty, to go into the workhouse the various times which you have enumerated? — He has suffered very much.

It was a fact that his youngest child was allowed to leave the workhouse in a state of absolute nudity? — I am so informed by various individuals.

When was it brought out of the workhouse? — My note says, "They all came out yesterday;" that is three weeks ago. . .

Data concerning the incomes and family budgets of three Bedfordshire Labourers before and after the Poor Law Amendment Act were given in an appendix to the evidence.

APPENDIX (B.)

STATE of THREE LABOURERS in Husbandry, in the Parish of Westoning, Union of Ampthill during 1834.

	John Carter.	William Odell.	Benjamin Cox.
1. Name of labourers	John Carter.	William Odell.	Benjamin Cox.
2. Age of ditto	25	37	41
3. Work employed on	Jobbing	Jobbing	Jobbing
4. Wife or not	Wife	Wife	Wife
5. Children living with parents	2	4	5
6. Age of oldest child	5	12	16
7. Age of youngest child	2	1	1
8. Weeks labourer was employed	10	17	12
9. Rate of wages per week	9s	10s	8s
10. Amount of wages of labourer at his employment	£4 10s	£8 10s	£4 16s
11. Additional for harvests	£2	£2	£2
12. Amount of earnings of labourer's wife and children	–	£10 8s	£16 2s
13. Additional for gleaning	10s	–	–
14. Allowance from parish for work and relief for labourer and his family	£13 18s	£14	£16 10s
15. Total income of family	£20 8s	£34 18s	£39 8s
16. Out-goings for rent and fuel	£6 18s	£6 18s	£6 18s
17. Net income applicable for food, clothing, soap, candles and other necessaries	£13 10s	£28	£32 10s
18. Number of persons in labourer's family	Four	Six	Seven
19. Average income per head for the year	£3 7s 6d	£4 13s 4d	£4 13s
20. Average income per head per week	1s 3½d	1s 9½d	1s 9½d

STATE of the same THREE Labourers during 1837.

21. Work employed on	Thrashing	Jobbing	Jobbing
22. Number of weeks employed	52	38	52
23. Rate of wages per week	9s	8s	8s
24. Amount of wages of labourer at his employment	£23 8s	15s 4d	£20 16s
25. Additional for harvest	£2	£2	£2
26. Earnings of labourer's wife and children	–	£10 8s	£10 8s
27. Additional for gleaning	–	–	–
28. Allowance from parish	–	–	–
29. Total income of family	£25 8s	£27 12s	£33 4s

30. Out-goings for rent and fuel	£6 18s	£6 18s	£6 18s
31. Out-goings for benefit clubs	–	–	–
32. Net income applicable for food, clothing, soap, candles and other necessaries.	£18 10s	£20 14s	£26 6s
33. Number of persons in labourer's family	5	7	9
34. Average income per head for the year.	£3 14s	£2 19s 1½d	£2 18s 5½d
35. Average income per head per week during 1837	1s 5d	1s 1½d	1s 1½d
36. Average income per head per week during 1834	1s 3½d	1s 9½d	1s 9½d
More per head in 1837 than in 1834	1½d	–	–
Less per head in 1837 than in 1834	–	8d	8d

The foregoing tabular statement shows, that in the year 1834 these three labourers (they, their wives and children numbering together 17 persons) were employed at their occupations, collectively, 39 weeks, for which employment they received the sum of £23 16s. The earnings of their wives and children, for the same period, amounted to the sum of £25 10s, making together the sum of £50 6s. The allowance from the parish for these three families for work and relief, during 1834, amounted to the sum of £44 8s, showing a total income of £94 14s for these 17 persons. The out-goings for rent and fuel amounted to £20 14s leaving a net income of £74 applicable for food, clothing, soap, candles and other necessaries for these 17 persons; an average of £4 7s 0½d for each, or 1s 8d per head per week; the lowest family having only 1s 3½d and the highest 1s 9½d per head per week.

In 1837 these same three labourers (they, their wives and children numbering together 21 persons) were employed at their occupations, collectively, 142 weeks, and received for wages £65 8s. The earnings of their wives and children were £20 16s, making together (all parish relief being withheld) a total income of £86 4s for these 21 persons. The out-goings for rent and fuel amounted to £20 14s, leaving a net income of £65 10s applicable for food, clothing, soap, candles and other necessaries for these 21 persons, an average of £3 2s 4½d for each, or an average of 1s 2½d per head per week; the lowest family having only 1s 1½d and the highest 1s 5d per head per week.

Thus these families, by being thrown on their own resources by the operation of the new Poor Law, have had their means of living reduced, in money, from 1s 8d per head per week in 1834, to 1s 2½d per head per week in 1837, notwithstanding the work of these three men has been increased, as independent labourers, from an aggregate of 39 weeks in 1834, to an aggregate of 142 weeks in 1837.

But take the command that money had over bread in these two years, the condition of these labourers is shown to be still more deteriorated; the average price of wheat being in 1834, 46s 2d per quarter, and in 1837, 55s 9d per quarter; so that the net income of these three labourers and their families, 17 persons, would buy them 32 quarters of wheat in 1834, being 965 pints for each person, or 18½ pints of wheat per head per week; whereas their net income in 1837, being then 21 persons, would purchase them only 23½ quarters of wheat, being 573 pints for each person, or 11 pints of wheat per head per week; that is, a reduction of 41 per cent...

Select Committee on the Poor Law Amendment Act.   *BPP 1837-8 XVIII Pt.II*

2.3.4   *Under the New Poor Law, Bedfordshire parishes were grouped together into Poor Law Unions for the administration of the Act. The Unions of Bedford, Woburn, Ampthill, Luton and Biggleswade comprised Bedfordshire parishes. The Unions of Leighton Buzzard and St. Neots included about half their areas in the county, the rest being in Bucks and Hunts respectively, while the border parishes of Holwell were attached to Hitchin in Herts, and Podington and Wymington to Wellingborough in Northants.*

Applicants for poor law relief had to supply information by means of a questionnaire giving information regarding occupation, marital status, health and occupation of land.

SILSOE
APPLICATION AND REPORT
1st week of quarter ending *20th June 1840.*

Name and Age of Applicant,	*Joseph Pedder* 50
Name and Age of Wife.	*Ann* 51 plaiter
Name and Age of Children under 16	*Thomas 12 – with Mr. Flint*
	Sarah 10 – plaiter
Settlement	*Silsoe*
Residence and amount of Rent	*do. 52/- near the old workhouse*
Calling.	*Works for Mr. Eve 12/- a week*
If occupying an allotment of land quantity and Rent	*½ an Acre 17/- a piece of Garden 40 poles 10/6*
Description	*Married*
If ablebodied	*Yes*
If not ablebodied, description of disability	
If receiving Medical Aid	*from his Club*
If receiving regular or temporary Relief or relief from Club, Pension, &c	*8/- a week from Club*
Cause of present Application	*Illness on the Club 3 weeks.*

| Names of Relations liable under 43rd Elizabeth, distinguishing those apparently capable of assisting the Applicant. | *Son Samuel – Mar. Labo*^r*. 2 Children*
Son Richard do. 1 do at home
Son John – Single – farm Servant to
Mr. Eve Ramrick
Daughter Mary 16 – with Mr. Hare
Gravenhurst |

Present weekly earnings or Income of
Applicant and Family.
Relief given in Kind by Relieving
Officer.
Relief ordered by Guardians – Money.   *Refused G R*
For what period Relief ordered.
Week when ordered.

Beds. C.R.O.   *P.U.A.R. 5/2*

. . .

1 Name of Pauper, and of Wife and Children (if any)	2 Age	3 · Date of Chargeability	4 Parish of Residence (1) and supposed Parish of Settlement (2)
David Peete *Wife*	*39*	*Octr* *9th* *57*	*(1) Maulden* *(2) Tottinghoe*

Date of Coming to reside	Period of Uninterrupted Residence in the Parish			Intervals of Time to be excluded in the Computation of the Time of Residence.			Period of Residence conferring the right of Irremovability.		
	Years	Mos.	Days	Years	Mos.	Days	Years	Mos.	Days
1826	*31*	–	–	–	–	–	*31*	–	–
Totals of Periods, etc.	*31*	–	–	–	–	–	*31*	–	–

. . .

e. Or has been a Patient in any, and
     what Hospital, and for what Period?   *not before his present accident*

. . .

Further Observations of the Relieving Officer.

the pauper states he was born at Tottinghoe near Dunstable, left at the Age of
8 and came to reside in Maulden with his Widowed Mother who received
relief for himself and 3 others until they were able to work, from the said

parish of Tottinghoe, that he never did any act to gain a Settlement in his own right,

I certify that the foregoing is a true Statement of the Evidence and Grounds on which I apply to have the abovenamed Pauper charged to the Common Fund of the Union, so far as I have been able to ascertain the same.

Dated this 21st day of Octr 1857

. . .

1.   Winter farmyard scene *c.* 1830.

2.   Building a hayrick at Turvey *c.* 1830.

3. Gleaners and thatcher, *c.* 1850.

4. Woburn sheepshearing and the Woburn shepherd, 1811.

5.   Three Ampthill labourers, Joel Stanbridge, Thomas Money and another,
     c. 1890.

6. Levi Williamson, shepherd, of Great Barford, photographed between 1864 and 1869.

8. Willington farm workers at haytime, c. 1900.

9.   Isaac Parker with his threshing tackle at Gt. Barford, c. 1905.

10.   Gleaners at Riseley, *c.* 1900.

11.   Farmer and his men at harvest time, Wakes Farm, Eversholt, *c.* 1900.

3. THE LIFE OF THE LABOURER

3.1 The Working Day

Farmers' diaries describe the work done each day throughout the year by the farm labourer. Few such diaries were made, and fewer still have survived, and the three extracted relate to Harlington, Upper Stondon and Chalgrave, and are for 1847, 1866-7 and 1880.

3.1.1 Throughout the nineteenth century members of the Foll family farmed at Toddington, Chalgrave and Harlington. John Warren Foll farmed 240 acres at Harlington, and the diary (entitled "Journal of Agriculture March 1st 1847") lasts for a little over a year. It was probably kept by a farm pupil. The extracts cover a whole week in March, four consecutive entries for June, and two for September 1847. John Foll employed about 25 labourers.

1847

March 12 T. Baker, T. Bushby thatching a hovel in Wickhearn. D. Ashby, Linger, J. Purser, Bushby draining as before. Hudson and boy, Worker and do., Lorman and do., with ten horses part of the day ploughing in 12 Acres, the rest of the day in Wickhearn. T. Ashby, .Bonner and Linger twitching. Harriss and J. do. shepherding. Cartwright gardening. M. Denton and J. Chance dressing clover seed. R. Martin began threshing peas and beans. P. Ellis, Jno. Purser cutting and faggoting as before. Harriss and J. Ashby thrashing as before. S. Ashby and J. Wilson seeing to stock. T. Chance drawing tiles in the morning, twitching in Wickhearn the rest of the day. A fine day with a little frost. Mr. Parker spent the evening here.

March 13. Bushel and ½ of barley, ½ do. beans, 2 bushel Linseed for cows, ½ bushel beans, 3 bushel of barley for pigs. Hudson and boy with three horses ploughing in 12 Acres. M. Denton faggoting do. Cartwright, Worker, Linger and boy drilling barley in Wickhern with three horses. Lorman and boy, T. Ashby and do. with four horses harrowing in do. P. Ellis and Jno. Purser faggoting in Berryfields. T. Chance with two horses drawing do. away. D. Ashby, Bushby and J. Purser draining as before. R. Martin thrashing beans as yesterday. J. Chance thrashing barley. Harriss and J. Ashby do. Wheat. Harriss and J. do. shepherding. Boy keeping crows in the New Field. A fine day with a little frost. Woodward picking stones in Wadlows.

March 15 A fine day. D. Ashby, Linger, Bushby, Jos. Purser draining in the Westfield. Hudson and boy, Worker and do., Lawman and do. with 10 horses ploughing in 12 Acres. Cartwright gardening. T. Chance drawing stones out of Wadlows. Woodward finished picking do. M. Denton faggoting in 12 Acres. R. Martin thrashing beans. J. Chance barley do. T. Ashby, Bonner and boy twitching in Wickhearn. T. Bushby and Baker thatching do. P. Ellis, Jno. Purser finished hedge cutting and faggoting in Berry fields. Harriss and Jo do. and Boy Shepherding. Harriss and J. Ashby threshing wheat. Self and Mr. Foll went to Luton in the afternoon. J. Wilson and S. Ashby seeing to stock.

March 16. A fine day, Hudson and boy finished ploughing with 4 horses in 12 Acres. Lawman and do. Worker and do. with 6 horses began ploughing in the Wadloes. Woodward spreading dung in the West Mills. T. Baker and T. Bushby thatching as before. T. Ashby, Bonner and Linger junior twitching in the Wickhearn. P. Ellis and T. Chance with two horses drawing thorns. Jno. Purser faggoting in Ley Close. D. Ashby, Bushby, Jos Purser and Linger draining as before. Harriss wheat thrashing as yesterday. J. Ashby absent. Cartwright do. J. Chance finished thrashing barley about 3 o'clock, the rest of the day helping Martin thrash beans. J. Wilson seeing to stock and twitching in Spinney Close. Harriss and Jo do. shepherding. S. Ashby seeing to stock. Mr Foll at Leighton. Began brewing. M. Denton cutting hedge in Vineyard.

March 17. A fine day. Hudson and 4 horses took 16 quarters 2 bushels of wheat to Buckmaster's mill. T. Chance and boy, Lawman and do., with 6 horses ploughing in Wadloes. Cartwright, Worker, T. Bushby, T. Ashby and boy with 2 horses cutting chaff. D. Ashby, Jo Purser and Bushby draining as before. Linger filling in do. Woodward spreading dung in West Mills. Harriss and Jno. Purser winnowing wheat at Town Farm. J. Ashby absent. T. Baker mending sacks. M. Denton cutting hedge in Ploughed Vineyards. P. Ellis do. in Ploughed Woods. J. Chance and Martin threshing beans. Harriss and Jo do. shepherding. S. Ashby and J. Wilson seeing to stock. Bonner twitching the Wickhearn.

March 18. A fine day. Cartwright, T. Bushby, T. Chance, J. Chance, Jno. Purser, T. Ashby and Linger junior taking in wheat at home 3 horses. Jno. Purser and J. Chance threshing mangel seed afterwards, M. Denton, R. Martin hoeing wheat in 4 Acres. P. Ellis cutting hedge in Ploughed Woods. Hudson and boy, Lawman and do., Worker and do., with 9 horses ploughing in Wadloes. D. Ashby, Bushby, Jo Purser draining in West Field. Linger filling in do. Woodward threshing peas. Harriss do. wheat. J. Ashby absent. Baker making picks. Harriss and Jo do. Shepherding. S. Ashby seeing to stock. J. Wilson do. Bonner twitching in Wickhearn. . .

3 June. Cartwright and Chance as before. Hudson and six horses harrowing with Norwegian harrow in 6 Acres. Ashby, Bushby and Purser hoeing beans in

Duckpits. Ellis and party twitching in Wadloes. Worker and party weeding as before. Harriss and Ashby do. R. Martin and M. Denton do. in 4 Acres.

4 June. Hudson harrowing with Norwegian in Wadloes. Cartwright, Lawman and party dunging do. Ashby, Bushby and Purser hoeing beans in Duckpits. Worker and party as before. Harriss and Ashby do. R. Martin M. Denton weeding in 10 Acres. Harriss, J. Ashby shearing.

5 June. Cartwright and boy drilling turnips in Wadloes. Hudson harrowing with Norwegian harrow in 6 Acres. R. Martin M. Denton weeding in 15 Acres. P. Ellis and boys twiching do. Ashby, Bushby and Purser hoeing beans in Duckpits. Harriss and J. Ashby straw drawing. Worker and party weeding in 10 Acres. Mr. and Mrs. Foll and self spent the evening at Mr. Parkers.

7 June. Hudson, Lawman, Cook and Chance at plough in Wadloes. Bonner at roll do. Cartwright at drill do. R. Martin, M. Denton weeding in 15 Acres. P. Ellis and boys twiching as before. Ashby, Bushby and Purser hoeing beans in Duckpits. Baker horsehoeing do. Worker and party finished weeding in 10 Acres and began in Vineyards. Harriss and J. Ashby straw drawing. . .

[The journal was neglected in Harvest Time]

August 4	10 Men began reaping in 10 Acres		
5	15	do	do
6	14	do	in 10 Acres and 4 Acres
7	6	do	in 4 Acres
9	15	do	in Berryfields
10	16	do	in 10 Acres

. . .

September 18. Cartwright sowing mustard in New Field. Hudson, Lawman, T. Chance, G. Cooke and 2 boys, T. Denton, Bonner J. Cartwright and 12 horses ploughing and harrowing do. Began plough in Ploughed Woods afterwards. M. Denton, J. Bushby finished dressing wheat at Home Farm setting up bean shocks afterwards. J. Purser, Jo Wilson, Bonner and 3 boys twiching in 11 Acres. Harriss and Jo Ashby absent. W. Ashby, J. Chance turnip hoeing in Wadloes. Worker twiching in Duckpits. J. Harris setting up shocks do. Harris senior shepherding. J. Woodward water-guttering in 6 Acres. R. Martin and party stubble mowing in 15 Acres. Linger stubbling in Vineyards. Ashby, Cartwright, Babbister sheep and pig keeping. J. Purser, S. Ashby, J. Cartwright seeing to shocks. Baker and boy thatching.

September 20. Monday. Cartwright, Jo Purser, Bonner, Jo Wilson, Jo Harris and four boys potatoe digging in Wickhearn. Hudson and party at plough as before. Linger stubbling in Vineyards. R. Martin and party do. in 10 Acres. W. Ashby and J. Chance threshing at Town Farm. M. Denton, Jo Bushby finished dressing wheat at home. Baker and boy thatching. Worker twiching in Meadow. Woodward waterguttering in 6 Acres. Cartwright and Babbister sheepkeeping. J. Cartwright J Purser, S. Ashby seeing to stock.

3.1.2   *Robert Long (who was aged 43 in 1861) farmed 280 acres at Ston-*
don Manor Farm situated on a low ridge of the gault clay in south east
Bedfordshire between Shefford and Hitchin. The farm was a mixed
one on land nearly all leased from the Wrest Park Estate at Silsoe. In
1861 the farm employed 16 men and 4 boys but it is impossible to
say with certainty how many people were economically dependent on
this farm. Upper Stondon was very small and most of the farm
workers lived in either Lower Stondon or in Meppershall, both within
a mile. Usually we possess only the surnames of labourers, and so it is
difficult to see who is meant from the census enumerators' records.
There are, for example, two Rainbows and three Dilleys, all within
easy walking distance of Stondon Manor. Nor is it likely that all the
families of these labourers were entirely dependent on the wages that
Robert Long paid them, for most labourers had wives and daughters
who were straw plaiters.

1866

27th January. Very mild, very still, and chiefly dull, yet we had some sun-
shine. On Monday the teams finished up all the ploughing we have to do at
present. Since then some of the horses carted dung from the yards, and two
days the teams went out with the wagon to Ickleford with wheat. All the
week the odd folks have carted dung from the yards and now we have a large
pressed heap of it just at home near the horse pond, as handy as could be to
the gate without damaging the roads, for all the time lately the ground has
been so very wet and soft we could not cart on the land without doing damage. Four men have been draining, two in Debditch, putting in some new
cross drains where the water stood in the hollows, and where some old
wooden drains had burst out. The pipe drains are all cut into and run well.
This Debditch field is now quite green in places after the steam ploughing and
dung on the surface. I expect we shall have to plough it again in some way or
other before the beans are put in, but we must have dry weather before that
can be done. It is terribly dirty now. Today I had chaff cut and meal ground,
and roots pulped with the engine. The garden job is not yet quite finished.
Two men have been most of the time at it again this week replanting the
flowers on the new borders . . . The old hedge at the bottom of the grass
meadow I have cut up this week, and hope the new quick fence behind will
be strong enough to stop the cattle now. . . .

7th July. Shocking wet weather it has been this week for the hay, yet to-day it has been fine all the day long, but we dare not move the hay for it threatened rain again so much. Every time we did so lately it got wetted. Nearly every day there was thunder, yesterday the most, and yesterday, as we could not get on with the hay, I had a stack of winterbeans thrashed, the one that stood close to home next to the Plantation. On Monday the men finished transplanting Kohl Rabi next to the Lucerne from the rows of plants between the Mazagan Beans in the Little Field. The rest of the time, when the weather would permit, the men singled out turnips on the bouts in Rust Hill Shot. The teams have been at odd jobs carting out dung and carting in gravel to the yards, and also to the New Close ruts that have been made larger lately since the weather has been so showery. Today I sent two carts to Hitchin for gas lime, the roads at home being too wet for carting, and I sent for a cart home from Bedford that had been 14 months waiting for new wheels. At the same time I had some new rope porters from Bedford for the steam cultivation, for several of mine are worn out . . . I am trying Thorleys food for the sheep in a small way . . . On Wednesday I served on the Grand Jury at the Quarter Sessions. Today I had the harness menders here. . . .

	£	s	d
4th August. First Week of Harvest			
Millard 3s 9d R. Dilley 12s S. Cobb 8s 6d Young 10s			
Thos. Hibbitt 10s	2	4	6 [sic]
Thos. Whitbread 6s Gazely 4s Shepherd 11s 11d			
C Whitbread 4s seeds 7d	1	5	7
John Dunham & Company Recd. on the Harvest	9	0	0
	12	10	1

Very showery for Harvest. Today it has been fine, and very windy, yet almost every day besides it has been rainy. The men have shifted several days from wheat to bean cutting. The Brickfield crop of winter beans is all cut, but not tied. All the Hardcastle white wheat I had cut first, and now they are cutting the Nursery sort in the Ladyleys. All the week the dirt has clogged on the men's feet, but it could not be avoided for now all the wheat wants cutting and must be done when the weather is not too bad. Today I have had the horse drag going between the shock rows. It has not before been dry enough. The pigeons today have been very troublesome on the Gravel Pit Piece. I am ob-liged to have a boy there constantly to keep them off. Two teams have been kept ploughing the clover ley on the Eight Acre Shot in Littlefield just above Debditch. It has been too wet for the cultivator wheels to run so we have not used it much this week. It has also been a bad time for the reaping machines. Several of our neighbours have got them in readiness this year but could not start them even, which was very disappointing, and no doubt has made the men chuckle over it rather, particularly now that labour is scarce and men have got so independent. I am sorry to say mine got colting again the first day of the month, a thing I have so often quarrelled with them about before. I always threaten to discharge a man who fetches beer from a public house, but in Harvest time when the corn wants cutting (and they know it) it cannot be carried out. I was only last week boasting that I had kept the same lot on ever since last Harvest and had got no fresh hands even now, but again I am sorry to say it, I have lost all confidence in them, and once again conclude they are not much better to be trusted than others. Now it rains again and the glass gets no higher. . . .

1st December. Mild altogether for the time of year, yet we have had frosty mornings. Two days were bright and sunny, yet in London those days it was a dense fog as bad as ever was known there, so the papers reported. Two days this week, after the frost, I had dung carted on the Ladyleys where I want to get some beet. Today it was put on Hempland corner, where I thought of growing some flax or linseed. On Monday I had a stack of old plump small beans thrashed, and have sold some of them for 34s 6d per load. These are not quite so good and dry as the other stack last week. I sold some for 36s per load to the same man. All the week we have been brewing to fill two of the great barrels up. Malt is now 10s per bushel and hops 2s per lb. On Saturday night last there was another fire at Langford at Mr C. Fowler's, a corn stack again, making now 3 in the family in a very short time. This last one happened in the middle of the night, and stood in the field, which proves it to be again the act of an incendiary. How sad it is to think about even, but very sad indeed where it does happen, for certainly there must be spite of some kind. This week R. Long junior planted a chestnut tree near the S.E. corner of the farm buildings, which I have had well fenced round to protect it. The fat sheep have just finished eating the white turnips on the Rusthill-shot, and have begun the kohl rabi adjoining the lucern near the Sandpit. Some poles I have had cut in the Spinney and brought home to keep the hurdle maker going. Four men are still draining on the west side of the Rust-hill-shot where the turnips are eaten off. The earth is very strong there. . . .

1867

	£	s	d
23rd March			
R. Dilly 11s Jn. Rainbow 10s 6d, Jn. Cobb 11s, Millard 3s 6d	1	16	0
A. Jenkins 4s 6d, Gazely 4s, G. Jenkins 11s 8d,			
G. Whitbread 3s 6d	1	3	8
Payne 11s, Abm. Rainbow 11s, Harris 3s 6d,			
Wm . Dunham 11s 4d	1	16	10
Jn. Dunham 11s 10d, Jas. Rainbow 12s 6d,			
Saml. Cobb 8s 6d	1	12	10

Thos. Whitbread 6s, expenses 2s 8d, Arnold 12s,
Shepherd 12s   1   12   8
Jackson 12s expenses 2s 4d, Jenkins 12s,
Whitebread & son 17s   2   3   4
    22, one unwell   10   5   4

Very winterly all the week. Three times this week the ground has been quite covered with snow. Today we had fog and rain. The snow has most of it gone hereabouts, yet we can see long streaks of it on the hills in the distance. The land and roads are very soft and dirty and set, as well they may be after so much snow. Most of the week we have been carting out dung from the yards, and have now made a very large heap just outside the gate near the Brewhouse. On Thursday it was fine and we began to take a wheatstack in, although the ground was all white with snow, for the chaff was all used up and we had none to go on with. The stack was the last from New Close. We have not been able to finish it yet, for the weather has been so bad, but all the straw that was thrashed I have had cut up into chaff, so now the barn is quite empty again, and I can stow away the brewing tackle there before it is filled again. We have been 10 days brewing this time, and have filled 3 of the large barrels in the cellar, and all the small beer pipes also in the Brewhouse. Today I sent a cart load of seed barley to Ampthill to meet a cart from Broughton, Bucks (Henry Pestells) and when he came back, I found him very dissatisfied with his wages. He had heard from the Bucks man about the strikes they have had there lately, and on the strength of it demanded 1s more per week of me, which I did not consent to. Was it likely when my neighbours are paying the same as myself? What very bad weather it has been for the lambs. They have been but very little in the fields for it has been so very much snowed up. 20 loads of old beans I sent to Hitchin this week and brought back coals from the station. Two men have been finishing the hedge stocking at the top of the sward meadow, and also moved the gate to the line of new quick hedge, which is to take the place of the old one just grubbed up. A new window I have had put in the barn wall on the yard side, so as to be able to put the straw out that way when we think proper. . . .

17th August. Very variable. The early part of the week was very hot, and it brought on thunder early on Thursday morning. Since then it rained heavily at times, but none today, although it is very stormy and cold. The men kept on wheat cutting when it was not too wet. Then they cut winter beans in New Close. Much of my white wheat is sadly blighted or mildewed. On the clover ley piece where I ploughed it up early and had mustard after, it was the worst, yet in Lady Kents Corner after winter beans it was not much better, although it is Chidham. The rest is Hardcastle, both white wheat, which are always more subject to mildew. The best I have is where it looked the worst all the Spring, and which I really felt ashamed of because it looked so pale and light. It was after mangolds [had been] drawn off. The men are cutting it today. It all stands and has ripened kind. The oats in Debditch were all carted on Tuesday morning, and now I have got them all thatched, but not before they had a wetting. On Tuesday afternoon after finishing oat cart, I set the odd men to cart dung from the yards to Debditch, and they kept on till the rain stopped them. Today I had some more mustard harrowed in on the Lawn Shot, Spinney side. The whole piece of fallow, about 34 acres, is now sown with it. I had also some cabbage seed drilled in the piece below the Grass Meadow on Wednesday. On Tuesday evening a Balloon passed over here and fell at Beadlow. Mr. and Mrs. Long went to tea at Lady Cowper's at Wrest Park on Wednesday, the very hot day before the thunder came. Four old men began to cut Masagan beans in the Chibley field today. I have bought a lot of 12 pigs this week of Cooper at 9s each. . . .

28th September. Very fine dry weather still. On Thursday the Debditch field steam cultivation was finished at noon, and the tackle all shifted to the Rust Hill Shot barley stubble, the home side, but as the dung was not spread, we were obliged to wait a day for it to be done previous to starting. This morning we made a fresh start, and broke the tine of the large cultivator on the carted part, and have sent it to Hitchin to have a new one fitted to it, for I find it is no use mending them where the strain is so great on them as it is now the ground has got so very hard. Today only we finished carting dung from the great heap near home to the Little Fields towards Lower Stondon, and the piece where the spring wheat was grown near the Sand Pit, and some on the top end of the Eight Acre Shot top of Debditch. All the empty carts this week were filled with gravel (that I bought of Mr. Watson) in the Sand Pit and loaded back home till today both jobs were finished, and a very fine time it has been for it. We kept on all day long. Yesterday 2 teams began to plough in some of the mustard on the Charlock Hill Shot. Today the crab harrowing was all finished after the skim plough in the Chibley Field, and some of it burnt. I mean the weeds that had been harrowed out. This morning one of the heifers calved before we expected it. This afternoon I have been to Ashwell to see a second hand harmonium which we think of purchasing for the school services at Lower Stondon. The sturks have been out in the field on the young clover plant every day this week. One hooved and we gave it a bullet which has apparently prevented its doing so again. I have often used them before with good effect. Mr. Dodwell's steam cultivating tackle was broken wilfully on Sunday last and has offered five pounds reward to find it out. . . .

26th October	£	s	d
Harris 3s 6d Millard 3s 6d G. Thompson 2s 6d J. Cobb 11s	1	0	6
G. Whitbread 12s J. Dunham and Jno. Rainbow ½ day each 2s		14	0
J. Dunham recd on winter bean setting	3	0	0
Shepherd		12	0
Saml. Cobb 10s Eli Gazely 4s 6d Payne 1s Wm Dunham 1s		16	6
Young		9	0
G. Jenkins 1s 10d J. Jenkins 11s & 2s on marking		14	10
R. Dilley 8s 9d J. Rainbow 5s 9d Thos. Hibbitt 7s 6d			
Thos. Whitbread 9s	1	11	0
Arnold 12s 6d expenses 2s Whitbread & son 17s 6d			
expenses 2s 6d	1	14	6
22 (pd. sheep dressers 50s, sieve menders 6s 6d,			
window mender 2s)	10	12	4

Fine, mild and foggy. The days have been very bright, but nights and mornings foggy. On Monday began to set winter beans in Debditch where it was steam ploughed, but it was very rough in places for the marking and harrowing. One team ploughed headlands, which were very hard. All the other teams were ploughing mustard land in Lawn Shot after sheep, and drilling oats, and on Wednesday, Chidham wheat in the lower corner of Lawn Shot. Yesterday I sent the wagon to Hitchin station for 6½ quarters of Nursery seed wheat which was fen-grown. I had no Red Wheat last year, and was sorry for it, particularly after the Broad Clover. The white wheat does not ever seem at home there -- I mean, it grows too rank and frothy, I think, always, and the past harvest more so. The ewes have been dressed to cure the scab which was breaking out, and the pigs have been rung to stop their digging. Two more cows have calved. One I had sold on Tuesday last, and one I sold Cooper of Lower Stondon. On Monday last, after attending a Turnpike Trust meeting at Shefford, I had a job to take two prisoners back, or rather, to go back again with two men to the Police Station at Shefford hand-cuffed to the Dogcart, and of course another man to assist. They had been assaulting a gamekeeper at Nun Wood on Saturday, and being at Meppershall again on Monday, the villagers followed them to my gate. Then Mr. Hull and I and my man Whitbread joined them in the chase. We took them on the Holwell bridle road after much threatening to be stabbed by them in the attempt to do so. On Wednesday, before the Magistrates at Biggleswade, they were sentenced to two months hard labour. Took out the charcoal which was put in in October 29th 1864 and cleared out the water tank at the end of the Fish Pond.

Beds. C.R.O.   X 159/3

3.1.3   Richard William Foll, nephew of John Warren Foll, farmed 540 acres at Chalgrave Manor Farm held of the Mercers' Company. In the 1871 census he was employing 23 men. The extracts are taken from an account book entitled: "R. W. Foll's Labour a/c from Mich. 1875 On Chalgrave Manor Farm, Beds." and entries continue to 1896. On the left of each double page is a list of men and their usual wage; then come four columns for four weeks' wages (with totals); then a column for "Remarks". The extracts begin with the wages paid on 2 Jan 1880, and continue with the "Remarks" for each month of the year.

1880

January 2nd. Dumpleton T. 14s; Turvey Jo 14s; son Wm 8s 6d Geo 7s 6d; Hide Jas 13s 6d; Bates H. (Toddington) 13s 6d; Baker T. 12s; son 3s 6d; Turvey T. 12s; Turvey Joe 12s; Tring Jo 12s; Hart D. 12s; Garritt W. 12s; Chapman 12s; Bates H. (Woodend) 12s; Ayres Jo 12s; Willis Jas 12s; Denton W. 12s; Bates T. 12s; Whitbread 5s 6d; Brown 5s; Holman 5s; Hart 5s and 6d; Sinfield 3s 6d; Kingham 3s 6d; Groom 3s 6d; Whitbread 2s 6d. T. Turvey settled thatching straw hay and harvest work see Page 170 £3 8s 6d...

1880

January. Remarks No Wheat up on Chalgrave Manor Farm few Kernels just coming through that was put in 29 October by the 1st January. J. W. Foll Harlington finished wheat sowing 3 January latest he ever remembered to be. No wheat up in this part of the county by 1st Jan. that I, R. W. Foll, know of, only small piece of Mr. Jo. Dover on Red Hill Farm. 4 January Tegs finished all Turnip & Rabi. Finished Wheat sowing 13th January 1880 began 29 October and none up so that can see the rows can hardly tell it wheat at all if did not know – about 120 acres.

February. Remarks 7th could just see rows of Wheat 1st time in New Ground that was drilled 29 and 30 October seems coming up well. 7th set Winter Beans Woodfield next New Mead 3a 3½ bushels per acre up furrows. Began setting spring beans 12 Feb Sorrys Close 4½ bushels per acre bad seed from Jas. Proctor very bad. Shepherd began having beer for night 17th February. Ring bell 6 O'clock at night and 6 morning 24 February 1880.

March. Remarks Finished plowing for Beans 3rd March. Finished setting beans 5 March if do not have to plow any more clover up and peas. 7th Mr T. Janes drilled top end of field opposite Slipe, wheat Red Lamas, 9 & 10 March and left bottom part for Spring wheat. Began penning Wheat off Moores thin end. 12 March folded tegs on at night 169 of them 12 by 12 hurdles in fold. 27 March finished plowing for Barley and began plow for Roots Mangels. Began drilling Oats 15a and 14a Dutch blues too wet could not go on 1 & 2 April.

April. Remarks Mr T. Janes drilled some April wheat in corner of field next Mercers Piece bottom corner 3 April. I began drilling oats 1 April wet could not get on finished 9 April I began drilling barley finished. Tilled beans up in Sorrys Close with Essex Mazagan, began 3 April, and finished 13 April. Heard Cuckoo first time 21st April in Great Wood. Ewe and lamb laid out 1st night in Olneys Close 21st April. Finished penning wheat off Bandyland 23rd April. Finished barley sowing 23 April.

May. Remarks Finished Harrowing wheat Moors 1st May been eat off with sheep — 18th first night any beast laid out and then only 7 of them, frost night and very cold sunny days. Parkins said they had 4s 6d per score for store and 5s for fat sheep shearing, & 4 or 5 pints beer each per day 6d per score, for use of brook 1s, & 2 pints beer per score if they washed them. 25th 1st night Cow laid out. Wind been so cold & frosty nights.

June. Remarks T. Janes men Harrowing & hoeing Lamas Wheat 1st June & afterwards only began Field the 31 May. Field opposite Slipe was finished 14 June. Mr Janes Men hoeing oats 16 June. Mr Jo Adams sowing seeds in & hoeing Oats & harrow seeds in 15 & on 22 June.

July. Remarks Began cutting Grass Watergait 12 July. It so showery or should have began before. Began setting Mangels out Coppice 10 July. Finished cutting [? Grass] 7 ac. 23 July. Cut about 3 ac. of clover Union & Hordon it missed eat it off with sheep & being so showery could not cut it before.

August. Remarks 2 Aug Began cutting Peas Common Sangster No. 1. I set them for picking-they never grew. Hay home except some round about, & ricks to make up. 6 Aug. Cut Trifoil & dutch seed 5, 6 & 7 Aug Ladys Hollow green Standing & when cut so hot & wet. Began cutting Wheat 21st Aug & grain Month 23rd Aug. Began cutting Dutch blue Oats 23 Aug & Tartan Blk 27 Aug. Began cutting Winter Beans set in February 31 Aug & Spring Beans same day only Greener. 31 Aug Began cutting Barley.

September. Remarks Began cutting Rurt Wheat 6 Sep the day we should have finished cutting other sort of Wheat only we went to oat cart 1 Sep instead. Mr T. Janes cutting his Wheat Opposite Slipe red Lammas that was Drilled 9 & 10 of March and some Spring Wheat drilled some time after say 3rd April all quite dead ripe. Very Poor crop. Did not blight quite so bad as some of it did this year. Finished cutting Barley 9 Sep and Rent about 10 Sep. Finished cutting Spring Beans 27 Sep. One Wheat cock and one Oat cock Long Ground that had the 4 wet days and the 2 very heavy rains on in the time before they were thatched heated and sunk tremendous and they were carried very dry and in good order. The rain came from 11th Sep to 18th or till after they were thatched.

October. Remarks Harvest Home 16th. Winter Beans cut Woodfield. Going to Dunstable morning 20 Oct J. W. Barnard at Wheat & Bean cart seemed to have lot of Wheat to carry 1 stack or more Rents. Began getting Mangels up 20 Oct say.

November. Remarks Began Wheat sowing 6 Nov in Lords Hill. Ewes laid in yard 27th 1st night. Finished carting Mangels off 29 Nov only had about 14 ac set swedes.

December. Remarks Finished carting Swedes off [   ] we ought to have had Mangels in Coppice 17 December. Had horses in yard and Dial Close to give them Hay 17th Night.

Beds. C.R.O.   X 52/71

3.2   Social Life

No single question is more difficult for the social historian of rural England to answer than to say whether or not a village community was a happy community. Surviving evidence does not give the impression of cultural richness or variety, and by modern material standards it was a harsh and barren existence. More to the point, contemporary observers such as Richard Jefferies comment on the lack of spiritual awareness, imagination or vision of the English countryman, even when compared with contemporaries among the European peasantry, who may have been no better off, but who still retained a strong cultural identity. Compared with the continental peasant, or even with the Celtic peasantry in Scotland, Ireland or Wales, the English countrymen had no strong traditions of national dress, oral heritage of legend or myth, or even distinctive cooking.

Even the sporadic outbreaks of unrest hardly amount to a tradition of colourful banditry to compare with the Scottish highlands or the peasantry of, say, Spain or the Balkans.

The social life of the English village was to a great extent a watered-down version of the social life of the upper echelons. Villages possessed small friendly societies and local charities. There was always the pull between what the labourers were prepared to do for themselves, and what their betters expected of them. 'Friendly societies' were always in two minds as to whether they were social clubs or merely mutual benefit associations managing a pension fund. Land set aside for the poor tended to become administered by landowners or clergy as a charity, rather than be available for the poor as of right. Village festivals and feasts were always under pressure not to be too exuberantly proletarian, nor to show too much working class high spirits. It would be exaggerating to say that the working classes were oppressed in Bedfordshire, but they were treated like children.

3.2.1   A Friendly Society. There were Friendly Societies or Benefit Clubs in most Bedfordshire villages, each with its own rules. The rules of the Eyeworth Friendly Society were printed by T.W. Spong, Printer, Stationer, etc., High Street, Biggleswade, 1869.

Articles of Agreement made and continued by A Friendly Society of Working Men, Held at the House of Edward Franklen, Ongley's Arms, Eyeworth, Bedfordshire. Instituted September 1849.

We, whose Names are entered in the Book hereunto belonging, for the promoting Christian Love, upon all just occasions, to assist each other, do bind ourselves by the following Articles.

IMPRIMIS. That our times of Meeting shall be on the last Saturday in every fourth week, between the hours of seven and nine from Lady-day to Michaelmas day, and between the hours of six and eight from Michaelmas to Lady-day; every member shall pay 1s 6d per month, and each member is to have one quart of beer, and the rest to be put in the chest provided for that purpose: and if any member neglect paying his payments at any of these meetings, if he appear in the club room, he shall forfeit one quart of beer.

II. That no person shall enter this Society without the consent of the senior members, that have been in the Society one whole year; and every person that enters himself shall be in perfect health, and not above 35 years of age; and if after his or their admission, he or they be proved to have any infirmity in body, or above age, before he or they entered, he or they shall be excluded this Society, without any return of money out of the chest: and every person that enters himself shall pay 2s for his entrance, 1s to the clerk, and spend one quart of beer.

III. That every member shall pay, or cause to be paid, all demands on every quarter night, which shall be the last Saturday before St. Michael, and the first meeting night before every quarter day in the year.

IV. That there shall be a New Steward chosen every month, who shall receive every member's money, and pay it into the chest, and every member who has been in this society one year, shall serve steward in his turn, or forfeit 1s, and on the said monthly night the old steward shall deliver up his accounts, keys, and books, to the assistant, who shall then become steward, and the next member on the list shall be appointed assistant in his room; which books shall contain all the money paid out by him, received in, and the balance of the said accounts.

V. That the steward for the time being shall attend every month, between the hours appointed, and if he be absent, he shall forfeit 6d for the first night, for the second 1s, and so double for his absence during his stewardship, except sick, lame, blind, or otherwise disordered; and during his absence the assistant shall act as steward; and if it should happen that both steward and assistant should be absent at any meeting night, the two first members that come into the room shall officiate for that evening, or forfeit 6d each, which said members shall be invested with the same power in every respect for that evening, as the steward and assistant, or if the steward neglects to send his key on the club night in due time, he shall forfeit 6d.

VI. No person shall be admitted into the club room without the consent of the majority, and if he partakes of what is spent he shall pay 4d to the house; but if any person brings an absent member's money, they shall have one pint and a half of beer out of the club room.

VII. No member shall receive any money from the stock of this society, until he hath paid all demands to the society one whole year; after which time, if any member becomes sick, lame, blind, or otherwise afflicted, so as not to be able to work, (except by fighting, drunkenness, whoring, or inoculation for the small pox,) he shall then acquaint the steward or stewards of the same, and if he continues so one whole week, he shall be allowed 8s per week from the box, and shall have the money paid him by the stewards for one year; and if his affliction shall continue after the expiration of one whole year, he shall be allowed 3s 6d per week, as long as such affliction shall continue; and if any member breaks a bone, as a leg, arm, &c., (except as before, by fighting, drunkenness, whoring, or gaming,) he shall receive 10s 6d the second club night after giving notice of the same to the stewards, over and above his week's pay, from the box; which sum shall be towards paying a surgeon for setting and curing his broken limb or bone, and every member shall pay 3d towards the same the first quarterly night after, and during the time any member receives money from the box, in his sickness or lameness, he shall keep his payments to the box.

VIII. If any member receives money from the box, for sickness, lameness, &c., and it be proved that it came by fighting, drunkenness, whoring, or gaming, he shall return all the money he received, or be excluded; and every member that is a soldier or sailor, except drawn by lot, or impressed, shall be excluded; but if drawn for the Old Militia, but not for the Local, he shall be allowed 40s.

IX. That if any member become sick or lame, or otherwise afflicted, as aforesaid, so that he be entitled to, and require the benefit of the box, he shall give notice to the steward or stewards, and one or both of the stewards shall visit him twice a week, and that on two working days, or forfeit, 1s, and the steward that goes to visit him shall be allowed 2d per mile, for three miles; and if any live above three miles from the box, and he be taken sick, one of the stewards shall visit him once a week, and that on a working day, and be allowed 2d per mile for six miles.

X. If any member becomes sick or lame, above six miles from the box, then any other person may receive the money for him, upon producing an order every week signed by the minister, churchwarden, or overseer of the parish he is in, certifying that he is unable to work.

XI. If any member demands money on pretence of being sick or lame, and shall be known to work during the time he receives his pay from the box, he shall be excluded; and if any member knows of any one to work during the time of his receiving pay from the box, and conceal the same, he shall be excluded.

XII. When any member dies, there shall be allowed from the box, for his funeral, and for the widow, or fatherless, or to whom he before his death shall leave the same, as follows: if he has been in the club one whole year, £1, two years, £2, three years, £3, four years, £4, five years, £5, but they shall receive for no more than for the whole years that he was in, which shall be paid the first club night; and every member shall pay 1s towards the same, on the first quarterly night after his funeral. Every member that attends at a funeral, must appear with hat-band and gloves, or forfeit 1s.

XIII. If any member's lawful wife dies after her husband has been in this society one year, the surviving husband shall receive 20s from the box, towards the funeral charges, if demanded, the first club night after her decease, and every member shall pay 6d towards the same. But if any one buries his wife, and receives the 20s as aforesaid, the said 20s shall be deducted from the sum allowed at his death.

XIV. If any member dies within three miles of the box, the person that buries him shall give notice to the steward or stewards two days before they inter him, of the time and place where he is to be interred, or forfeit 5s, and the steward or stewards shall give notice to those of the society that reside within three miles of the box, or forfeit 1s, except the person died of the small pox, and all the members that have notice and do not attend the funeral, if within 3 miles, shall forfeit 6d.

XV. The members of this society agree to have one feast every year, which shall be on the first meeting in May, and every member shall pay, or cause to be paid, 1s if required, towards a dinner, or be excluded if not paid on the feast day, and that dinner be ready at 2 o'clock in the afternoon.

XVI. That the chest shall not be broken or shared so long as three members will hold to a society, who shall be invested with the same power to hold it as such, as the whole body; and if any member propose to share the money in the chest, he shall be excluded.

XVII. That if any member of this society, at any of these meetings, swears, curses, gives any abusive language to the steward or stewards, or their representatives, or offers to fight, quarrel, or challenge to fight in the society room, he shall for every such offence forfeit 5s, or if any member shall quarrel or challenge to fight on the club night, or on the club feast day, he shall for every such offence forfeit 5s, or if any member keep not silent when three times commanded by the stewards or their representatives, to pay 3d, and for every oath 2d.

XVIII. If any one lays wagers, or gambles in the society room, he shall forfeit 1s, or if he offers to lay a wager, to forfeit 2d.

XIX. It is agreed that this society shall not be removed from the house aforesaid, without a just reason, and with the consent of the majority, and the club room to be ready at the hours aforesaid, on the meeting night, or the master of the house to forfeit 5s to the box.

XX. If any member be cast into prison for debt, he shall be freed from all payments, and shall not be allowed to pay or receive while in prison, but shall be received when he comes out, without cost or charges, into this society again. And if any member be convicted of felony, to be excluded for ever.

XXI. That all forfeitures and payments due from any members shall be paid into the chest, towards increasing the stock, and the books entirely discharged therefrom, on every quarterly night on which the same shall become due and payable, and every member so neglecting or refusing to discharge the same, shall be forthwith excluded.

XXII. That all debates and disputes that arise in this society, shall be decided by the major part of the members then present, except it be any matter touching these articles, which shall be decided at the general quarterly meeting; and if any member refuse to abide by the decision of the said majority, he shall forfeit 1s.

XXIII. That no stock is to be lent out without lawful interest and approved security.

XXIV. Every assistant steward is to see that the proper allowance of beer is bought into the club room, and that every member has his proper share. JOHN HUMBERSTONE, Steward; JESSE JARVIS, Book-Keeper.

Beds. C.R.O. CRT 130 Eyeworth 1

3.2.2 *A Parish Charity. Eyeworth also had a Poors' Charity estate. In 1864 most of the land was let to a single tenant, but the four who leased small amounts of land also received doles from the annual income.*

Eyeworth Poors' Charity

Dr. A List of Recipiants to
the Poors Charity

Date & No. March 28th 1864	Names	No. in Family	Amount £ s d
in Town	Samuel Sole	4	6 4
"	John Sole	2	3 2
"	John Humberstone	2	3 2
"	Widow Chandler	1	1 7
"	George Hall	5	7 11
"	William Carter	6	9 6
"	Benjamin Chandler	6	9 6
"	James Carter	3	4 9
"	David Bartle	5	7 11

Date & No. March 28th 1864	Names	No. in Family	Amount £ s d
in Town	Widow Humberstone	1	1 7
"	Edward Franklin	2	3 2
"	Franklin	6	9 6
"	Joseph Morley	2	3 2
"	John Osborn	1	1 7
"	Thomas Nicholdson	2	3 2
"	William Morley	2	3 2
"	George Carter	3	4 9
	Carried Forward	53 .	4 3 11

Cr. Tenants of the Charity

Date March 26th 1864	Names	Tenants who pay the rates	Amount £ s d
	Simeon Lee		10 " "
	George Hall	1/4	10 "
	Benjamin Chandler	1/4	10 "
	David Bartle	1/4	10 "
	Jer^h. Franklin	1/8	10 "
	Carried Forward	5/8	12 " "

Beds. C.R.O. P. 19/25/1

3.2.3   Drunkenness and Feasts. The labouring classes were constantly being rebuked for drunkenness, and as far as possible the gentry and clergy restricted or reformed occasions for celebration, such as harvest homes or village feasts, that were likely to lead to excesses.

The Rev. Stephen Fawcett, Vicar of Eaton Socon, published two pamphlets for the benefit of his parishioners.

TO THE HARVEST LABOURERS OF THE PARISH OF EATON SOCON. I have been told that it is a custom among you to get drunk on the first day of being hired for harvest. Now I have heard many of you say that you look forward to the harvest as the best time in all the year for making a little money. Can you possibly expect God's blessing on your labour by running wilfully at the first start into a deadly sin? When you see God so faithful to His promise, that "whilst the earth remains seed time and harvest shall not cease," how diligently should you thank Him, instead of calling down His curse upon you, and making yourselves more stupid and senseless than the dumb animals. Some of you may perhaps say, "Oh it is only once in a way that I so far forget myself." Suppose at that very time God should call you to your last account, what would that excuse do for you? ...

The drunkard is not his own enemy only – Oh! he has much to answer for – he sins against his family by beggaring them, and still worse, by setting an evil example, and so endangering their souls; – he sins against his neighbour, – his country, – and indeed it is not possible to say where the effects of his wickedness end. Cursing and swearing proceed from his mouth, – he calls his neighbour a fool, (and the Bible says, he is in danger of hell fire who calls his brother a fool) – Quarrels ensue, and often end in murder, – and how the love of drink leads to breaking the fourth Commandment; for to spend a Saturday's Evening in a public-house is a dreadful preparation for the holy Sabbath-day. And I warn you, that at the awful day of judgment you need not think to plead you did not know what you were about; for the excuse of drunkenness will only make your case the worse. God says, "The drunkard shall not inherit the kingdom of God," and again, "Take heed to yourselves, lest at any time your heart be overcharged with surfeiting and drunkenness, so that day come upon you unawares." ... Remember you must not resolve to do better in your own strength, you cannot make yourself clean; – go then to the only Fountain for Sin, and for uncleanness, and may the Saviour exercise his pity toward you, and make a way for you to escape, that you may not be taken captive by the devil at his will.

This is the prayer of a faithful friend. July, 1848.

TO THE GLEANERS. Since writing the foregoing, three years ago, I have much wished to say a few words to the Gleaners in this large parish; – when I see you all assembled together, the thought arises, "How many of this great number of women and children will be able to answer at the Great day of account, with their Master in Heaven, for their sayings and doings in the gleaning field?" The owners of the fields kindly allow you to glean, therefore you may be supposed to go forth with grateful thanksgivings to the Almighty Giver of every good gift; for surely the corn you get is a good gift, – and you take your children with you, so that all anxiety about them is spared you; – the sweet fresh air, the pleasant exercise does you good: – do you feel thankful for these mercies? Some of you I believe do. But of too many, the scolding tongue, – the scandal, – the angry disputings, – evil example to the young ones around you! all to be heavily accounted for. How the Word of God warns us against such sins.

The time of harvest should especially remind us of the Great Harvest of all, – the end of the world – it will come upon us suddenly, for the Bible says, "of that day and hour knoweth no man," and feeling deeply anxious that your souls may be saved, I remind you again, that Gleaners have a great call to examine into the states of their souls, and see if they can really look unto God as their reconciled Father in Christ Jesus, and make this an occasion to edify one another: of shewing kindness to the aged and infirm: of instructing their little ones in the ways of honesty, not suffering them to pilfer even a grain of corn that does not belong to them, or to use a bad word, or to be rude and quarrelsome, but "to cherish a meek and quiet spirit, which in the sight of God is of great price," and to make them feel the awful trust that we never can be one moment out of God's sight, for his blessed book says, "The eyes of the Lord are in every place, beholding the evil and the good;" and as every thing is appointed by God, I would beg of you to check all murmurings about the quality of the corn, or the weather, or any other thing which may not be exactly as you like, but (as the Bible teaches us) giving thanks always for all things to God.

I will now only say that I hope you will receive these few words in the same kindly spirit in which they are written by Your faithful friend and sincere well-wisher. July 31st, 1851. Tomson, Printer, St. Neots.

Beds. C.R.O. CRT 130, Eaton Socon 2.

Quarter Sessions moved to restrict village feasts.

Bedfordshire Mercury 24 October 1859.
Bedfordshire Michaelmas Quarter Sessions. Second Day — Wednesday. The court met this morning at ten o'clock, and precisely at that hour the proceedings commenced. T.C. Higgins, Esq., occupied the chair: W.L. Smart, J. Tucker, W.H. Beauford, G.P. Nash, H. Littledale, Esqrs., and Captain Moore were also on the bench ... There was one other matter he wished to bring before them, and it was one that was of great interest to every person in every parish in the county. There had been a custom grown up, and it was now of a very serious character he was sorry to say, that at feasts and fairs (and all their villages had one during the year) a number of persons entered the place, put up their booths, kept them standing for two or three days, much to the harm of the interests of the public, and very much to the injury of respectable tradesmen in the neighbourhood. It tempted young people to spend their money, and it only tended to increase the selfish emoluments arising from public-houses, for it was there that the harvest was made. If they had any influence in their respective parishes he trusted they would exercise it in order to put a stop to these stalls being left standing for such a time. No person had any right to erect a booth, at all; but they were not desirous of dealing too rigidly with them. It was an absolute permission only, and not a right that these parties could claim. There might be some places in the county in which the lord of the manor had the power to give permission to hold a fair and to erect booths, but these instances were exceedingly rare, in short he only knew of one in the whole county. If they allowed the parties to erect their booths on one day he thought that was quite sufficient, and as much as they could reasonably expect. The magistrates in this division had given strict orders to the police to acquaint the parties with the fact that they would be allowed to erect their tents for one day, but that they must be taken down by the next. He was quite sure it would be conducive to the morals and well-being of the poor people in these villages to come to such a determination. He liked to see cheerful merry faces and kind looks, but he never witnessed a fair or any kind of feast (and there was one held now in connection with a friendly society, so that there were in some villages three or four feasts held during the course of the year), but what he saw drunkenness to a very great extent. It was extremely distressing to see these numerous cases of drunkenness; a holiday in a village ought to be for the benefit of the poor people, and not to suit the selfish purposes of those persons who keep public-houses. It was almost wrong that they should reap the harvest at the expense of the pockets of the poor people.

Bedfordshire Mercury 24th July 1860.
SHARNBROOK. THE FEAST — The principal event in this rural village during the past week, has been its annual feast. This festival always occurs on the first Sunday after Old St. Peter's day, St. Peter being the patron saint of the parish church. The object of holding the feast is to commemorate the dedication of the church to its noble purpose. Whether the mode of celebrating the anniversary of such a dedication be worthy of an enlightened christian people, is a question, that many scrupulous persons dispute. This, however, we may safely aver, that the greater number of those persons, who take part in holding the feast, think very little either of its original institution, or of its avowed object. In these modern days it is simply observed as a secular rural holiday. As usual the first day of the feast was marked by a considerable influx of visitors, some from

neighbouring villages came merely pursuant to established habit, some from the lower motive of having a pint or two of ale, on such occasion, at the public inns, and others from a higher motive of visiting the relatives, acquaintances, or friends. The nearness of the railway to the village, was no doubt an inducement for many to pay a visit to Sharnbrook on that day, as was testified by the unusual number of persons hurrying to and fro, when the trains arrived and returned. From the natural love that the human kind, especially the young, (which sometimes lasts to latest age) have for holidays, we may infer that such is in accordance with the design of the beneficent Author of human nature. At any rate, their tendency is to cheer and exhilarate the drooping spirits of thousands of persons, whose lot is one of constant and monotonous toil. To the harassing and wearying round of labour they afford a pleasing relief, and awaken up and invigorate the generous impulses of the heart. Unwise persons, misapply the opportunities, and abuse the privileges that holidays afford. This is ever to be regretted. Of late years the character of the feast has undergone a great change. The public houses unusually close at 12 o'clock at night, and the stalls, regulated by the police, are permitted to remain only one day, at these festivals. In accordance with that regulation, Monday was the only day which wore the face of a thorough holiday. The stalls presented their usual attractions in the form of nick-nacks, gingerbread, &c., to the rustic lads and lasses and longing youngsters, to whom these "tempting wares" always possess a peculiar charm. Groups of well dressed persons at times thronged the streets. Of course Bacchus had his devotees, and the vigilant Tempter his votaries. Some members of the County Constabulary were there to preserve order, and to see that the regulations relating to the public houses, and the removal of stalls, were observed. With some small exceptions, the feast, as it has done of late years, passed off quietly.

Bedfordshire Mercury 25 August 1860.
BLETSOE. PETTY SESSIONS, August 14 1860. Present: W.H.W. Gery, J. Tucker, C. Alston, B.H. Starey, R. Orlebar, H.W. Beauford, and J. Gibbard, Esqs. **THE RIGHT OF ERECTING STALLS AT VILLAGE FEASTS** — Mr. J. Stewart, of Keysoe, licensed hawker, was charged by police-sergeant J. King, with erecting his stall by the side of the turnpike road at Risely on the 31st ult., being the second day of the feast at that village. It appeared from the evidence that the police-sergeant, acting under orders from his superintendent, had requested the defendant to take down his stall on the second day of the feast, in accordance with orders that had been issued from one of the divisions of the county, and which had been recommended by the Chairman of Quarter Sessions (vide Quarter Sessions report, October 24, 1859), but the defendant refused to comply with the police-sergeant's request, alleging that his stall stood on ground belonging to the public house, and he had the landlord's leave to stand there, consequently the police had no authority to remove him. On the part of the police it was admitted that the stall occupied a space in front of the public house, which, probably, was private ground, but that a part of the stall reached over the boundary line between the road and that ground. The object of the police was, to ascertain how far they would be justified in interfering in such cases, and whether the bench would lay down any rule for their guidance in regulating the erection of stalls at village feasts. The room was ordered to be cleared, and on the re-admission of the public, the chairman said the bench had decided to dismiss the case, on the ground that the stall did not stand on any part of the turnpike road. At the same time, the bench informed the defendant that it was unlawful to erect a stall upon any part of any turnpike road, or highway. No other orders were given to the police.

3.2.4 Royal occasions. At Sharnbrook the celebrations on the wedding of the Prince and Princess of Wales in 1863 have a more festive feel than those on the occasion of the Coronation in 1911.

SHARNBROOK. REJOICINGS ON THE OCCASION OF THE MARRIAGE OF H.R.H. THE PRINCE OF WALES. A DINNER Will be provided, in the Yard adjoining the School, for all the Men and Boys over 15 years of age who reside in the Parish of Sharnbrook. Each Person to bring his own knife and fork.

Dinner will be on the Table at Half-past One precisely, and the Tables must be cleared at 3 o'clock.

At 4 o'clock, TEA will be provided for all the Women and Children and Boys under 15 years of age who reside in the Parish of Sharnbrook. EACH PERSON TO BRING A CUP AND SAUCER.

At three o'clock in the afternoon the following GAMES will be commenced:—

3 o'clock — A RACE FOR WOMEN over 50 years of age; 60 yards. 1st prize, Half a pound of Tea; 2nd ditto, Quarter of a Pound of Tea.

3.15 — A RACE, open to Girls under 20 years of age: 150 yards. 1st prize, Two Pairs of Scarlet Stockings; 2nd ditto, One pair of Scarlet Stockings.

3.30 — A Grand WHEELBARROW RACE, open to all ages. Each Competitor to be Blindfolded. 1st prize, a Digging Fork; 2nd ditto, a new Shovel.

4 o'clock — A FLAT RACE FOR MEN above 50 years of age; 100 yards. 1st prize, a new Spade; 2nd ditto, a new Hoe.

4.15 — A FLAT RACE FOR MEN between 30 and 50 years of age; 200 yards. 1st prize, a new Spade; 2nd ditto, a new Hoe.

4.30 A FLAT RACE FOR MEN from 15 to 30 years of age; 200 yards 1st prize, a new Spade; 2nd ditto, a new Hoe.

4.45 — A RACE FOR BOYS under 15; 200 yards. 1st prize, 2s; 2nd ditto, 1s.

5 o'clock — A RACE IN SACKS, open to all ages; 30 yards. 1st prize, Half a Bushel of Flour; 2nd ditto, One Peck of Flour.

5.30 — A PIG of the value of one sovereign will be the prize of any person who can fairly catch and hold him by the tail. N.B. — The aforesaid tail will be plentifully greased.

There will also be several other races open to Children only.

A GREASY POLE WILL BE CLIMBED FOR A LEG OF MUTTON. No Irons, Cords, or Sand allowed.

It must be distinctly understood that the Dinner, Tea, and Sports are open only to Persons actually residing within the Parish of Sharnbrook.

At Dusk a Grand Display of FIREWORKS, After which will be Kindled the BONFIRE.

[1863] C.F. Timaeus, Printer, Bookseller, Stationer, High Street, Bedford

Beds. C.R.O. X. 25/42 [printed]

SHARNBROOK CORONATION FESTIVAL, June 22nd, 1911. Programme
of Sports to take place in a field kindly lent by Mr. Thomas, commencing
with the Races for Children at 4.15 o'clock.

Events

		1st	2nd	3rd
1.	To the Lady for the Best Decorated Cycle in the Parade (comic or otherwise)	Value 7/6	5/-	
2.	To the Gentleman for the Best Decorated Cycle in the Parade (comic or otherwise)	7/6	5/-	
3.	30 yds. Race for infants under 6.	Sweets		
4.	50 yds. Race for Boys under 9 years of age.	3/-	2/-	1/-
5.	50 yds. Race for Girls under 9 years of age.	3/-	2/-	1/-
6.	100 yds. Race for Boys under 12 years of age	3/-	2/-	1/-
7.	75 yds. Race for Girls under 12 years of age	3/-	2/-	1/-
8.	100 yds. Race for Boys under 15 years of age	3/-	2/-	1/-
9.	100 yds. Race for Girls under 15 years of age	3/-	2/-	1/-
10.	Sack Race 50 yds. (open)	4/-	2/-	
11.	Three-legged Race, 50 yds. for Boys under 14.	4/-	2/-	
12.	Three-legged Race, 50 yds. open.	5/-	4/-	
13.	Hurdle Race, 120 yds. over 8 flights, open	5/-	3/-	
14.	Wheelbarrow Race (competitors to wheel a barrow blindfolded).	5/-	3/-	
15.	Quarter-mile Flat Race for Men, open	6/-	4/-	2/-
16.	Race, comic open	5/-	3/-	2/-
17.	Egg and Spoon Race, open only to married women and widows	calico.		
18.	100 yds. Flat Race for Men over 40	5/-	3/-	2/-
19.	75 yds. Flat Race for Men over 50	5/-	3/-	2/-
20.	100 yds. Flat Race for Men open	5/-	3/-	2/-
21.	50 yds. Flat Race for Women, open	calico.		
22.	Donkey Race, first past the post to win	4/-	2/-	
23.	Donkey Race, last past the post to win	4/-	2/-	
24.	Women's Hammer and Nail Competition	calico.		
25.	Tug-of-War, Married v Single	tobacco.		

Balloons and Fireworks at Dusk. "God Save The King".
The above Races are open only to persons who reside in the Parish of Sharnbrook. No competitor can take more than one first prize nor more than two
second prizes. All Entries to be made to Mr. Prince Evans, at the School, during the morning of Coronation Day from 10 to 1 o'clock. C. Saunders, W. J.
Hales, Secretaries

Beds. C.R.O. A.D. 1073 [printed]

124 *The Bedfordshire Farm Worker*

3.2.5   Agricultural Societies. The Bedfordshire Agricultural Society, founded in 1801, gave prizes to labourers in husbandry, and to female servants on farms.

1835 Labourers and Servants in Husbandry in Classes 1, 2, 3, 4, 5, 6.
THE UMPIRES appointed to inspect the Certificates to determine the respective Premiums of Candidates under Classes 1, 2, 3, 4, 5, and 6 having inspected and taken the same into consideration Do report and adjudge as follows:
Class 1.
   To James Sudbury of Ridgmont he having brought up 10 children upon the earnings by labour of himself and family only without parochial relief the premium of £2. 10. 0.
   To John Randall of Stotfold he having brought up 10 children in the same manner and under the same circumstances the premium of £2. 10. 0.
   [These 2 Candidates having brought up an equal number of children and maintained themselves and families without parochial relief the 1st & 2nd prizes are divided between them.]
   To Thomas Swanson of Bedford having brought up 9 children in the same manner and under the same circumstances the premium of 1½ Sovereigns.
   To Charles Lee of Northill he having brought up four children in the same manner and under the same circumstances the premium of 1 Sovereign.
Class 2.
   To James Facer of Houghton he having maintained himself and family 60 years without parochial relief and without having applied to the parish Officers for work the premium of 3 Sovereigns; and also the sum of 16/- being one years interest upon £20 lodged in the hands of Thomas Times Esq. a late Secretary by John Lee Esq. L.L.D. for this purpose.
   To James Odell of Stagsden he having maintained himself and family 40 years in the same manner and under the same circumstances the premium of 2 Sovereigns.
   To Charles Lee of Northill he having maintained himself and family 34 years in the same manner and under the same circumstances the premium of 1½ Sovereigns.
Class 3.
   To Thomas Allbone of Southill he having worked as a labourer 45 years on the same farm without intermission the premium of 3 Sovereigns.
   To James Sudbury of Ridgmont he having worked as a labourer 44 years on the same farm without intermission the premium of 2 Sovereigns.
   To Henry White of Sharnbrook he having worked as a labourer 40 years on the same farm without intermission the premium of £0. 16. 8.
   To John Holdstock of Streatley he having worked as a labourer 40 years on the same farm without intermission the premium of £0. 16. 8.
   To John Finch of Houghton Conquest he having worked as a labourer 40 years on the same farm without intermission the premium of £0. 16. 8.
   [These 3 Candidates having worked the same number of years on the same farm without intermission the 3rd and 4th prizes are divided between them.]
Class 4.
   To Robert Cannon of Great Barford he having lived 36 years in farming service on the same farm with the same Master the premium of 3 Sovereigns.
   To Thomas Coles of Eastcotts he having lived 7 years in farming service on the same farm with the same Master of premium of £1. 15. 0.
   To John Knight of Chalgrave he having lived 7 years in farming service on the same farm with the same Master the premium of £1. 15. 0.

[These 2 Candidates having lived the same number of years in farming service the 2nd and 3rd prizes are divided between them.]

To William Giltrott of Hockliffe he having lived 6 years in farming service on the same farm with the same Master the premium of 1 Sovereign.

Class 5.

To Sarah Boon of Sandy she having lived 20 years as a hired servant on the same farm the premium of 3 Sovereigns.

To Sarah Rae of Potton she having lived 11 years as a hired servant on the same farm the premium of 2 Sovereigns.

To Sarah Bland of Marston she having lived 5 years as a hired servant on the same farm the premium of 1 Sovereign...

Beds. C.R.O. X136/3

The text of a speech made at the Annual Meeting of the West Bedfordshire and East Buckinghamshire Agricultural Association held at Leighton Buzzard on 25 Sep 1846. The speaker was Major Gilpin of Hockliffe, the President of the Society, who had presented prizes to deserving labourers and farm servants.

Bedfordshire Times 3 Oct 1846.

. . . As soon as the prizes had been distributed, the Chairman addressed the labourers, servants, and children. He said this was an occasion on which he had the pleasure of giving prizes to the deserving competitors; and he congratulated them on the success which had attended their exertions and good conduct. Since this Society had been formed, it had given away, in this manner, no less a sum than £400 (cheers). There was one class of recipients which it gave him great pleasure to see, and that was the servants who had lived so many years with the same families. He recollected, upon one occasion, there was a man who had been 50 years in the same service; and this day there were some present who had continued their service above 40 years (cheers). Nobody could witness this without being gratified at the good conduct thus displayed, and he could only say, whilst addressing those of the labourers who were parents, that the Society would lend its aid, to the fullest extent in its power, in enabling them to bring up their children in the same excellent manner; but they must remember that the principal training rested with them at home. They must teach them that they might become useful members of society if they did their duty in that station to which they were called, whatever that station might be. In conclusion, he wished them all health and success.

3.2.6. "The Good Old Times". At the time of the 1910 election, there were letters in the "Bedfordshire Times" about the advantages of Free Trade, and the paper offered a prize for the best account of life in the 1840's.

Bedfordshire Times 8 April 1910.

The 'Good' Old Times. The following descriptions of what life was like in Bedfordshire about 70 years ago have been sent in by readers in response to our recent invitation. We offered prizes of 10s and 5s for the two best accounts sent in. There is no question as to who takes the 1st prize . . . Mrs. Emma Thompson, 38 Houghton Road, Bedford.

I can well remember Protection days, as I was born at Cardington in April 1823 . . . Well, I can tell you when I had two children I never washed my tea pot out only once a week, for if I got a half a ounce of tea in a week I thought I had done wonders when bread went up to 1/0½d.

We used to buy matches tied up in little bundles, and then we had a tinder box and a piece of rag and two flint stones, and I had to sit and clink the two stones together to get a light. Sometimes it would take half an hour before I could get a light. At this time my husband's wages were 8/- a week. My children have many a time cried over night to know if they should have a bit of bread in the morning. I can tell you the chief of their living was bread soaked in water and a little salt in it, and vegetables. Meat we never thought of. If we ever got a piece, I had to make a crust an inch thick round it, no suet in the crust those days; we had to get a piece of bread and toast it, and boil some water and pour over it to drink for our tea.

Men got a pair of corduroy trousers and they was dressed. If one did manage to get a pair of cloth britches and leggings they thought he was a gentleman. I well remember free trade coming and cheap corn. I have a plate with a picture on it of the boat when it brought cheap corn; it has on it "No monopoly! Free Trade." . . .

And in those days if people sent letters, those that sent them could not afford to pay postage, and them that receive them if they couldn't afford to pay they didn't get the letters; and if they did get them they couldn't read them. They had to go to the Clergyman and perhaps he was busy, and then they would have to wait till after dinner. And then a newspaper; poor people never thought about such a thing. The parson only got one a week, and if we wanted to know any news they used to say we must go to the parson and hear what was in the paper. Then see how poor people from the Workhouse was used, and the poor children. I often shed tears when I think about it. I often tell my daughter I can see the weals on the poor children's arms if they didn't get their days work done. I well remember seeing a little boy flogged, and he died in three days.

Who is it brought all these good laws that we enjoy to-day? Why it is the Low Party as we used to call them. Of course we had a good squire in our village. He would often make the farmers find work for some of the people. Of course if they did anything wrong they had to go to the squire not come to Bedford as people have to do now. Then the men had to go what they use to call their rounds – that was to go round to every farmer every morning to see if they could get work; and then if they couldn't get work, they were allowed a little, not much. The last time my husband worked for a farmer he had 6/- a week for wheat hoeing . . .

Well I am so glad there is still a lace man, as I am sure poor people were glad of a lace man when I was a child, and since I have been a woman we were almost starved and we should have been quite if there hadn't been a lace man. It doesn't matter what sort of lace man . . .

I could tell a lot more as my grandmother was a shop keeper in the days of Sir Frederick Howard's grandfather. He use to call at my grand mother's once a month. I knew the Addington who had to be hung for setting fire — he was the last that had to be hung for fire at Bedford. Well in those days it didn't take long to make Jam and marmalade, as we couldn't get the sugar, neither did it take long to clean our furniture, as we only got a round deal table and about three chairs and an old stool or two, and no grates; it was wood hearths and a few bricks packed together with some old bits of iron across the bars. I can tell you I use to get all done and ready for the lace pillar at nine o'clock when the coach would come by at that time . . .

Mrs. Thompson afterwards sent us the following:—

Sir, — I see you want to know how people use to be accommodated for room. When 80 years ago I well remember three families living in one house, and two families, and only one fire place. When I was first married I had one room to live in and sleep in. They had big families them days. And then I got a house, one bedroom and one room downstairs. The bedrooms walls use to lean right over, so I tell you we didn't get much air — one little window in it. I had ten children born in that house; seven I brought up to be men and women. The people who lived in it first brought six children up in it; no fire grate.

About parish relief — the relieving officer use to call at my house; I remember six different pay men. He called at my house fifty years. I have known as many as 30 people come to my house on a Monday, sometimes more. I have known ten men who were able for work, but could not get it; but when they began to allow a little for these people the farmers soon found them some work. When a poor old woman could not work they would allow her 1/- and a loaf of rye bread; and a widow woman who was left with children, she would get sixpence a head; and then as times got a little better if any one was very ill they would give six pennyworth of mutton, sometimes 9 pennyworth but they had to come to Bedford to fetch it or send for it and many a time when they got it they could not eat it as it would stink. That butcher was a brute to poor people. I have brought it right back many a time for the people.

I have seen the poor old people lay on Cardington Green filthy dirty. The Union was on the green; some of it is standing now, only they made houses of it. The boys had to go in the chimneys to scrape the soot down, and the girls had to make lace. It was disgraceful the way poor people were used. They wasn't used nor fed half so well as cats and dogs are now a days. I got married when I was 24 years old and then I went to Cotton End to live, so that is where the parish people use to call at my house. Well about 42 years ago at Cotton End there was still such a lot of young men out of work, and didn't know how to get a piece of bread so Miss Bessie Whitbread of Cardington paid for a lot of them to go to America, and they had to pay her back when they got work. Some did and others never did; but the Whitbreads were always good to the poor of their Parish. They never asked whether you was high party or low party — we were all served alike.

I lived at Cotton End 59 years, Cardington 21 years, and Bedford 7 years. I helped to make a piece of lace to trim Queen Victoria's wedding dress. The lace man use to live at London and come once a month to the Fountain Inn at Bedford to buy work, and I can tell you the farmers them days didn't like the lace man. As time went on the lace kept making more money, and it got so as women earned more than the men, and then came Joseph Hart [Arch] and he quite upset the farmers. He was a good man to help to improve things for the poor people.

Then we used to have to pay toll along the roads. I remember when we had to pay toll if we took a horse and cart over the Old Bridge, and you would not go far along the roads before you would have a toll gate, I do wish I could make the people understand how we had to suffer years ago. I do hope they will never lose free trade. I remember when the Clergyman only had a paper once a month, and then one a week. I well remember when they use to sell people's beds if they owed a little and could not pay. They don't do those things now. I wish I could get about. I would tell the people to stick to low party . . . I wonder what they would say to rye bread now.

4. MIGRATION AND EMIGRATION

The most obvious way to improve one's lot in Victorian rural England was to leave it. The fact that most larger towns and villages grew in population while smaller villages usually went into decline after mid century in spite of a high birth rate and a declining death rate, indicates that people did leave in considerable numbers. Most of those leaving Bedfordshire villages left for local towns and for London. There was some attempt to encourage families to migrate to the industrial north, although some contemporaries complained that it was difficult to get men to go even as far as Northampton or Birmingham. Those who did move found that wages were on the whole better in the north, but some were caught out by unforeseen troubles, such as the cotton famine during the U.S. civil war.

Emigration overseas was frequently in the foreground of attention. The poor law authorities encouraged farm labouring families to emigrate to the United States and, later in the century, there was an increasing official emphasis on Canada and on the Australian colonies and New Zealand. Australia, however, had to overcome a deep seated prejudice because of its past association with transportation. Emigration was one issue where both the civil authorities, such as the poor law unions, and the farm workers' own trade unions saw eye to eye, and which both promoted as a means of reducing the chronic over population of rural districts.

4.1 Migration

4.1.1 The incumbent of Cranfield encouraged unemployed labourers to move to Mellor in Derbyshire. James Kay, M.P., reported on their changed conditions, 1836.

Mellor, in Derbyshire. Mr. Clayton's mill.

Mr. Clayton expressed great satisfaction with the docility and good conduct of his new work-people. He would not have one Irish-man at Mellor on any account. His mill is in a secluded situation, and he has taken great care to select good hands. He thinks he could not keep Irish workmen in subordination, and considers them decidedly inferior workmen. His new hands from Bedfordshire are very gentle in their manners, and have acquired a knowledge of their employment with great rapidity. Mr. Clayton is quite satisfied with their whole demeanour. The Mill is situated in a most romantic valley, and the cottages of the work-people are scattered over the neighbouring hills, in very healthy situations.

Philip Peddor, aged 39; migrated from Cranfield, near Bedford, with his wife and six children, five of whom are here. The family earned, respectively, in Bedfordshire, as follows:

	s	d	
Philip (the father) as farmer's labourer	7	0	per week
His wife, in lace-making	1	0	per week
Mary, aged 19, in lace-making	1	6	per week
Sarah, aged 16, in lace-making	2	6	per week
Thomas, aged 14, as ploughboy	2	6	per week
Betsey, aged 9, in lace-making	0	10	per week

Philip, aged 4, nothing.

Henry, aged 22, was married, and lived separately from the family. His rent in Bedfordshire was £3 a year. He had a large garden, also, for which he paid £8 annually, but he thinks he did not make money by it. His cottage was ruinous; it was thatched, and had a rough broken brick floor. It contained four rooms, and was built on "the waste," with wood. Fuel was very scarce indeed in Bedfordshire, but is very plentiful and cheap here.

	s	d	
He now earns, as a farmer's labourer	12	0	per week
His wife is in the factory, and obtains	5	0	per week

Mary, aged 19, is deformed and feeble; she keeps the house clean, cooks the meals, and employs her leisure in picking cotton, by which she can now earn 1s per week, but when she has acquired more skill will be able to earn more.

	s	d	
Sarah, aged 16, works in the factory and earns	5	0	per week
Thomas, aged 14, works in the factory and earns	4	6	per week
Betsey, aged 9, works in the factory and earns	2	6	per week
Total earnings of family	30s		per week

He pays 1s 8d weekly rent for a large cottage, containing three lofty rooms, which are provided with every convenience he requires. Provisions are about the same price here as in Bedfordshire. Furniture is rather dearer; but clothes and fuel are much cheaper. He was nearly starved in Bedfordshire, but all the family have plenty to eat and drink here. He says he would "rather cross the sea than go back into Bedfordshire." He feels much stronger himself, but does not see so much progress in the rest of the family. He has written to Cranfield to induce his friends to migrate, and expects that 12 of them will come over very soon. He told them, when he wrote, that "if they would not come, they deserved to be starved in Bedfordshire." He says, he has heard that some very foolish reports have been spread in Bedfordshire concerning their condition here, but that the family was never so happy before . . .

William Rogers, aged 37; migrated from Cranfield, Bedfordshire, with his wife, aged 24 and two children. He earned in Bedfordshire 5s per week, as a farmer's labourer; and his son John, aged 12 (by a first wife), earned 1s per week; Mary, aged 11, could get about 4d a week at the lace pillow. He paid 1s per week for a pretty good cottage. The family now earn as follows:

	s	d	
William (father), as a farmer's labourer	12	0	per week
John, at the factory	4	6	per week
Mary, at the factory	3	0	per week

His wife is ill, and keeps the house.

He pays 1s 6d weekly rent for a comfortable cottage.

He says, "The parish officers gave me 50s to pay for new furniture when I came here, but if they would take me back free of expense, and give me 50 sovereigns when I got into Bedfordshire, I would not go; for I was starving, and I have now plenty of food and a good master to work for."

He has written to his friends to induce them to come and hopes that some of his near relatives will. Mr. Clayton gave all the families a load of coals on their arrival, and charged them nothing at all for the first nine days' rent. He also offered to lend them money to enable them to buy furniture.

First Annual Report of the Poor Law Commissioners 1836. p 324

4.1.2 *The Rev. James Beard, Rector of Cranfield, report on his efforts to encourage the migration of labourers and their families, 1836.*

Letter to E. Chadwick, Esq. from the Rev. James Beard, Rector of Cranfield, Beds. on the Results of the Migration of Labourers, under the Amended System of Poor Law Administration.

Sir,   Cranfield Rectory, Woburn, Beds., 1 June 1836.

From the courtesy I have received from the board, and the interest I have always taken in the poor laws, I am induced to write a few lines, showing how the amended system has operated, as connected with migration, in this parish, as well as in this Union (Ampthill) at large. To enter into full detail would take up too much of your time, but as I have been one of the individuals who have long publicly advocated migration, I cannot avoid making a few remarks now I have tried the experiment. . . .

Being aware of the disparity of wages in the agricultural and manufacturing districts, I gave public notice in my parish about nine years since, that I was ready to send away 10 labourers to good places, as our soil was daily sinking in value from the destruction caused by poor-rates; 12 men applied, who were sent by the overseer, and the first question asked of me, was, "What beer do they give in that country you wish us to go into?" I desired them to return to their places of idleness, viz., the gravel pits, and when next I endeavoured to induce them to migrate and amend their condition, I would have another law to enable me to carry my wishes into execution. . . . At last the change came; one year has passed since we were embodied as a Union, and I then explained to some good working labourers with large families what would be the effect of the Bill; I recommended them to migrate into the manufacturing districts, in consequence of which 19 families, about 130 souls, have migrated; generally speaking, they write in the most gratifying manner, but some of them having fallen ill of small-pox, they have been forced to call upon us for temporary assistance. Looking, however, to the operation of migration throughout the Union, I find this to be the result: Farmers appreciate their servants far more than they did; servants value their places and get better paid; the labourers in this parish are better off than I ever saw them, although the rates have been reduced one half; and sanguine as I have always been as to the moral effect of the change upon the people, it has far exceeded my earnest expectation. I now see the boy taken out to work with the parent in the field; I see mothers remaining in their houses teaching their children to make lace, &c.; I see industry where there was idleness; I see sobriety in the place of drunkenness; I see, in short, a desire amongst the labouring classes to assist themselves, and gratitude for any kindness that may be bestowed upon them. If the poor are temperately reasoned with, I have scarcely met with one that attempts to vindicate the old system; they know the rates were prostituted to the worst of ends, and they saw but too well how many industrious people were brought to penury by the payment of them. For many years I have advocated strongly a change in the administration of the poor laws, and this I have done, not so much as regards pecuniary matters only, but as relating to the moral condition of the poor. Everything about us was paralyzed by pauperism; the land was cultivated by it, the children were nursed and rocked in the parish-cradle, and mendicancy was the first thing they were instructed in, by clothing them in rags and turning them upon the high roads without restraint. The farmers said, "if we cannot manage the poor, I wonder who can;" and the overseers were so alarmed by anonymous letters, and the constant dread of fire, that they dared not, in most instances, refuse a sturdy pauper's demand. . . .

I must not, however, further trespass upon your attention; I will briefly conclude by adding, that the land is better cultivated, the labourer better paid, the children under better control, and I hope, ere many years have passed away, that the English labourer will be restored to what he was before 1796; that bees and poultry may be attended by the wife, the cottage garden cultivated in surplus hours by the husband, and we shall then have our places of worship fillled with woman dressed in red cloaks, the men in good coats with nosegays in their buttonholes; and I am sure the general feeling will then be to help those who help themselves.

I am, &c.

James Beard.

To Edwin Chadwick, Esq.

Second Annual Report of the Poor Law Commissioners, 1836, pp. 545-7

4.1.3 When paupers had migrated they might still need help. Biggleswade Poor Law Union sent money to the Agent for Migration at Leeds for the use of Joseph Lovell from Blunham.

Board Room Wednesday June 21 1837 At the Meeting held this day . . . The Chairman then read to the Board a Letter he had received from Mr Baker the Agent for Migration resident at Leeds stating, that Joseph Lovell of Blunham who had migrated to Leeds last summer was in great distress at Halifax for want of employment, and requested the Board to send him £5 to relieve his present necessities as his Master had promised to give him the first chance of re-employment, and the Relieving Officer was directed to send Mr Baker that amount with instructions to apply it as economically as possible. . . .

Beds. C.R.O. PUBwM. 2

4.1.4 Some of the labourers and their families who had migrated to the cotton manufacturing areas suffered in the distress caused by the American Civil War 1861-1865. This printed circular is among the Eversholt parish records. The Mellor near Stockport to which help was sent is the Mellor in Derbyshire where Cranfield families had gone to find work in the 1830's.

Mrs. H. Veasey Gratefully acknowledges the following Sums Received for the DISTRESSED OPERATIVES IN LANCASHIRE.

RECEIVED	£	s	d
In Shillings and Pence	1	4	1
Mrs & Miss Veasey, Froxfield	1	10	0
Mr. & Mrs. H. Veasey	1	0	0

Rev. G. S. Whitlock, Milton Bryant Rectory	1	0	0
Mrs. Baker, Eversholt Rectory	1	0	0
Mrs. & Miss Gascoyen, Birchmore		15	0
Mr. Fowler, Woburn	1	0	0
Anonymous from Miss Gascoyen	1	0	0
Mrs. Wolfe	1	2	0
Mrs. Cumberlege	0	5	0
Mrs. Sanders	0	5	0
Mr. & Mrs. Clarke, Woburn Abbey		10	0
A Friend, Woburn Abbey		3	0
Mrs. Mossman, Battlesden	0	10	0
The Misses Clarke, Park St.		3	0
Mr. Sergeant	0	3	0
Miss Daniel	0	2	0
	11	12	1

EXPENDED

58 yards of Flannel	2	18	0
48 yards of Lindsey for Women's Dresses	1	0	0
Remnants for Childrens' Dresses etc.	1	0	0
Sent to the Rev. J. M. Freeman, for his Parish, Mellor, near Stockport	1	14	0
To the Rev. H. Byrth, Bardsley Parsonage, Ashton-under-Lyne	5	0	0
	11	12	0

Two Casks of CLOTHING, Old and New, were sent to, and Gratefully acknowledged by the Rev. J. Wilson, St. James' Parsonage, PRESTON.
One Cask of CLOTHING, Old and New, were sent to, and thankfully acknowledged by the Rev. H. Byrth, Bardesley Parsonage, ASHTON-UNDER-LYNE. These Packages were conveyed free of Cost, through the kindness of Mr. SANDERS.
Mrs. VEASEY begs to thank Messrs. GILBY & SLINN for their Presents in Clothing, as well as for the liberal Deduction made in the Price of their Goods.
Mr. J. CLARKE kindly undertakes to Print this Circular.

Woburn, January 1863

J. Clarke, Printer & News Agent, Woburn

Beds. C.R.O. P.42

4.2   Emigration

4.2.1   The Duke of Bedford's agents saw the necessity for emigration before it was generally accepted as the best if not the only solution to the problem of over-population and poverty. The following four letters were from Thomas Bennett, the Steward at Woburn, to the estate's Agent-in-chief in London.

4.2.1.1   Woburn May 17 1833
. . . Capt. Radcliffe agrees as does Mr. Platt to join The Duke in their share of the expense of sending the Family from Ridgmont to Canada. I have yet no reply from Mr. Smith, the only proprietor of any consequence besides those two, nor do I expect he will assist. I have determined to send the Man, and if we can get Mr. Smith's share of the expence, we will; if not, we must do without it. The whole expence of the Man his Wife and Five Children will be above £50; the Duke's share including Col. Macqueen's Estate will be about £40, Capt. R. £8 10, and Mr. Platt 30s. . . .

Beds. C.R.O. R 3/3758

4.2.1.2   Woburn Sept 7 1834
. . . Mr. Pickering of Risely (Lord St. John's leading tenant) applied to me yesterday to solicit The Duke's assistance in sending out some emigrants who are at this time in the mind to go out: Lord St. John has offered to pay one half the Expense. I told him if the people were in the Mind to lose no time and send them off. As neither The Duke nor yourself were at present in the country, I could not say any thing positive, but that I thought His Grace would be ready to contribute his share in proportion to Lord St. John's subscription according to the relative value of the different Estates — and this is all they expect, the remainder to be paid out of the Rate by the occupiers — and I think when land-owners unite to do so it is very well, for the outlay to a yearly Tenant is such, as often to make them treat applications for emigration as a thing they have nothing to do with . . .

Beds C.R.O. R 3/3813

4.2.1.3   Woburn November 30 1834
. . . I am glad you have seen Mr. Lefevre and that he is willing to allow we have a surplus population. Mr. Adey was not willing to allow we had, and said he thought the Commissioners were of his opinion; and without some means can be devised to dispose of this redundancy, the Workhouse system will fail; (at least such has always been my opinion). However if this is admitted we must turn all our thoughts to the subject of emigration. If there is work in England we must endeavour to get them sent where it is, in preference to sending them abroad; but I am pretty sure that in those districts where Agricultural Labourers are most wanted it is only for the Hay and Harvest Months, as in the Fens and some of the Northern Counties, and there is always plenty of Irish (who are a Migratory Class, ours are quite the reverse) ready and willing to come over for that purpose. It is out of the question to think of ever getting a Married Labourer to move himself and Family 50 or 100 miles. By pinching the Young Men, they will be more likely to go having no encumbrance, and now that the Law of Settlement is altered, farmers will be more ready to engage them, but still the owners of the Soil can never look to any permanent relief until a considerable part of the population will leave the country altogether. But many well meaning people object to emigration because by doing so, they say, we get quit of so many of our consumers. But if, by getting quit of a proportion,

those who remain are placed in a position to obtain better wages, which would enable
them to live better, the smaller number would consume quite as much as the present
large number does, for we know they are not hoarders, but circulate all the money they
earn . . . We cannot expect to get many of the Married people to go, and the only way to
get the young ones to start will be as I said before, by hard pinching and herein is a great
difficulty, for we must either have two sorts of Work (parish Work I mean) or two prices
for the same, which is just going back to where we were, paying a Man for his family and
not for his Labour, because I find by Keeping all at Work at one price the Married Man is
hard pinched, and the single man is so much better off that he will not look for any
thing better. . . Where you have another opportunity, I wish you would draw the Commissioners attention to this point . . .

Beds. C.R.O. R 3/3830

4.2.1.4   Park Farm, Woburn, 1840 November 27
. . . If we could get into a plan to induce the Young Men to emigrate, the want of means
would be easily got over, because parishes are enabled to raise money upon security of
the rates for this purpose, to be paid off in five years (under directions of the Poor Law
Commissioners 4 & 5 Wm 4 cap. 76 sec. 62) and where a Landowner has the whole
parish, or where different Landowners can agree to assist beyond the Sum raised by the
Occupiers, Relief to any extent might be had. The great difficulty to get over would then
only be the unwillingness to start. As to fitness for emigrating, good health and a willing
Mind are the best qualifications. The adjoining parish of Milton Bryant has been wonder-
fully improved by the joint endeavours of the occupiers, and Sir Robert and the Misses
Inglis. The accounts from the first lot are so encouraging that they sent another huge
family last spring. Great good was done at Oakley nine or ten years ago, by sending off 3
or 4 large families. . .

Beds. C.R.O. R3/4314

*4.2.2 At Riseley the Vestry agreed to help the emigrants referred to in
4.2.1.2 above.*

Riseley August the 25th 1834 Select Vestry Assembled . . . John Tebbott,
James Neall, W. Kirk, John Dickins, Job Smart and Wm Arnold and Hen.
Fairy apply to be sent to the United States of North America they wish for 2
Sovereigns a piece when they have landed. Resolved that they be sent with his
Lordship's approval and assistance. . .

Riseley September 8th 1834 Select Vestry Assembled . . . Job Smart applies
for a pair of Shoes and some shirts. Allowed with the proviso that they be put
into the Ship and that after he has set sail for America he may have possession of them. . .

Beds. C.R.O. P50/8/3

4.2.3 Wilstead Vestry gave moral but not financial help to a deserving case.

Wilstead Vestry: At a Vestry Meeting duly called and assembled June 14th 1854, The Rev. Mr. Passy in the Chair.

The case of Daniel and Samuel Wightman who have expressed a wish to emigrate to America was taken into consideration, and from the very vague and unsatisfactory manner they answered various questions, it was unanimously agreed that their application could not be entertained by the meeting for the present. . .

At a Special Vestry Meeting held in the School Room April 7th 1854 for the purpose of receiving Tenders for gravel carting etc. . . . .

Mrs Rogers applied for some assistance owing to her husband having left her and gone to America. The meeting permitted her to remain out of the Union House with her Eldest and youngest children, the other two to remain in the House for a time, with a distinct understanding that this is not by any means to be considered a precedent. . .

At a Vestry Meeting held in the School Room April the 13th 1854 for the transaction of Parochial business, and also to consider an Application from Sarah Rogers who wishes to join her husband in America.

. . . The application of Mrs Rogers was fully considered, and the Vestry not being satisfied that they could appropriate any of the poor Rates to such a Purpose; but owing to the excellent character of the applicant as an industrious woman, the Meeting sanctioned her making a personal application to such of the parishioners as she might deem fitting in her present emergency, she having received £20 from her husband in America to defray a portion of her passage and that of her four children. . .

Vestry Meeting . . . April 19th 1854 . . .

. . . The case of Mrs. Rogers was considered, and Mr. Thomas Armstrong said he had no objection to going to London to see her properly started under certain conditions. . .

Beds. C.R.O. P22/8/1

4.2.4 After 1835 the poor law unions encouraged emigration. The printed statement of returns for 1844 and 1845 show that most assisted emigrants in those years were from the centre and north of the county.

Statement of the Number of Poor Persons who have Emigrated, and of the Sums which the Poor Law Commissioners have authorized to be raised or borrowed, from the 1st January to the 31st December, 1844
County: Bedford

Number of Poor Persons who have Emigrated

Parish	Amount authorised to be raised or borrowed £ s d	Males [over 14]	[7–14]	[under 7]	Females [over 14]	[7–14]	[under 7]	To what part Emigrated
Bletsoe	80 0 0	8	0	3	3	0	4	South Australia
Bromham	10 0 0	1	0	0	1	0	1	South Australia
Ridgmont	40 0 0	1	1	0	1	0	3	Canada
Riseley	121 0 0	10	1	4	5	0	0	South Australia
Wilshamstead	40 10 0	3	0	1	2	0	1	Canada

11th Annual Report of the Poor Law Commissioners, 1845.

[as above 1st January to the 31st December, 1845]

Parish	Amount £ s d	Males [over 14]	[7–14]	[under 7]	Females [over 14]	[7–14]	[under 7]	To what part Emigrated
Barford, Great	38 0 0	1	2	1	2	1	2	South Australia
Bolnhurst	80 0 0	6	1	3	4	1	3	South Australia
Cardington	19 0 0	0	0	0	1	0	0	Cape of Good Hope
Colmworth	47 0 0	2	1	4	2	1	3	South Australia ‑
Milton Ernest	105 0 0	0	0	0	0	0	0	
*Sharnbrook	46 0 0	4	2	4	4	1	1	South Australia
*Stevington	70 0 0	15	4	8	11	3	7	South Australia

*Omitted in 11th Report

12th Annual Report of the Poor Law Commissioners, 1846.

4.2.5 This printed leaflet is in the Bedford Poor Law Union papers.

CLOTHING REQUIRED FOR THE VOYAGE TO AUSTRALIA

The Emigrants must bring their own Clothing, which will be inspected at the Port by an Officer of the Commissioners; and all parties are particularly desired to observe that they will not be allowed to embark unless they provide themselves with a sufficient supply for their health during the voyage. The lowest quantity that can be admitted for each Person is as follows:

For Males	For Females
Six Shirts	Six Shifts
Six Pairs Stockings	Two Flannel Petticoats
Two Pairs Shoes*	Six Pairs Stockings
Two complete suits of exterior Clothing	Two Pairs Shoes*
1 Pair of Sheets	Two Gowns
3 Towels	1 Pair of Sheets
	3 Towels

* Shoes or Slippers are more convenient for use on Board than Boots

As a general rule, it may be stated that the more abundant the stock of Clothing, the better for health and comfort during the passage. The usual length of the voyage to the Australian Colonies is about four months, and at whatever season of the year it may be made, the Emigrants have to pass through very hot and very cold weather, they should therefore be prepared for both.

By Order of Her Majesty's Colonial Land and Emigration Commissioners S. WALCOTT, Secretary.

9 Park St. Westminster, 1st June 1847

[in manuscript] A Comb and Brush, and 3 lbs of Marine soap for each person

Beds C.R.O. PUBC 2/6 p.473.

4.2.6 *By 4 & 5 Will. 4, c. 76, s. 62, parish vestries could raise a fund to pro-mote emigration, and several did so. The Haynes fund continued up to 1909.*

4.2.6.1 Bolnhurst Vestry Book

At a vestry meeting held the 20th day of March 1845, It was agreed that a sum of Money should be raised for the purpose of Emigrating such families belonging to the Parish as should be agreed upon at the meeting to be held on Monday March 24th. W. Wade Gery, Rector, Wm. Green, Joseph White, John Whitmee, Joseph Sharman, Mark Warmesley

. . .

At a Vestry Meeting held the 16th March 1845 it was agreed that the sum of £80 be Borrowed of Government for the purpose of defraying the Expences of sending Jacob Newal, Ben. Carter, Beecher Busby and Families to New Holland

R. Kilpin

Beds. C.R.O. P46/8

4.2.6.2 Silsoe Vestry Book

Parish of Silsoe. Ampthill Union. County of Bedford.

At a meeting of the Rate payers of the above Parish and owners of Property therein, entitled to vote pursuant to the provisions of an Act passed in the fifth year of the reign of His late Majesty King William IV intituled "An Act for the Amendment and better Administration of the Laws relating to the Poor in England and Wales" held at the Vestry Room in this parish on Thursday the 4th day of February 1848 pursuant to Notice of such Meeting duly published and given on Sunday the 30th day of January. Thos. P. Ferguson Chairman

It was resolved That the Churchwardens and Overseers shall, and they are hereby directed to raise the sum of twenty pounds as a fund for defraying the expenses of the Emigration of poor persons having settlements in this parish, and being willing to emigrate, to be paid out of the rates raised and to be raised for the relief of the poor in this parish and to be applied under such rules orders and regulations as the Poor Law Commissioners shall in that behalf direct.

A List and description of the persons desirous of emigrating from the parish of Silsoe in the county of Bedford

	Age	
Edmund Squire	26 years	married — Labourer — no parish relief during past year, emigrating to S. Australia
James Bryant	8 years	emigrating to S. Australia — son of Edmund Squire's wife
Elizabeth Squire	28 years	married — emigrating to S. Australia — wife of Edmund Squire
Susan Bryant	6 months	emigrating to S. Australia — daughter of Elizabeth Squire.

Beds. C.R.O. P54/8/1

4.2.6.3 Haynes Emigration Fund papers
Notice of Meeting to consent to raising or borrowing Money for Emigration purposes. Hawnes Parish. Ampthill Union. Bedford County.

Notice is hereby given that a Meeting of the Owners of Property in this parish legally entitled to vote, in person, or by proxy, and of the Ratepayers therein will be held at the School Room Church End in this parish on Thursday the thirteenth day of January next at Ten in the forenoon for the purpose of considering whether any and what Sum or Sums of money, not exceeding half the Average yearly Poor Rate for the three years now last past, shall be raised or borrowed as a fund for defraying the expenses of the Emigration of poor persons having settlements in this Parish, and being willing to emigrate and of giving directions for raising or borrowing such Sum or Sums to be paid out of or charged upon the Rates raised or to be raised for the Relief of the Poor in this Parish, and to be applied under and according to such rules, orders, and regulations, as the Commissioners for administering the Laws for Relief of the Poor in England, shall in that behalf direct. Dated this Eighth day of January 1848   *Beds. C.R.O. P6/24/1*

P6/24/2 "Emigration Rate for the Parish of Hawnes" April 1852 shows that the sum of £69 9s 10½d was raised. P6/24/6, the first surviving Savings Bank Book, shows that the sum of £33 17s 8d remained in May 1880.

Explanation. I came to Haynes in July 1895, and know nothing of the £5 withdrawn in November 1891.

In May 1904 the sum of £5 was withdrawn and given to Arthur Allen who emigrated and went to South Africa for a short time in search of work, but failed and returned home again.

In July 1906 the sum of £20 was withdrawn. £10 was given to Charles Adams, his wife and three children, and £10 to William Brunt (£5 to be repaid by him) all of whom emigrated to Canada under the auspices of the Church Army. The £5 was repaid by W. Brunt, and replaced in the Savings Bank in February 1907. £8 was withdrawn in August 1907 and given to John Woodcroft, who emigrated to Canada, £3 to be repaid. £8 was withdrawn in April 1908 and given to Percy Wood who emigrated to Canada, £3 to be repaid by him. £3 was repaid by John Woodcroft in August 1908, and replaced in the Savings Bank on September 2nd 1908 (see new Bank Book). Wm. C. Browne, Vicar of Haynes. September 3rd 1908.

£3 was repaid by Percy Wood in May 1909 and replaced in the Savings Bank on May 25th 1909. W. C. Browne.

Beds C.R.O. P6/24/4

4.2.7 *Throughout the century public spirited individuals continued to help the poor to emigrate. This subscription list at Eversholt in 1874 includes a donation from the Agricultural Labourers' Union.*

Subscriptions received to enable William Odell and Family, Abel Chew and Family, and Thomas Valentine and Family (19 in all) to emigrate to Ontario Canada. 15 June '74.

Received	£	s	d
Duke of Bedford	15	0	0
Baroness Rothschild	1	0	0
Rev. W. S. Baker	1	10	0
W. L. Smart Esqr. per Rev. W. S. Baker	3	0	0
Trustees of Eversholt Estate	12	0	0
J. Green Esqr.	1	0	0
Parker Esqr.		10	0
Mrs Gisborne		5	0
Mr. Stannard		5	0
Mrs. Pearson		2	0
Labourers' Union	7	5	0
Mr. Sprague		2	6
Mr. Dimmock		5	0
A Friend		2	6
A Bricklayer			6
Mrs. Sandys for Flannel	1	2	6
Miss Sandys		10	0
Miss M. Sandys		5	0
Miss Saunders		5	0
Mr. Sandys	3	0	1½
Total £47		10	1½

Paid

Agent Canadian Govt. for Passage	21	17	4
Railway Fares	8	12	9½
Carriage to Ridgmount		5	0
Expenses of B. Valentine from London		5	0
Paid for Flannel 12 yards each family	1	2	6
Cash to purchase necessary articles in Liverpool etc.			
£5 2s 6d each family	15	7	6
Total £47		10	1½

Examined and found correct. William S. Baker 15 June 1874.

Beds. C.R.O. P42

5. HOUSING

5.1 'Open' and Close' Parishes.

*The system of 'open' and 'close' parishes (as described in the Intro-
duction) meant that the landlords of 'close' parishes were able to res-
trict numbers, so as to reduce the burden of rates from inhabitants
who might become paupers, and labourers wanting houses had to
move to adjoining 'open' villages. Thus farm workers often had to
travel a considerable distance to work. In Bedfordshire the system was
investigated in 1865 by R. Hunter, a doctor employed by the Privy
Council. Hunter found that the system of open and close parishes was
most marked in an area of East Bedfordshire in the Poor Law Union
of Biggleswade. He showed that the neatness of the well administered
'close' village had been bought at the price of creating rural slums in
larger villages and country towns. Hunter took the extreme view that
farm workers should not live in country towns at all.*

**Details concerning House Accommodation in different Counties of England arranged in
the Alphabetical order in Counties.**

BEDFORDSHIRE.
Bedfordshire as being the chief scene of the straw plaiters' labour has a large adult population; for the most part it is very inadequately supplied with cots. They are few and
small, and their condition is often a mere precarious holding together of rotten materials;
the stitch in time has not been applied, and there are hundreds on which no repairs can
now be bestowed with advantage.

The new cots are very poor, small, or dear. I saw four at Wrestlingworth which were
only a few years standing, they might have been built for £100, they were let for £13 a
year, a proceeding of which no one can complain, the fault if any lying with those who
having waste bits of land lying idle still allow their servants to seek lodging by competition among those who pay dearly for every yard they get to build on, and have no
interest in the people beyond their rent.

There are numerous houses of the worst character; sometimes a boarded partition
would make two bedrooms of one, but when the outside measurements were only about
15 feet by 11, this was a questionable improvement.

The discomfort was eased by a bed being placed in the little kitchen, but this room
was sometimes only 5 feet 6 inches high; sometimes a second bedroom was got for a
large family by taking both chambers of a pair of cots and leaving the kitchen only for
an old couple next door. The ground plan of one house was only 11 feet by 7 feet 6
inches, the kitchen was 6 feet high; the family, five adults and a child, slept over the
kitchen of this and the next cottage.

Rents were about £3, tenants have to build their own privies, the landlord providing
a ditch or hole. As soon as one builds the rest use it; there are very few privies, and these
may be removed any day.

One house called Richardson's could hardly be matched in England for original meanness and present badness of condition. Its plaster walls leaned and bulged very like a lady's dress in a curtsey. One gable end was convex, the other concave, and on this last unfortunately stood the chimney, which was a curved tube of clay and wood resembling an elephant's trunk. A long stick served as a prop to prevent the chimney from falling. The doorway and window were rhomboidal.

A few yards from this cabin stood two of the most ridiculous new model cottages ever seen. The money wasted on these two would have built a third of equal size and convenience, and the cabin might no longer have remained to disgrace the country.

I visited 17 houses, only four of them had more than one bedroom, and these four were full. The single bedroomed cots contained three adults with three children; a married pair with six; with five; or with four children.

In only four parishes of Bedfordshire had cots been destroyed in the decennium 1851-61, in the teeth of an advancing population. Of these cases Potton is one, and not a remarkably bad one. It is a small poor town full of labourers' cottages containing, one or two, and never three bedrooms: but, dear, gardenless, and every way unfit as they are, every one is and was wanted. With such houses the population stood below five to a house in 1851, and wanted no further pressure; they are now above that figure. A group visited on the Gamblingay road had gardens, privies, and a draw-well. They were outside the town. The largest family was one of three adults and four children in two bedrooms.

Cockayne Hatley was almost a close village; the few residents had good gardens, draw-wells, privies, low rents and allotments; but though the houses were large and over full, it was plain there were not hands enough in the parish, and labour was obtained from Gamblingay or from Wrestlingworth. Three cots stood together, in whose three bedrooms slept 11 adults and 13 children. Double chambered cots are very few.

At Eyworth there is more comfort and decency, and there are gardens to nearly all; but this state is artificial, the place belongs to one owner, and many men who belong to and work in Eyworth are obliged to live in Dunton and wretched Wrestlingworth; thus long walks are added to their other miseries, and Eyworth tidiness is dearly purchased. I visited 6 single bed-roomed houses at Eyworth, they contained 13 adults and 12 children. Two old parish houses stood in the village disemplastered and abandoned while two excellent new houses a world too wide for the shrunk income of a farm labourer, had been built beside them.

High rents are among the errors of Dunton. Outside the village a new row of 10 cots containing 2 bedrooms each, were taken before completion at £4 5s rent. Men's wages were only 10s, but the families hoped to pay their way by straw plaiting. Whatever may be the example set them, it does not seem to be the legitimate mission of Bedfordshire cottage speculators to force an industry into any particular neighbourhood or out of another, they will do right when they simply obey the demand; still if they look around at the history of the other village trades, they will see that straw plaiting is a precarious matter to invest in, and will perhaps only anticipate an inevitable future if they confine their building to the towns. The social duty of building for farm servants does not belong to them, and as an investment, loss and disappointment will follow the erection of such high rented houses in the villages. The higher the rent the larger the number who must combine to pay it. The six adults who with four children sleep in one bedroom at Dunton pay for it £3 10s. Other families far too large for the accommodation pay similar rents, have no garden and have long walks, as for instance to Abington, to their work. The cheapest house seen in Dunton measured outside 15 feet by 10, and was let for £3, at least double its value. Only one of 14 visited in the village had two bedrooms. A little outside the village stands what is, as far as my experience goes, the worst inhabited house in England in point of condition. The owner condescended to receive 25s a year for it until August 1864, when he was induced to part with it to the present squire. There being no privy the tenants dunged against the house side. The lower nine inches of the door having gone through sheer rottenness, a few bricks were ingeniously drawn against it from within after shutting, and a bit of matting hung on the inside. Full half of one window was gone, glass and framework too. Here without furniture, huddled three adults and five children. Futile is the agreement to repair which a labourer tenant is always ready to make and seldom able to keep. The owner might have known that if he got his sixpence a week he must expect no more, and that if the house was to be maintained no one but he would do it.

Dunton is no worse than the rest of Biggleswade Union, indeed it is much better than some of the villages visited.

In Biggleswade rents were oppressively high, Fountain Cottage in Beech Street and others letting at 2s a week without garden; in one of these a privy and cesspool were actually within the house; it was a half-drained street, full of stinking gullies. Many five pound houses had no back openings and a mere closet for a second bedroom. Palace Yard, now more suitably named Jail Yard, was found to contain eight single chambered houses. In one bedroom slept six adults; in another four with two children; in another four with four children; and no wonder, when these people were paying 20 per cent. on the value of the houses, sometimes so much as 2s a week, if they combined means to the greatest possible extent, and with corresponding squeezing. They had no gardens, but they had gullyholes and their wells in the yard. Biggleswade though a small place is a town, and the farming man here is not wanted, and is out of his place as in all towns. Far better than building for him here would be to induce landlords to allow him to live in his natural habitat.

Sutton has been described at page 146. The rents were so low as £2 2s and £2 12s 6d, but have a tendency to rise.

Most of the Dunstable houses have two bedrooms. A row on the Houghton road was visited. The houses had a passage from front to back, a draw well, small garden, and sufficient privies. Some were crowded with adults. In one were seven adults and four children, in another seven adults and one child. The rents were about £6.

Houghton Regis also had something of this disagreeable feature of the straw plait country. The men were seen doing unusual feats of house work, while the women were earning a living for the family. With the families always at home the people complained that one privy to eight houses was insufficient, it was "always" occupied. Gardens and out-houses were rare. The water was got from draw wells. A few cots stood to let at 1s 6d a week without rates to pay. The material was brick and slate and there were few thatches. About half the small houses had two bedrooms. In one single bedroom house were five adults with four children, in another four adults with two children.

I heard at Tilsworth that in that part of the county farmers protected their servants, by taking some into the farm house and taking cots for others. Wages were about 10s, and it seemed necessary to combine to pay the rents, although these were not always high. 1s, 1s 3d, 1s 4d, 1s 6d a week were various rents mentioned, varying rather with the gardens than with the cots, which were much alike and all bad. In one a brick floor was broken down to the size, but not the regularity of Roman tesserae, and an old man said they had been exactly so for 50 years, a proof of the wisdom which so arranged the floors of the antique villas. In cots nominally of two bedrooms one was often a mere closet or back kitchen; the privies often unfit for use. In one, £3 10s was paid where an old thatched roof sprang direct from the bedroom floor, and the underside of the thatch was bare to the room; but here was a good garden full of plums. The water supply was insufficient everywhere. New houses had been built, but unfortunately old houses had been pulled down. In single bed-roomed houses were found families of 3 adults with 5 children; of 5 adults with 1 child; 3 adults with 3 children; 4 adults with 1; 5 adults with 2; 6 adults with 5; 2 adults with 5, and 7 adults with 4; the adults being usually of both sexes and the room-floors about 12 feet by 12.

In Standbridge are some very small redbrick modern cots in rows. There are also some thatched roofs with single bed-rooms; the floors generally of tile; the rents 1s 3d or 1s 6d. In 10 double bed-roomed houses visited lived 26 adults.

Leighton Buzzard is much neglected in sanitary matters. A nasty black open drain runs in front of some of the houses; Mr. Theobald's for instance, in Hockliffe Road.

There is at Eggington a new row of very bad cots, called Southam's houses, eight in number, back to back, without garden, with built up uncovered cesspools. They have but one bedroom each, in which sleep 22 adults and 12 children. Many of the older houses are miserably bad and the gardens worthless. The new houses, although usually spouted, are so poorly constructed that the spouts get out of repair in a year or two and are seldom worth mending.

BPP 1865 XXVI pp 148 - 151

5.2 The Landowner and Housing

5.2.1 In 1861 A. W. Peel bought the Ongley estate at Eyeworth, and in 1864 his agent made a survey of the cottage accommodation.

Eyeworth Estate: Account of the Cottages
Old Farm House in three tenements: old but not requiring any immediate repair.
1. George Carter. Kitchen, pantry and 2 bedrooms, no garden.
2. William Morley. Kitchen, pantry and 2 bedrooms with small garden.
3. Mr. Tilcock's waggoner has the old Brewhouse and one bedroom over, no garden.
Double Cottage mud walls and thatched roof very poor and old but repairable.
4. William Brim. Kitchen, pantry and one bedroom over with good garden.
5. Thomas Humberstone. Kitchen, large pantry and 2 bedrooms over, with good garden.
Double Cottage brick and tiled in good repair, built by Lord Ongley.
6. Jesse Jervis. Kitchen, pantry and 2 bedrooms with Barn and good garden.
7. James Sanderson. Kitchen, pantry and 2 bedrooms with Barn and good garden.
Old Farm House in four Tenements, brick walls, roof thatched, thatch out of repair.
8. William Finding, an old Brewhouse, used as Kitchen and pantry. Two bedrooms, one on the floor and the other over Kitchen; with good garden.
9. John Lowe, Kitchen, pantry and two bedrooms one on the floor and the other over Kitchen: with good garden.
10. John Morley, Kitchen pantry and two bedrooms, with good garden.
11. Widow Sole. Kitchen, pantry, 1 bedroom on the floor and another large one over — with good garden.
New Double Cottage Let with Mr. John Lines' farm
12. William Hall, Kitchen, back Kitchen, pantry and 2 bedrooms over, with Barn and good garden.
13. Joseph Carter. Kitchen, back kitchen, pantry and 2 bedrooms over, with Barn and good garden.
Double Cottage brick and tiled in good repair with an old Cottage behind used as a barn.
14. Samuel Sole. Kitchen, back kitchen and 2 bedrooms over, with good garden.
15. Widow Clarke. Kitchen, back kitchen and 2 bedrooms over, with good garden.

New Double Cottage in very good repair, brick and tiled.

16. Elizabeth Chandler, parlour, Kitchen, pantry and three bedrooms over with good garden.

17. George Hall parlour, Kitchen, pantry and three bedrooms over with good garden.

Single Cottage William Carter mud walls and thatched roof in fair state of repair.

18. Kitchen, parlour, Closet and 2 bedrooms, with Barn and good garden.

Single Cottage Benjamin Chandler, mud walls and thatched roof in fair state of repair.

19. Kitchen, lumber room, with leanto pantry and two bedrooms over, with barn, pigstye and garden.

Double Cottage mud walls and thatched roof, old but repairable.

20. James Carter. Kitchen, cupboard and one bedroom over, with Barn and very small garden.

21. Widow Humberstone. Kitchen, pantry and one bedroom, with barn and a very small garden.

Ongley Arms Public House. Edward Franklin, good mud walls and tiled; Parlour, Kitchen, pantry, washhouse and cellar, 3 bedrooms. Gighouse and barn, boards and tiled, with Parish oven, Pigstyes behind the house, in a very poor state of repair and too close to the house, with garden.

Three Tenements, mud walls and thatched roof. Pigstyes in bad repair and too near road.

22. Joseph Morley, Kitchen, pantry and 2 bedrooms over with barn, – pigstye and good garden.

23. John Osborne Kitchen, pantry and 1 bedroom over with barn, pigstye and good garden.

24. Thomas Nicholson. Kitchen, pantry and 1 bedroom with barn, pigstye and good garden.

General Remarks Of these 24 Labourer's dwellings –

8 of them Viz Nos. 6, 7, 12, 13, 14, 15, 16 and 17 are nearly new, and good Cottages in every respect.

7 of them Viz Nos. 1, 2, 3, 8, 9, 10 and 11 have been made out of two farm houses.

9 of them Viz Nos. 4, 5, 18, 19, 20, 21, 22, 23 and 24 are old mud Cottages, that may be kept in repair for many years to come.

The repair necessary in the present season is the thatch of Nos. 8, 9, 10 & 11 and the Doors, Windows and thatch of Nos. 4 and 5.

There is also the old Workhouse, mud walls and thatch behind Nos. 17 & 18 which might at a very small expense be made into a widow's or old mans Cottage, if such a thing is desired.

Charles Couchman, Temple Balsall, Birmingham. 4 March 1864.

Beds. C.R.O. X 344/3

5.2.2 *A tabular statement of the number of cottages built by the Duke of Bedford from 1843 – 1861 and those now required, drawn up in February 1862 [Beds C.R.O. R 4/194/1] see Plate II.*

5.3 Housing and Health

The Public Health Act of 1872 set up Rural Sanitary Authorities, which later became the Rural District Councils. The Medical Officer's journals show that health was closely related to water supply.

Bedford Rural Sanitary Authority – Medical Officer's Journal No. 3

1889 April 22. I visited **Kempston Up End** and **Kempston West End**, on making inquiries at the house at Up End where A. Breed was in service I cannot ascertain the former or recent existence of any case of Enteric Fever either in the family or neighbourhood. At Breed's West End I found the house to be a new cottage one of a block of two, there is a well but the water is alleged to be brackish (see my last Annual Report with respect to the well waters of this neighbourhood) and, in addition, it is much too near to a privy cesspit; the water of the pond, which both families have been in the habit of using as a beverage, appears to be liable to pollution at certain times by soakages from the privy and ash hole; the outbreak of fever is attributed to these sanitary defects, but the chain of proof is not quite complete at present. I have requested Mr. Turnbull to visit and to report. . .

May 2 **Risely** . . . Several misuses were observed, respecting which Mr. Turnbull will report. At Boot yard the house occupied by Jesse Gammons his wife and six children sons aged 16, 12 and 6 daughters 23, 20 and 18 consists of only two rooms a living room 13 ft x 10 ft and a sleeping room over it in which there is next to nothing in the way of furniture; this house requires cleansing and is so overcrowded as to be a nuisance and injurious to health.

May 4 **Kempston West End.** I was present at the removal of two fresh cases of Enteric Fever from the house already alluded to. The patients on this occasion were the father of the family and a little boy of four years old. I afterwards saw these patients at the Fever Hospital. . .

1893 July 3 **Renhold** visited. At the School I found a full attendance and no epidemic disease known to be in the village.

At houses near the Church and occupied by Widow Gurney Widow Brown and others the well has been out of order and unusable for some time, water for all purposes is obtained from a pond. At the East end of the village ponds are generally in use and they are more full than might be expected after the long drought. A well which was originally intended for a public supply is out of order and cannot be used. At Salph End the well which was made under the auspices of this Authority is in good condition and the supply abundant.

Beds. C.R.O. RDBV 4

A STATEMENT OF THE NUMBER OF COTTAGES BUILT BY HIS GRACE THE DUKE OF BEDFORD ON THE BEDS AND BUCKS ESTATES FROM 1843 TO 1861 AND THOSE NOW REQUIRED.

District	YEAR	1843	'45	'46	'47	'48	'49	'50	'51	'52	'53	'54 Girls Sch.	'55	'56	'57	'58	'59	'60	'61	Total	The following are required.
WOBURN DISTRICT	Woburn	1	11		5	16	16	26	9							14	4	5		92	
	Aspley																				2
	Crawley									12	19	21	9		2					63	20
	Eversholt							6												6	
	Flitwick													2					2	4	
	Houghton Regis				2	5			3					2						12	12
	Lidlington					1 Sch		5										4		10	20
	Maulden				2	2														4	20
	Milton Bryant																				2
	Ridgmont								2			1 Sch	1	3		6			3	7	20
	Steppingley				7	3			2 Sch				12							28	16
AMPTHILL	Ampthill	1				3		1				Sch			6	6				15	20
	Houghton Conquest																				24
	Marston Moretaine																				4
	Millbrook					4 1 Sch	6					3				10			6	27	24
BEDFORD	Cople		2		4		2					2	4	18						37	30
	Goldington														2					2	10
	Knotting					2		3											6	11	20
	Oakley				6			6			6	3			2			1		18	30
	Souldrop									1		12								13	16
	Steventon																				2
	Willington					4					3				10	1				15	20
	Chenies				2	8				3	3									16	24
TOTAL	Cottages	1	13		22	22	42	43	14	16	28	41	26	25	18	31	4	10	17	374	
	Schools & dwelling houses					1	1		2			2								6	
	Total	1	13		22	23	43	43	16	16	28	43	26	25	18	31	4	10	17	380	+ 336

= 716

Note, It is proposed to renew the 336 Cottages at the Rate of 20 per Annum taking the worst ones first. B. 26 Febry 1862

Beds. C.R.O.   R 4/194/1

PLATE II

6. ACCESS TO LAND

The question of labourers' access to land in the nineteenth century was fraught with controversy and myth. It is not now generally thought that the process of land enclosure robbed the self sufficient peasantry of their land and reduced them to a landless class of employees. During the main period of parliamentary enclosure in Bedfordshire – from 1750 to 1830 – most Bedfordshire countrymen had little or no access to any land of their own. Nevertheless the applications for poor law relief even in the 1840's indicate the presence of a small minority of land holders among this depressed section of the community. Some allotments were made available to the poor at the time of Swing riots of 1830. Parishes were able to provide land for the poor under the Poor Law Amendment Act of 1819 (59 Geo. III cap. 12).

. Some Bedfordshire landowners and administrators such as the Russells of Woburn and Henry Trethewy, the Cornish-born steward of the de Grey estate at Wrest Park, Silsoe, took the lead in providing the labourer with allotments, which, orginally an adjunct to the Poor Law, became a fringe benefit to encourage farm workers to remain within the village community.

The agricultural depression of the 1870's called into question the whole basis of what had been assumed was a prosperous and successful rural social system. Perhaps the concentration on the middle-acreage, tenant farmer had after all been ill advised. Land reform, i.e. the re-creation of a self-supporting peasantry with its own small holdings, and recruited from the ranks of the hitherto landless rural workers, was, after all, the route to rural prosperity. In some other countries in northern Europe, in Scandinavia and even in backward Ireland, the way forward was increasingly seen as involving a revived peasantry rather than an extinct peasantry. In England the advanced radicals like Joseph Chamberlain and Jesse Collings took up the call for land-reform in the 'unauthorised programme' of the Liberals in 1885.

In the event, it was the Conservatives who won the 1886 election, not least because they had the support of the land-reforming element among the liberals, who had deserted Gladstone over the issue of Irish Home Rule. The Allotment Act of 1887 closely reflected the ideas of the benevolent landowners in rejecting all suggestion of land reform, or the break-up of estates. It concentrated instead on the provision of small allotments that the labourer might be able to work in his spare time. Under this act, the new rural sanitary authorities (later the rural district councils) could make land available to the poor but only in such quantities as would alleviate their lot as employees, rather than give them the opportunity to become economically independent as smallholders. Nevertheless, the Rural Labourers' League, the Birmingham-based organisation of the land reformers, made the best of things and provided encouragement and assistance to groups of labourers who wished to petition for allotment land, as they did in many Bedfordshire parishes during the 1880's and 1890's.

6.1   Theory

6.1.1   This pamphlet on the provision of allotments at Toddington was printed in 1832.

1832. On the Allotments made to the Labourers in the Parish of Toddington, in the County of Bedford.

As the system of making small allotments of Land to the labouring Poor, is extending very much, and great good is found to result therefrom, not only to the Poor themselves, but also to all those who are in any way interested, either as contributors to Parish Rates, or in the quiet and orderly behaviour of the labouring Class; it has been thought that it might be beneficial to relate what has been done on this subject in the Parish of Toddington, in Bedfordshire.

This Parish, as appears by the last census, contains 1926 inhabitants, of which 306 are employed in Agriculture.

In common with many other Parishes, the quantity of agricultural labour has greatly exceeded the demand, and for want of a regular, well managed plan, for the employment of the extra hands, they have been turned on the high roads in gangs of 20 or 30, not to work, but apparently to give them an opportunity of forming plans for midnight depredation. The consequence was as might have been forseen, a great demoralization of the men, and an increase of the rates. Under these circumstances, W. D. C. Cooper Esq., the principal Proprietor in the Parish, resolved to make the experiment, whether this sad state of things might not be ameliorated by making small allotments of Land, to the labourers.

In November 1829, six allotments of half an acre each, were made to six men well recommended for their good conduct, and having large families — The Land is a free-working gravel, and at the time, was a Wheat stubble: it was let as from the 29th September preceding; but as no profit could accrue to the people for the next half year, their rent was not to begin before the 25th March following. It was not supposed that they would attempt to put in any Wheat, however, they each by some means or other, collected sufficient manure for a small part of their Land, and sowed it with Wheat. The rest of the Land was in spring, set mostly with Potatoes, with some Peas, Cabbages, Turnips, Scarlet Beans &c. The men took great pains and kept their Land very clean — they were repayed by good Crops, which caused them to redouble their exertions to procure manure; so that the streets were cleaned of whatever could be made convertible to this end. As a proof of the benefit which was derived, one of the men having a very large family, and who had heretofore been obliged to go to the Overseer for money to pay the rent of his Cottage, was able to pay it himself, to his no small satisfaction.

This experiment seeming to succeed so well, the labourers generally, were very importunate also to have Land; accordingly, at Michaelmas, 1830, a large field was divided among 41 labourers, in pieces varying in size according to the Ridges into which it was accustomed to be ploughed; giving the larger portions to those with the larger families.

This Land too was let upon the same terms with the former; but as it was for the most part extremely foul and out of condition, very little Wheat was put on it; and indeed it was feared in the Spring, they would hardly be able to get their Potatoes in: but the Men turned to with hearty good will (they were working for themselves), and the Farmers having ploughed the Land in the Autumn, they set most of it with Potatoes and some Corn and Vegetables – their crop of Potatoes has been abundant; some having from 60 to 80 or 90 bushels.

That the people receive benefit from these allotments is evident from the labour they bestow, not only in getting out the twitch grass and other weeds, but also in their actually making good and substantial hollow drains; it is further evidenced, by their good and orderly conduct. In Summer evenings, instead of idly lounging about the place, or doing mischief; they are occupied on their Land. It is a heart-cheering sight to see from 40 to 50 persons, after their master's work is done, labouring in their allotments; weeding and cleaning the Crops till daylight fails, and then going quietly home, doubtless, with the pleasing anticipation of their labour eventually making them independent of the Parish, as their Fathers, or rather Grandfathers had been formerly.

In addition to the 47 allotments already spoken of, and two good gardens; 34 more pieces were allotted last Michaelmas: making a total of Eightythree, which will nearly meet the demand.

The rules and terms upon which the Land is held, are very few and simple, and cannot be misunderstood or forgotten: In the first place, the rent is to be paid punctually on each quarter day, under a penalty for default, of immediate loss of Land and the Crop on it: secondly, if any of the Men are convicted before the Magistrate of any breach of the Law, the Land and Crop are in like manner forfeited: lastly, it is particularly insisted upon, that they shall be very watchful over the morals of their families, and regularly frequent some place of Public Worship: and especially that the children be not permitted to be idling about the Streets after nightfall.

In granting the allotments, of course regard was had to the characters of the applicants; and house who were notoriously bad, were objected to: this rule was all well enough to begin with, but upon reflection, it was thought right to give those whose characters did not stand very well, a chance of retrieving themselves; as one of them said "I know, Sir, that you have not a very good opinion of me, but give me an opportunity of honestly employing my time and you shall see that my Land shall be as well cultivated as the rest, and no fault shall be found with me in other matters:" – he has hitherto kept his word: he has hollow-drained his Land, and bestowed as much labour and pains upon it, as if it were his own freehold. G. A. January, 1832.

Beds. C.R.O. A.D. 531

6.1.2 *Henry Trethewy, the steward of the de Grey estate, Wrest Park, Silsoe, read a paper on "The Allotment System" to the London Central Farmers' Club in November 1858. It attracted much attention, and the account in the club's journal was reprinted in the report of the Royal Commission on the Employment of Children, Young Persons and Women in Agriculture, 1867. The text below consists of extracts from Trethewy's paper.*

THE ALLOTMENT SYSTEM

Mr. Trethewy. – It may be said that the subject which I have the pleasure to introduce to you this evening is one more calculated for the consideration of landowners and those concerned in the management of estates than for discussion at a farmers' club. A little reflection, however, will show us that it is one involving, if possible, even more the comfort and prosperity of the occupier than of the owner of the soil; for it cannot be denied that much of the success of the farmer depends upon the class of labourers he may have about him, whether steady, industrious, and skilful, or otherwise. Any system, therefore, having a tendency to elevate the moral character of the labourer and to improve his condition must be worthy of encouragement; and therefore I think the committee have exercised a proper discretion in selecting this subject for an evening's discussion, for it is one upon which much prejudice exists, and not without some reason. Like many other useful schemes, the allotment system has suffered from the injudicious zeal of its advocates, some of whom have taught people to expect too much from it, and who themselves have regarded it almost as a panacea. Hence it has in some instances been carried to such an extent as totally to alter its character, and therefore the prejudice which I have just alluded to has arisen against it. A desire for the occupation of land is inherent in the human mind. No wonder then that the labourer, whose very existence is identified with vegetable life, should participate in this feeling. And when we consider how influential this feeling often is in diverting his attention from places and objects having a tendency to demoralization, surely it is the duty of every one interested in his well-being, so far as is consistent to promote his wishes. How many hours, which might otherwise be passed in the alehouse, may thus be spent in profitable occupation! But here it is possible I may be met by an objection which I have sometimes heard made, that if the labourer does his duty to his employer during the day he can have little desire to work afterwards. In other words, that he employs strength and exertion on his own land which of right belong to the farmer who pays him for his day's work. To this I would reply that if the day's work is done (and I apprehend no employer would keep on a man who habitually failed in doing it), to restrain him from devoting his leisure hours to his own pursuits would be to reduce a labourer to the lowest degree of serfdom. Upon this principle the cottage garden must go uncultivated, and all recreation would have to be given up. I do not, however, for one moment anticipate such an objection at the Central Farmers' Club in the nineteenth century, and it is therefore scarcely necessary to advert to it. About the year 1830 a number of noblemen and gentlemen, "to meet the pressing exigencies of the times," formed a society called the "Labourers' Friend Society," having more especially for its object the obtaining a small portion of land for the labourer at a moderate rent in addition to the "fair price of his labour." One cannot but feel thankful, after perusing some of their reports, and comparing the state of the labouring population of those days with that of the present generation of labourers, for the great improvements which have taken place, both in the social and moral point of view. Various causes have operated to accomplish this end: education, improved dwellings, and, although last, not least, an alteration in the poor laws. In Bedfordshire allotments were laid out on the estates of the Duke of Bedford and Earl de Grey in the year 1829. In that year it appears that on the former estate, in the parish of Maulden, 18 acres were divided into parcels of from 20 to 40 poles each; while on the latter estate in the same year 30 acres were set out in parcels of from one rood to two roods each. Other proprietors soon afterwards followed these examples until garden allotments became very general. I would, however, here observe, that it is not my opinion that allotments are suited to all districts, and that it does not follow that because they answer well in one locality that they will succeed in another. It would be a task far beyond my power to point out and describe such districts, residents being by far the best judges in the matter. I would merely observe that where labourers live in villages, as in the midland counties, the system would be more practicable than in those districts where they more generally reside on the farms they work upon. In selecting ground for allotments, the principle points to be attended to are situation and soil. It is of the utmost importance that they should be within an easy distance of the dwellings of the poor. The nature more than the quality of the soil has to be considered; for it is astonishing how much poor thin land is improved by spade husbandry, while strong heavy clays are wholly unfit for the purpose of allotments, no matter how well they may be drained. Of course the rent would be in proportion to the quality. And now as regards the quantity for each occupier. My experience convinces me that a rood is sufficient under almost any circumstances; and the greatest error that has been committed has been the allotting of too much land to one individual. To dwell upon the evils arising from such a proceeding is scarcely necessary, as it must be obvious that without sufficient capital the occupation of land cannot be attended with profitable results. Some instances in confirmation of this view have come under my own observation, and I can confidently assert that instead of the position of such men having improved, it has retrograded. Occupied nearly the whole of their time upon their own land, they can no longer be classed under the head of labourers, and they actually injure regular workmen by throwing their labour into the market at seasons of the year when the demand for it is unusually depressed. If it be argued that the restriction of the system would have the effect of preventing a labourer from improving his condition, and effectually debar him from rising in the world by his own industry, I would answer that I am not now discussing the relative advantages of large and small farms, but am confining myself to the agricultural labourer in the broad acceptation of the term. Every employer knows, and every man of common sense must feel, that it is as important to the farmer to have his regular men at work at all times as it is to the manufacturer or tradesman, and that the business of the farm could not be carried on without such regularity. I regard it, then, as a fatal error for the labourer to follow any pursuit that would at all interfere with the claim of his employer upon him; for be it remembered, that it is upon hired labour that the working man must chiefly depend for his subsistence, and any scheme that has a tendency to interfere with this, his chief capital, must very shortly end in disappointment and distress; but any plan that can be devised which will improve his condition, without interfering with his free labour, must be hailed as a great boon. Such I believe the allotment system properly managed to be. That there always have been, and that there always will be, men to raise themselves by their own industry above their original position, no one can deny; nor would any man of common justice and generous feeling attempt to prevent such an occurrence; but such men have always risen gradually, and not at once jumped from the one state to the other. Whenever a man shows himself superior to his fellows in intelligence, skill, or application, he will be sure to push himself, and by obtaining higher wages, the natural result of his superiority, gradually improve his position. And it often happens that such men, after saving a little money, are assisted by their former employers, or by others who have watched their career, in accomplishing the object of their desire, whether a small occupation or otherwise. By the sweat of his brow man must ever live, and so long as society exists there must be rich and poor.

I will now say a few words upon rents and managements. There is no reason, that I am aware of, why the labourer should have land at a lower price than others would give for it; nor do I see upon what principle he should be asked to pay more. After all, it is not a question of rent, so much as to have the allotment ground on a convenient spot. If situated near a village, as it should be, the land may assume the value of accommodation land, and should of course be paid for accordingly. On the estate of the Right Hon. the Earl de Grey, in Bedfordshire, with which I am connected as agent, the rents vary from 32s to 72s per acre (or from 8s to 18s per rood), including all rates and taxes, and the gates, fences, ditches and watercourses are kept and maintained for them, so that they have nothing to pay but the rent. Of course, many of those rents are higher than are paid by the farmer; but, as I before observed, they are many of them accommodation lands, and would readily let at the same prices to others. It is to me a matter of peculiar gratification to be able to testify to the punctuality with which those rents are paid. Including a few market gardeners, there are on his lordship's rent roll, in Bedfordshire, some 750 tenants. The collection occupies five days, and it rarely happens that there are any arrears. Below is a tabular statement, showing the acreage and the number of allotment tenants in a few of the parishes where the principal portion of the Wrest estates are situate.

Parish	Population per Census of 1851	Area of Parishes	Number of Allotments	Acreage of Allotment Land
		Acres		Acres
Silsoe	755	2,067	78	24
Clophill	1,186	2,317	180	55
Flitton	656	1,020	163	140
Pulloxhill	688	1,584	131	51
Upper Gravenhurst	357	895	66	24
Lower Gravenhurst	58	757		

Many of those, especially in the parishes of Clophill, Pulloxhill, and Flitton, which are what are termed "open parishes" i.e., parishes where the cottages belong to several proprietors, have no ground whatever belonging to their dwellings. Hence it may be easily conceived what an advantage an allotment must be to them. Indeed, so anxious are they for it, that whenever a vacancy occurs numerous applications are sure to pour in. No restriction as to cultivation is imposed, except such as are common to the farmers. Some people have an objection to cottagers being allowed to grow wheat, but I cannot say that I have ever found any inconvenience to have arisen from it. I see no reason whatever why such a restriction should be imposed; for a crop of wheat is as much a change to the soil as any other crop, and at times no doubt as profitable; while the straw comes for litter for the pig, and returns to the ground in the shape of manure. It is not found that the privilege is abused by excess of cropping, and therefore the practice has not been prohibited. In every parish on Lord de Grey's estate, where there are allotments, a barn is provided for the use of these tenants alone for the purpose of thrashing, &c., and they generally agree pretty well among themselves, so that it is seldom necessary to interfere with their arrangements as to its use. The early promoters of the system seem to have been very much prompted to it by a pressure of the poor rates. It was a very general impression for a few years before the passing of the Poor Law Amendment Act, in 1834, and indeed for some time subsequently, that great relief would be given to the ratepayers by the introduction of allotments; but I have not been able to learn that such was, or has been, the case to a very great extent. I would here notice a curious circumstance in connexion with this part of the subject, which occurred in a parish with which I am acquainted. It contains about 650 inhabitants, nearly all of whom would be engaged in the cultivation of the soil; and in consequence of so many labourers being out of employ, the poor rates at one time amounted to nearly 16s in the pound. In this fearful state of things the largest occupier gave up his farm, saying he could manage to pay his rent, but that the rates would ruin him. A considerable portion of his occupation was then let out to the labourers in parcels varying from one to five and ten acres each. In a few years the rates were considerably reduced; but whether this improved state of things was to be traced to the division of the land as described or to the operation of the new poor law, is a point which is yet open to speculation; for both causes, as well as one or two others of a local nature, were in operation at the same time. My own conviction is that to the legislative enactment the credit principally belongs. The original allottees were allowed to remain in possession of their land till they were removed by death or became incapable of managing it; but it was not considered good policy to continue this system; but rather, when one of the little holdings became vacant, to divide it into allotments of a rood each, thus affording land upon a sounder principle, and providing for the necessities of greater numbers. The rates are now about the same as in the adjoining parishes similarly situated. There may be a difference of opinion as to whether it be more desirable that each man should have a garden of sufficient size for his wants, or whether a piece of ground should be set apart for the whole village, in the shape of an allotment. The latter scheme offers advantages peculiarly its own. They are, first, that a spirit of emulation is excited when all are brought into a kind of friendly competition, as is the case in an allotment field. If one man succeeds beyond the rest in raising any particular crop, it will be sure to be noticed, and his system most probably adopted. Every man has the advantage of the experience of the whole field, whereas in a garden there are not those opportunities. I believe example has a strong influence in promoting good and clean cultivation among all classes of occupiers. With a view to encourage it amongst the allotment tenants of the district, a society, called the "Silsoe and Ampthill Labourer's Friend Society," was established about seventeen years ago. It offers several prizes annually for competition, and great interest is excited among the exhibitors. This society is under the patronage of Earl de Grey, and has Lord Wensleydale as president, while the stewards consist entirely of tenant farmers, who thus evince their sense of its usefulness. The subscribers comprise the clergy and gentry of the neighbourhood, and the exhibition is invariably fully attended. In fact, all classes unite to promote the object it has in view; and the result is an exhibition of fruits, vegetables, &c., that would surprise any one who had never before witnessed it. Some persons have an objection to prizes being offered for length of service; but I cannot conceive that any opposition can be offered to the encouragement of good cultivation, whether on a small scale or on a large one. Upon the latter part of my subject I have little to say. The chief abuse of the system (to use the word on the card) consists in giving the labourer more land than he can manage consistently with his usual occupation. Every scheme must be kept within due bounds – every system must have a limit. To extend the allotment system beyond its legitimate bounds would have the effect of completely changing its character, and turning that which was intended to be an auxiliary into a leading pursuit.

BPP 1868-9 XIII

6.2   Practice

The printed rules for Harlington allotments, c. 1832.

RULES AND REGULATIONS Respecting the Allotment of Garden Land for Labourers, In the Parish of HARLINGTON.

I.   The Rent is to be paid half-yearly, on the 1st of April, and the 1st of October.

II.   No Occupier will be suffered to re-let his Allotment.

III.   No Person shall be employed on the Land who does not belong to the Parish.

IV.   No Occupier will be allowed to Plough his Land, but be required to cultivate it solely by Spade Husbandry.

V.   If any Occupier is found neglectful in the cultivation of his Land, he will not be permitted to hold it after the current year.

VI.   No Occupier who is at work for the Parish, or for any Employer, will be allowed to work upon his Land after Six o'Clock in the Morning, or before Six in the Evening without permission from his Master.

VII.   No Occupier will be suffered to trespass upon another's Allotment.

VIII.   All Occupiers will be expected to attend regularly at Divine Service; to conduct themselves with sobriety at all times; and to bring up their Families in a decent and orderly manner.

IX.   Any Occupier, who may be convicted of any Offence against the Laws of the Country, will be deprived of his Allotment, and the Crop growing thereon forfeited.

N.B.   Take care to suit your Crops to the size of your Garden, keeping in mind the Roots and Vegetables most in use in your Family, and observe that the produce of the Garden will be in proportion to the care taken of it; do not therefore waste anything that can be converted into Manure: keep your Hog-sty clean, the Hogs improve more and the Garden is enriched. To the Dung-hill from the Sty, add the decayed Leaves of the Vegetables and what the Hogs will not eat; the Soot and Ashes from the Chimney and Fire; the Suds from the Washing tub; the Sweepings from the Floor of the House; all Dirt and Rubbish, and cuttings of Weeds from the Roads, Banks, and Hedgesides; with all other Articles which will make Manure. Thus, at the same time that everything about you is kept clean and tidy, you will be paid well for your care by the produce of your Garden, abundantly assisting in the support of your Family.

W. FRANKLIN, PRINTER, AUCTIONEER, &c. AMPTHILL.

Beds. C.R.O. X 21/510

6.3   Local Government involvement

The Allotment Act of 1887 in operation at Kempston.
Bedford Union Rural Sanitary Authority Minute Book   18th February 1888

Kempston Allotments,
The Clerk read a representation under the "Allotments Act 1887" which he had received purporting to be signed by twelve Labourers residing at West End Kempston.

It was resolved that the persons whose names were appended be invited to send a Deputation to attend the next Meeting of this Authority and the Clerk undertook to make enquiries as to the existing Allotment Land in the Parish.

Beds. C.R.O. RDBM 1/1

7.   EDUCATION AND THE FARM LABOURER

The provision of village schools in Bedfordshire is to be dealt with by Mr. D. W. Bushby in a future volume, but there are some aspects of rural education that should be in a study of the farm worker. Although the motives and enthusiasm of the gentry and clergy who promoted voluntary schools in the 1830's and 1840's were probably the same in Bedfordshire as in other counties, the reception given to the new schools was gravely distorted here by the peculiar strength of domestic industry: lace in the north and straw plait in the south of the county. This hindered the attendance of girls in particular, and helped to reinforce a strong tendency towards illiteracy among females in rural areas. In the comparatively small areas where the labour of small boys was in demand – the market garden region in East Beds. – the school attendance figures are reversed, although it is not yet clear what effect if any it had on working class literacy.

The correspondence of the Bedford estate steward at Woburn indicates that in the 1840's a demand for village schools was being voiced by the labourers themselves, and was not merely a concern of their well-meaning betters.

After the establishment of parish School Boards under the 1870 Education Act, school attendance was made compulsory parish by parish. Before that date the working class families of the county had been divided in their attitude to education. The Victorian 'new working class' of occupation – policemen, railwaymen and the like – invariably sent their children to school. The 'traditional' working class in rural areas were far less uniform in their support for education, and more dependent on child labour in lace-making or straw plait. The Bedfordshire farm labourers come into the second category.

7.1   Duke of Bedford's involvement

7.1.1   Letter from Thomas Bennett, the Steward at Woburn, to Christopher Haedy, the estate's Agent-in-chief in London.

Park Farm Woburn August 18th 1840.

Dear Sir,

I have today called upon Mr. Pearse the Vicar of Westoning, to make some further enquiries of himself as to the proposed school. Mr. Pearse stated that the Children who now come from Prisley Farm to his Sunday School are

Children of Dissenters — that the Dissenters having no resident Minister, their Sunday School is badly managed, and that many Dissenters have begged as a great favor that he would receive their Children to his School and that several of the Labourers both in his own and adjoining Parishes have asked him to endeavour to get a day School for them.

There has in former times been a School at Westoning but the Masters have been a bad sort — and done no good either to themselves or their Scholars — the fact I dare say is — that the population is too poor to pay a Master sufficiently well, to insure a man of decent conduct. Mr. Pearse proposes that the Scholars shall pay a part and the rest made up by a Subscription: he further says that when his day school is established he has no wish that the Children of Dissenting parents should attend Church Sunday School against the inclination of the Parents.

His first application was only to build a School room, which was estimated at £180 but he finds to make the Master comfortable he must also have a Dwelling to adjoin the School — and he now wants the sum of £300. The Site for the building will be given and conveyed to the Clergyman for the time being in trust for the use of a School. Mr. P. expects at least 20 Boys from Flitwick when the Day School commences. The Duke is not a proprietor of Cottages in Flitwick beyond the Cottage at Prisley — but he is the owner of about one third of that Parish.

When I mentioned £10 as a Subscription I was not aware that Mr. Pearse intended to go beyond the School Room, but for the School House also I think His Grace might add £5 or £10 more — Westoning was one of the most pauperised parishes we had, and the population most notorious Poachers &c, the farmers are a Class only a little above the Labourers and no better educated. None of the Proprietors have taken any interest in the Parish so that, it is not to be much wondered at, the state of ignorance the people are in —

In self defence the adjoining Proprietors should be glad to assist, in order that the present race of Children may have an opportunity of learning something to counteract the example of their elders.

I am Most faithfully yours Thos. Bennett

Beds. C.R.O. R 3/4285

7.1.2   An account of the Duke of Bedford's expenditure up to January 1855.

Cost of Schools built by the Duke of Bedford & Donations by His Grace in aid of School Building.

Beds and Bucks.
Schools built:
Woburn Boys School and Master's Dwelling   500 '' ''

Woburn Girls School	407	” ”
Millbrook Infant School and Mistress's do.	260	” ”
Lidlington do. do.	340	” ”
Steppingley do. do.	210	” ”
Ridgmount New Schools at	723	” ”
Oakley Boys School and Master's Dwelling	480	” ”
Cople do. do.	320	” ”
Souldrope, a Cottage converted into do.	40	” ”
Chenies Boys School and Girls School and Dwelling for Master and Mistress	900	” ”
	£4,180	” ”

Donations in aid of School Building:

Ampthill National Site and	Site and	100	” ”	
do. do. Infant	do.	20	” ”	
do. British and Foreign	do.	100	” ”	
do. do. Infant	do.	10	” ”	
Aspley Guise National		160	” ”	
Chesham Infant		10	” ”	
Flitwick National		66	” ”	
Hawnes		6	” ”	
Chenies, alteration of schools		37	” ”	
Houghton Conquest National		100	” ”	
Keysoe British and Foreign		10	” ”	
Marston Moretaine National		100	” ”	
Maulden National — the site and Materials from the old School and		192	” ”	
Rickmansworth		5	” ”	
St. Cuthbert's Bedford		20	” ”	
Thurleigh		25	” ”	
Westoning		20	” ”	
Toddington, towards erecting new Schools		20	” ”	
Tebworth, towards erecting new Schools		5	” ”	1,006 ” ”
				£5,186 ” ”

January 1855

Beds. C.R.O. R 4/661/3

7.2   Help from a farmer

Robert Long was a substantial farmer at Upper Stondon, though most of his men came from Lower Stondon or Meppershall. He kept a weekly journal of wages paid and work done.

1861 30th March The weather this week has been cold, and at times showery, yet some days have been very fine and pleasant. The horses have this week been ploughing in New Close, where it had been done previously since Christmas in the contrary direction. All the piece too had been dunged in the winter and now in some parts it seems too wet for ploughing, yet I want to get it done and harrowed so as to be able shortly to drill in some mustard seed for a crop to be eaten off green by the sheep as soon as it will be ready. I have done so before in the beginning of April, and found it very useful food at the time of the year when the other keep begins to get shorter in supply. This week some of my labourers have been working at Lower Stondon where the new school is to be. They have been excavating the earth for a cellar to be made under the part to be used for a dwelling house for the Mistress. I have of late, too, carted a quantity of bricks to the spot for the building, and much of the top soil I carted away, besides having the stones sifted out of the soil for the purpose of concreting the foundation. Mr. Hull too has carted materials. The bricks were purchased early last year and stacked in Cooper's Yard before we had quite decided on the spot to build the school. This week I have had a cart colt broken into work. It is one of my own breeding, and at present it works pretty well. Lately I sold two horses, and shortly again I want to try the Steam Ploughing and then for a time I shall not want to use so many horses.

Beds. C.R.O. X 159/3

7.3   School log-books

Extracts from the log-books of six schools have been chosen to illustrate the schooldays of labourers' children in the second half of the century. Young children had previously attended lace or plait schools, and this continued, sometimes with the children as "half-timers". The Factory Act of 1867 attempted to prevent children under 8 from working, and allowed children between 8 and 13 to work only on condition that they attended school for 10 hours a week, although a child over 10 could leave for work if he had attained a specified standard of education. This act became effective when there were sufficient Factory Inspectors, who are here seen at work, for example at Odell. School fees could be charged until the 1891 Education Act led to free education, and the fees were an added burden on parents at a time when there was strong pressure towards compulsory attendance.

Roxton National School log-book. *Roxton was a village which had both straw-plait and lace schools, and boys and girls were employed also in the market-gardening industry.*
1864 18 Jan Four Girls left to go to Straw-plaiting school — three of them have just entered the first Class. 1 Feb Two girls sent to plaiting school, 1

from 3rd, and 1 from 4th Class. 22 Feb Eleven Boys and Girls gone to field work today. 13 Apr Several away Bird Keeping.

1870 16 Mar Several Girls gone to Lace School. 21 Mar Several Boys away "Bird Keeping". 24 Mar Five Boys and Girls away "dropping" etc. 31 Mar Many away at Field Work. 22 Nov Several Boys away "plant dropping".

1877 28 Sep Reopened School on Monday after six weeks holiday. Many children away still gleaning and picking up potatoes.

1878 3 May Several boys away to mind horses by roadside.

1885 29 May School resumed work after holiday with a poor attendance. Charles and Agnes Jeffries were sent home for School money and failed to reappear again during the week.

1887 14 Oct Attendance poor this week several children away potatoe picking. Out of 47 children on books over 7 the average is 31. 21 Oct Attendance again is very bad owing to potatoe picking.

Beds C.R.O. S.D. Roxton 1

Shillington National then Board School log-book.

1866 3 May Attendance poor in the morning it being wet and there being a wedding. 22 May Hitchin market affects school. 26 Jun Hay making. Big boys away. 28 Sep Our school treat. About 250 present. 1 Oct Some children leave school now feast is over. 2 Oct Plaiters away at Hitchin market.

1867 14 Feb Not many at school being Valentine's Day. 21 Oct Several boys picking weeds. 4 Nov Some boys who were working returned. 18 Nov Most of the big lads still engaged in weeding. 16 Dec Not so many at school today several of the bigger ones having gone to see a fox hunt.

1868 12 Feb Great many away at a wood sale in afternoon. 2 Apr Small pox – some school children attacked. 3 Apr Only about 20 in the large room this afternoon, the rest staying away for fear of infection. 24 Jul Great many away gleaning in the afternoon. 12 Oct Many children absent, some have gone to pick up acorns.

1869 3 Sep Very poor attendance still owing to the gleaning. 9 Sep A good school during the morning, but small during afternoon owing to a "Harvest Home" being in the neighbourhood. 29 Sep Three infants taken with the scarlet fever.

1870 3 Jun School closed for one week owing to the Measles being so prevalent in the village.

1871 4 Jul Several of the boys absent that were present on Monday, having been sent to attend the Hitchin market. 6 Jul Several girls absent plaiting. 6 Oct Very few girls attend School, in proportion to the number of boys. This is attributed to the existence of "Plaiting Schools" where girls are taught to plait straw which they sell.

1874 25 Sep Attendance low: average only 92.4. Weather wet; the fair on

Wednesday; also three Sunday School children's Teas in the village to keep them from going to the Fair. This accounts for small attendance. 9 Oct Several children absent "twitching".
1875 15 Jan Admitted 17 children this week: some came without their school fees. On the Tuesday I sent them home as they said their parents said "They would not pay".
1877 9 Feb Average attendance this week 151; this is the highest yet attained. Some of the parents have obeyed the order of the Board and taken their children from work and sent them to school full time; others are still sending their children only half-time to school. Her Majesty's Sub-Inspector of Factories called to ask the Master what steps the Board was taking relative to the children of school age attending plaiting schools. 23 Mar Attendance still on the decline. This is caused in part by children leaving for work who have reached their eleventh year; but some of school age are still sent to work part time. 29 Jun The attendance has again been very bad this week; girls are kept at home plaiting and boys are going to work.
1879 9 May Many children of 11 years of age have left, and are still leaving, as soon as they attain the age of 11 years, even in the 1st Standard.
1882 1 Dec Children under 10 years of age are asking to leave school; because they have passed in the three subjects of the Third Standard. 33 children under 10 years of age passed in Reading, Writing and Arithmetic in the Third Standard; and are therefore, by the Bye-Laws, at liberty to leave school as soon as they attain their 10th Birthday.
1883 12 Oct Attendance very bad in the upper standards, as the parents know they are not compelled to send their children when they have passed the III Standard. The Boys have been picking up potatoes and gathering fruit.
Beds. C.R.O. S D Shillington 1

Odell National School log-book
1872 14 Jun Harry Goodman has returned to school this week, after an absence at work of 7 weeks. 1 Jul Admitted Naomi Line aged 7 years and 11 months — she cannot read. We have had a very small school today, many having gone to Harrold Feast. 2 Jul A little better attendance today, but much below the usual number. Admitted Elizabeth Foskett as a half-timer. 5 Jul The numbers have been much reduced this week by Harrold Feast. 29 Jul Odell Feast a half holiday. 2 Aug We have had only about half our usual number this week. The Factory Inspector visited the school today in reference to the Half-timers.
1873 24 Dec Christmas Holidays commenced. The attendance has been rather small this week, because some of the parents are unwilling to pay a penny for three days, and it was a very wet morning on Monday, which prevented some of the little ones from coming.

1877 13 Jul Visit from Factory Inspector respecting the half-timers. I am requested to divide them into 2 divisions, and have a division mornings one week and afternoons another. I am thankful for this as I shall have a better chance to bring them on. 16 Jul This morning the half timers did not turn up till 10, and when I questioned them as to the reason, they replied "Mrs. Coleman, the Lace Mistress, would not let them come". As the Inspector said I was not to make any difference with the half timers and to let him know if they did not attend the full 3 hours, I at once wrote to him. 23 Jul Received a letter from the Inspector of Factories to the effect that the half-timers were to attend the full 3 hours, and that he had officially informed and cautioned Mrs. Coleman.

1886 26 Nov Received an order from the Bedford Guardians for Kate, Ada and Walter Headland to attend school, their fees to be paid by the Board up to February.

1888 9 Jan "Plough Monday". Many absentees among the elder children. 10 Jan Attendance Officer called and took notes of absentees. 26 Jan A worse attendance today. Several absentees have gone "sticking", much wood having been blown from the trees during the past night. 27 Feb Mrs. Gell, who lives over a mile away, beyond the Wood, called to say that her daughter Annie would not be able to attend school while there was such a depth of snow. The track is almost impassable for her, and for many other "long distance" children. 6 Apr A large number absent. Paltry excuses given, e.g. "Not ready when bell rang"; "A Club Walk" to take place; "Pig being killed"; etc. 18 Apr Very small school today. "Primrose gathering" is the general excuse for the present, and probably will be for some time to come. 1 May 33 children absent, most of them are "Maying". 2 May "Cowslipping" is the common excuse today for absentees when sent for. I fear it is an utter impossibility for me to drag the school up to anything approaching "efficiency" if the present (and past) system of *non*-attendance prevail much longer. Here is nearly ¼ the School Year gone, and about one third the children (supposed to be attending) absent. 6 Jun The Attendance Officer called this dinner-time and requested Master to sign certificates as to non-attendance of 3 children with a view to the prosecution of their parents. 22 Jun Three parents (or guardians) have been summoned for not sending their charges regularly to school. On looking over the Registers I find the three children's attendances to have been as follows during the past school year. School open 417 times:—

Herbert Ashton	202 attendances	Away 215 times
Lewis Line	294 attendances	Away 123 times
Edith Peck	304 attendances	Away 113 times

3 Jul "Harrold Feast" still keeps many away, in spite of the prosecutions for non-attendance on Friday last. 17 Jul Many of our children are absent this afternoon having gone to Sharnbrook to a "Tea-drinking" of a Temperance

Society of which several are members. 18 Jul The attendance this morning is much worse than yesterday's. Several are pea-picking.

Beds. C.R.O. S D Odell 1

Biggleswade National Girls' School log-book. *In Biggleswade the market-gardeners employed girls to peel onions in the onion sheds, and the girls also peeled osiers for basket-making.*
1876 8 May The attendance not so good, owing to the "Osier peeling".
1877 11 May Smaller average again, owing to several of the girls being sent away, by order of the Managers, because their money was not brought. 8 Jun 3 Girls sent home because *no* money brought, by order of the Managers. The average therefore is less, as they do not come any more that week and some not at all. 3 Aug A very poor school today. The onion peeling has begun. The numbers from Monday to Friday have gradually sunk from 103 to 71. We have had far greater control over the children this week, though there are still a few outbreaks. 14 Sep There has been a very poor attendance this week, the bulk of the children being away peeling onions and gleaning. 26 Oct The average this week has reached to 102, highest number present 115 with 141 on the books. The children have been most unruly, due to the return of so many onion peelers.
1880 6 Aug The average this week has again sunk, so many children away peeling onions. Mrs. Carr has paid me 4 visits in one day to get a certificate for Lizzie Carr. She could not or would not understand she was not eligible, having failed in reading in Standard III, and threatened to take her from school, as she did not consider she was properly "teached" – (taught).
1884 10 Oct So many children lose their marks because they cannot get back in time in the afternoons from carrying their parents' dinners.
1885 18 Sep Gave half holiday in the afternoon being the Statute Fair. Children still away gleaning and onion peeling. 16 Oct School still very badly attended, but I find the onion peeling will close on Wednesday next.
1886 10 Sep The school has been very badly attended this week and it is just the height of the onion peeling. Sent in a list of 51 to the Officer to visit. 17 Sep We are giving a half holiday this afternoon being the "Statute Fair". The improvement in the attendance has been very trifling. I wrote a note to the Officer to visit the onion sheds yesterday. He did so this morning and found a quantity of children illegally employed. Took the names of some and cautioned the employers.
1891 10 Jul Onion peeling has begun. The average is going down frightfully.

Beds. C.R.O. S D Biggleswade 2

Bletsoe National School log-book *Bletsoe had an unusually bad health record due, apparently, to defective water supplies.*

1897 4 Jan School re-opened this morning after Xmas holiday. Jesse Laughton still unable to return and Mary Partridge, Joseph and Charles Wildman also away ill. 18 Jan Minnie, Percy, Charles, Mabel and James Cranfield unable to attend school on account of there being diptheria in the family. 19 Jan One death has occurred from diptheria in the Cranfield family. 20 Jan Dr. Prior from Bedford came today and has ordered that Ethel Coleman, being resident in the same block of houses as the Cranfields, must not attend school again until the doctor says it is right. Beatrice Savage also suffering with bad throat and therefore her brother, Oscar, obliged to absent himself from school by doctor's order. 22 Jan Joseph Brown, Louisa, William and Rose Eleanor Robinson certified by doctor to be unable to attend school, also from throat disorders. Emma and Mary Partridge still away also Jesse Laughton, Harry Coleman and others. 21 Apr Opened school again this morning. Minnie Cranfield returned to school after an absence of three months. 22 Apr Mabel Cranfield returned today having been absent the same time as her sister. 14 May James Cranfield has not yet returned to school, his legs being too weak to walk far. 17 May James Cranfield returned to school this morning. 24 May Lucy, Edith and Thomas Armstrong forbidden (by the doctor) to attend school as Lucy has a mild form of Scarlet Fever. 25 May Mabel Cranfield went home at 12 o'clock being ill. 26 May Georgina Brown, suffering with measles, unable to attend school. The five Cranfields forbidden to attend school until Mabel's throat is better. 28 Jul Walter Coleman taken away to the Fever Hospital suffering from Diptheria. Percy Homes and Charles Wildman away ill. 5 Aug School closed today by order of Dr. Collins — order received about 8 p.m. yesterday evening. Cause for closing is that Maggie Wells is very ill with diptheria. Dr. Prior, however, came this morning and said there was no reason why the school should be closed, therefore it will be opened again tomorrow. 6 Aug School reopened but only 32 children present, as their parents fear the infection, the children having to pass by the house of Mrs. Wells. 9 Aug Attendance very low as the parents are still doubtful as to whether the school is free from infection. 13 Aug Amy Laughton away suffering from sore throat also Leonard Pettit and Edith Armstrong. Maggie Wells and Walter Coleman still progressing favourably. Attendance very low for the whole of the week, there being 55 on books, but only an average of 34.6. 1 Oct Maggie Wells has been brought home from the Fever Hospital during this week, but is not yet sufficiently strong to return to school. 8 Oct Walter Coleman and Maggie Wells still away from school, being too weak for work yet or even much walking. Louisa Robinson no better and Arthur Duncombe suffering from Debility.

7.4   A School Board

1874 At an adjourned Meeting of the Elstow School Board held at the Office of the Clerk No. 6 St. Paul's Square, Bedford on Saturday the 23rd day of May at 5 p.m.

Present: T. A. Macan Esq: In the Chair; Mr. Benjn. Prole; Rev. J. Copner; Mr. Risley.

. . .

Scale of Fees.

Mr Copner proposed that the following scale of Fees per week be adopted

For Labourers	1 Child 3d	2 Children 5d	3 Children 6d
		if more 1d	each child after 3
For Artizans	1 Child 4d	2 Children 6d	3 Children 8d
		if more 2d	each child after 3
For Farmers		6d each child.	

Seconded by Mr. Prole and carried unanimously.

At a Meeting of the Elstow School Board held at the Office of the Clerk No. 6 St. Paul's Square, Bedford, on Friday the 26th day of June at 5 p.m.

. . .

Bye-Laws

The following Bye-Laws were proposed by Mr. Copner and seconded by Mr. Prole and carried unanimously.

1. Every child of not less than five nor more than twelve years of age is required to attend School unless there be some reasonable excuse for non-attendance.

   Any of the following reasons shall be a reasonable excuse, namely:—
   (a) "That the child is under efficient instruction in some other manner."
   (b) "That the child has been prevented from attending School by Sickness or any unavoidable cause."
   (c) "That there is no Public Elementary School open which the child can attend, within a distance not exceeding three miles, measured according to the nearest road from the residence of such child."

. . .

5. That in case one of Her Majesty's Inspectors of Schools shall certify that any child between 10 and 12 years of age has reached the 5th Standard of Education mentioned in the Code of Regulations of the Education Department made on the 20th day of March 1874, such child shall be totally exempt from the obligation to attend School, and any such child who has been so certified to have reached the 4th Standard of Education mentioned in the said Code shall be exempt from the obligation to attend School more than 12½ hours in any one week.

. . .

7. Every parent who shall not observe or shall neglect or violate these Bye-Laws, or any of them, shall, upon conviction be liable to a penalty not exceeding five shillings including costs, for each offence. . .

Beds. C.R.O. S.B. Elstow.

8.   THE FARM LABOURERS' UNION

The local newspapers contained many reports on the Labourers' Union and meetings in the villages, which were often reprinted from the union's own papers: "The Labourers' Union Chronicle" and "The English Labourer".

Bedfordshire Mercury 18 May 1872
Beeston. The Agricultural Labourers assembled on Monday at the above place to agitate for an increase of wages and we hear that the proceedings were of a riotous character. It is high time the farmers of the county should meet . . .

Bedfordshire Mercury 15 June 1872
In connexion with the South Beds. and Herts. Agricultural Labourers' Union a meeting was held on Thursday evening week at No-Man's-Land, a common about three miles distant from St. Albans . . . There was an enthusiastic gathering of about 500 labourers . . . it appeared that the rate of wages in Hertfordshire is from 10s to 12s per week, with a few exceptions. A farm labourer named Joseph Allen stated that until lately he had been paid 11s a week only, but now received 12s; of that amount he had to expend 4s in rent, firing and candles, leaving 8s for the maintenance of himself and a numerous family during the week. He reckoned that his wages allowed 2½d a day for each member of his family to live on . . . In harvest time, however, he managed to earn a few shillings extra, which enabled him to purchase some clothing for the children . . . A resolution pledging the labourers to join the Union . . . was carried amid deafening cheers.

Bedfordshire Mercury 10 August 1872
Biggleswade. Harvest operations have commenced in this neighbourhood . . . The crops generally are very good. The question of labour is this year a serious matter, and from what we hear there is a difficulty to get the reaping done, except at the most exorbitant wages, one pound per acre being asked without hesitation by the labourers.

Bedfordshire Mercury 5 October 1872
Luton. Bedfordshire Agricultural Labourers Union: Demonstration of Labourers.
A demonstration of labourers took place at Luton on Wednesday. About a thousand labourers residing around Luton are members of a Union known as the Bedfordshire Agricultural Labourers Union, and they have recently affiliated with the National Union . . . In the evening a largely attended meeting was held in the Water-Street Plait-hall, Henry Wright Esq. of Luton in the chair. He was supported by Mr. Arch, and Mr. Taylor (Secretary of the Union); Mr. Henry Brown, senior, Mr. Butcher of Sharpenhoe, Beds., and the Rev. Mr. Austin . . .

The Chairman, who was greeted with loud cheers, said . . . In the *Times* newspaper of last week it was stated that the wages of the agricultural labourer immediately after the harvest, had been reduced to 9s per week . . . I think it is shameful for men to be paid such wages . . . It is said . . . that labourers receive many perquisites . . . Here they consist for the most part of beer, (a voice: You mean swash, and laughter) . . . What is the real value of the beer that is given to the agricultural labourers at the end of the week; would it amount to 3d ? [Wright strongly opposed women and children working full time in the fields to make up the wages] As a rule your cottages are ill-ventilated, ill-drained, and without sufficient bedroom accommodation, especially for your children . . . I do think, and I know any serious minded man thinks, that the closet arrangements of the working classes are not consistent with the common decencies of civilised life . . . I say it is a shameful and disgraceful state of things when horses are better fed and housed than men . . .

A labourer (on the point of emigration) was then called upon to speak . . . the agricultural labourer had just got in the harvest; they had spent many a weary hour in cultivating it; and now they wanted a taste of it . . . But the farmers . . . now threatened to lock them out (shame). He had made a speech at Noman's Land some time back, and on that account his master had turned him out [and he had not been able to get other work, because of what his former employer said of him] . . . Their masters thought they could bring up a family on ten shillings a week when they had to pay four shillings out of it for rent, fire and candles . . . Somehow he had managed to do it, and had brought up six children. After working seventeen years for one master, he was turned off on that accusation, viz., of speechmaking. That farmer had got 373 acres of land which was not occupied at all, and produced nothing this year but thorns and thistles. Why didn't he cultivate it and pay the labourers more money with the profits. The fact of it was, the price of the produce they raised was so high, and the cost of cultivation so low, that they didn't want to go to the cost of tilling it . . . Why didn't they turn it over to the men, and let them have three or four acres of it at a cheap rental. With their wages, and what they could make, they could grow enough to live very comfortably.

Bedfordshire Mercury 12 October 1872
Beds. Agricultural Society Dinner . . . The Vice-Chairman [Mr. E. Crouch of Cainhoe] said . . . I believe, however, we have had no strikes in this neighbourhood, nor have we any serious apprehensions of anything of the sort. The fact is the Duke of Bedford's labourers live in houses that are fit to live in . . . Mr Frederick Street said . . . While some districts have been much agitated, we have been free from it, and the question may well be asked, Why is it so? I think on great reason is the adoption of a plan which has been carried out for years and years – I mean piece-work. The grand mark of the agitators is this: to bring all men to a dead level . . . Give a man his place according to his merits, and reward him according to his deserts. . . .

Mr. Partridge [of Wellingborough] responded on behalf of the judges . . . The labourers are striking for an increase of wages of from 12s to 15s a week, and as a tenant farmer I cannot afford to pay this if I continue to keep the same number of labourers. A few noble landlords have endeavoured to meet it by various means . . . The effect of these Trades' Unions is to place all men on a level, and the man who is only worth 10s a week is to be raised to the level of the labourer who is worth 18s, and that is not right . . .

Bedfordshire Mercury 16 November 1872
Letter from Canada. Contractor's Office, Central Prison, Toronto, Oct. 24th, 1872. Sir, I believe on my departure from England in September, 1869, I promised to write to you, describing Canada as a field for emigration . . .

Agricultural labourers can always find plenty of work here at wages at least three times as much as they get in the old country. Emigrants intending farming can get free grant lands in the bush, very fertile, but they must not expect to find homes already made for them. No; they have to work hard . . . before they can get a comfortable home . . . Richard Roe, jun., late of 65, Well-street, Bedford.

Bedfordshire Mercury 23 November 1872
Tingrith. Canadian Emigrants – The Misses Trevor, Tingrith House, have at different times during the past few years sent out upwards of 100 men, women and children to

Canada, and that these emigrants are doing well in the land of their adoption a very pleasing proof has just been furnished. Two young men who went out in April 1860 to Ontario, came over recently on a visit to Tingrith, and we learn that they have given the most favourable account of the prosperity of the "Tingrith Colony" in that region. They took their departure on the morning of Wednesday fortnight, accompanied by two other young men, whom Miss Trevor, with her usual generosity, sent out at her own expense. . .

Bedfordshire Mercury 1 February 1873
Beds. Agricultural Society . . . Mr. James Howard, M.P. on Impediments to the Development of British Husbandry.
. . . The demand for labour, judging by the past, is far more likely to increase than diminish; to keep a full supply of labour in our rural districts sufficient cottage accommodation must exist and this of a superior kind to be found in most of the villages of England; as the people become better educated they will demand better homes; and if not forthcoming the labourers will go where they are to be obtained. The noble example set for so many years past by the Dukes of Bedford in cottage building has has an immense influence throughout the country, upwards of 1,000 new cottages have been erected during the past 25 years upon these estates, besides enlargement of old ones. If the Duke of Bedford is of opinion that his estate is deficient in good cottage accommodation, . . . which his Grace told me it was . . . how lamentably deficient the greater part of England must be . . .
The allotment system, so admirably carried out upon the estate of the Countess Cowper, by Mr. Trethewy, I cannot pass over, it being so eminently calculated to bind the labourer to his village, and to beget in his mind contentment and kindly feelings. The game question . . . does not excite so much interest in this county . . . simply because the estates on which over-preservation is carried on, are comparatively few . . .

Bedfordshire Mercury 22 February 1873
Beds. Agricultural Society. The Labour question as it relates to Agriculture. . . . Mr. William Stimson [farmer of Church End, Marston Morteyne] read the following paper . . . I am old enough to remember the time when it was usual for a farmer to keep several servants boarding and lodging in his house, and, so to speak, forming part of his family; and if he did his duty to them, caring for their morals and promoting their education, a feeling of attachment was created, which they cherished through life. Many and many a time have I heard men who had lived as hired servants with old Mr. Bennett of Tempsford (and father of the late Mr. Samuel Bennett of Beckerings Park) give expression to such feelings, in long after years. The fact that this system has now quite gone out of fashion (except in the north) goes far to explain, in my opinion, the altered state of feeling of many of the labourers at the present time. With no one to watch over their morals, with the public-house invitingly open to receive them, and the trash contained in the revolutionary publications of the day, available to mislead them, it is no wonder that the young labourers of the present day are wanting in that feeling of respect for, and attachment to, those above them, which characterized their forefathers. Many of the old-fashioned customs, too, which used to identify the labourer with the progress of his master's work have died out. When I was a boy, and lived in the fens of Cambridgeshire, all the labourers on the farm used to have a supper of furmenty at the end of wheat sowing, and of seed cake and ale when the sowing of the spring corn was finished . . . One after another the habits and customs which brought the master into social and friendly intercourse with this men have become obsolete, and the way has been prepared for the introduction of what is called the commercial principle . . . Mr. Samuel Morley, M.P., in a letter to the editor of the *Daily News*, . . . says "It is not because the farmer cannot afford it, that he refuses to pay higher wages; but because there are num-

bers of labourers ready and willing to accept the lower wages" . . . About a hundred years ago, according to Arthur Young, the wages of a labourer at Biddenham, near Bedford, was (exclusive of haytime and harvest) four shillings and sixpence per week, and the price of a bushel of wheat was at that time four shillings and ninepence – so that his weekly wages would not purchase a bushel of wheat. Wages since then have gradually increased, and in this neighbourhood for many years have averaged . . . a sum equal to the value of a bushel and one-third of a bushel of wheat weekly. And at the time of the commencement of the agitation in Warwickshire, wages were equal to the price of a bushel and a half of wheat; now the labourers want more than the other half bushel, and this the farmers cannot afford to give . . . Higher wages also means the substitution of machinery for human labour, at least to some extent . . . A farmer, living near Ampthill, last harvest agreed with 12 men for a certain price per acre, and for so much beer per day, to get in his harvest: on the 5th day 7 of them left and did not return. The farmer purchased a reaping machine, his sons worked it, and the harvest was got in. Now if a farmer could thus do with less than half his men in harvest time, he could at any other time . . . Many of [the labourers] in our parish occupy their own freehold cottages. It has been my privilege within the last three years to make more than one or two conveyances of freehold cottages for men working on our farm, without, as far as I know, any of the purchase money having been borrowed . . . Thanks to his Grace the Duke of Bedford, and others, the labourers in our parish have allotments of garden ground at moderate rents . . . In some few villages there are reading rooms, well lighted and warmed, where the labourers may obtain a cup of coffee or tea for a small sum, and may improve his mind, and pass away the long winter evenings much more profitably than at the public house . . . But what can we, as farmers, do to promote still further the well-being of our labourers? I say pay them well for the work they do, and you will get a good day's work for a good day's wage. Men won't work hard, even at piece work, if they think they are badly paid . . .

Captain Polhill – Turner said he was glad to find that Mr Stimson in his paper had not dealt hardly with the landlords . . . Anyone inspecting an agricultural village at the present day must at once be struck with the comfortable appearance of the cottages . . . It was stated that the average pay of the labourers of this county was about 12s, but when they took into consideration their perquisites, and the amount earned by the family, they must calculate that their weekly wages very often amount to about 28s or 30s . . . Agriculture had improved in proportion to the increase of the population. There was a time when an acre produced four bushels – now it yielded 27 . . .

Mr Crouch [of Cainhoe] said . . . The labourer was not in the position in which he ought to be. No doubt his position had been considerably improved during the last twenty years, but he would attain to a still higher position . . . About the year 1850 they paid their labourers from 7s to 8s a week; they now paid them 12s. They were told that 12s now did not go so far as 7s would go in times gone by. The price of bread was about the same; pork was as cheap as ever; and tea, coffee, sugar, and other household commodities, were also cheap. True, fresh meat was much dearer, but they could hardly look upon that as one of the actual necessaries of life. There was a great deal of piecework in this county, by which the men were able to earn 14s or 15s a week; that was all he, as a tenant farmer, was able to afford (hear hear). If they were called upon to pay more, they must resort to machinery, and pay off some of their men. He had . . . often told the younger hands to migrate to other places, and leave a thinner population. He did not believe in emigration. He considered there was ample employment in this country, and considered emigration a mistake . . .

Mr. W. Armstrong [of Haynes] said . . . he strongly approved of emigration wherever practicable. A great many labourers that had once been in his employ had gone abroad, and were doing well. It was most necessary, in fact, for the good of the country that there should be an outflow, or the population would be too large for the country . . .

Mr. A. Rogers [Bromham] . . . did not think farmers could much shorten the hours of labour, for the hours of labour now would not compare with those of twenty years ago, when men worked from early dawn till late at night. The "allowance of beer" question was one which caused great dissatisfaction to the men . . . many of them would rather have its value in money.

Bedfordshire Mercury 1 March 1873
Potton. Great Meeting of Agricultural Labourers. A meeting of agricultural labourers, under the auspices of the National Agricultural Labourers' Union, was held on Tuesday evening at the Crown Assembly Room . . . it being estimated that upwards of 400 labourers were present. Not many farmers were noticed in the room, but there was a fair attendance of the tradesmen of the town . . . The Rev. R. Hoskin, Independent minister, who happened to be in the room at the commencement of the meeting, was unanimously voted to the chair, but he made no remark save that he simply took the chair to see that order was kept, and that the meeting was properly conducted. Mr. Lane, the founder of the Union in the three counties . . . called upon the labourers to imitate their brethren of Biggleswade, and join the Union . . . As soon as Mr. Lane sat down a vote of thanks was passed to the Rev. chairman, and the men commenced enrolling themselves. Mr. David Brown, tailor, of Potton, was appointed secretary, and we hear that nearly 100 joined the Union.

Bedfordshire Mercury 8 March 1873
Sandy. Meeting of Agricultural Labourers. On Wednesday evening last a meeting of the Sandy labourers was held on the market-hill . . . They . . . got the bellman, who at the close of the meeting joined the Union, to go round the village and announce the time and place of meeting. About the same time someone obtained possession of the keys of the church, and set the bells ringing . . . The chief speaker of the evening, Mr. Lane, . . . was said to be the founder of the Union in this and the sister counties. His opening remarks were somewhat personal, in fact nearly his whole speech was a series of attacks upon the clergy, churchwardens, Dukes, and "donkey" . . . About 50 men signed their names, and one-third that number paid their money . . .
Letters addressed to the Editor: Our Labourers.
Mr. Editor — It must be admitted that we live in an age of progress when we hear of gentlemen taking up the question of the agricultural labourer. I really cannot agree in thinking their condition is so satisfactory as some of the speakers would have us believe . . . The speakers . . . seem to pass over the one thing that would most benefit that most deserving class of people. If every labourer had an acre of arable land at the same rent as the farmer does, I sincerely believe in ten years time poor rates would be a thing of the past . . . What prospect now has a young labourer before him but hard work and poor fare until he is worn out, and then about half-a-crown a week at the Workhouse . . . One of the speeches said there were labourers having thirty shillings per week. I think for every one such case there could be brought a hundred that don't have a pound, and more than fifty that don't . . . have fifteen shillings per week . . .

I am, Mr. Editor, yours respectfully, Thomas Ruffhead

Bedfordshire Mercury 22 March 1873
Meeting of Agricultural Labourers. On Monday evening a meeting of agricultural labourers was held at the Working Men's Institute, Harpur-street, being convened in connection with the National Agricultural Labourers' Union. Henry Wright, Esq., of St. John's College, Luton, occupied the chair, and there was a pretty fair attendance.

The Chairman said that the object of the meeting was to take into consideration the condition of the labourer . . . he had not kept pace with the prosperity of the times and shared in the improvement of the shopkeeper, the clerk, the artizan, and the farmers themselves (hear,hear) . . . How could this improvement be effected? The labourers said that it should be brought about by combination; but the farmers, who . . . had not made any proposition to the men on their own part, looked upon the unions with suspicion and . . . with an unnecessary degree of unfriendliness . . . Mr Stimson read before the Agricultural Society of Bedfordshire a paper on this subject . . . Mr Stimson referred to the labourer with generosity and great kindness, but still no results followed the reading of that paper . . . [Wright connects the conditions of the agricultural labourers with Tenant Right and reform of the Game Laws] He would tell them what he saw coming from Luton that day. The land was very ill-drained, and, although there had been much wet lately, it might be turned away instead of its being on the land and the wheat and barley being starved . . . Turning to the objects of the labourers' union, Mr Wright said that it was not only to obtain higher wages that the union was formed, but to assist the labourer to migrate from one part of the country to another, when there was a scarcity of work in his own district, and to enable him to emigrate if he thought fit to do so. On the 1st of May next, a benefit and sick club would be started in connection with the society (hear, hear). A time would come, was fast approaching, when the working men would be in power in this country, and he did not want to see in England the miserable mistakes which had been committed on the Continent. He hoped therefore the working man would be put in a comfortable position, and not have to look to the parish in his latter days. Above all, he desired the working man to respect himself, and to leave off so much guzzling and drinking at the public house (hear, hear). Did not the labouring man think that a pair of nice new boots or a new frock would look quite as well on his wife as on the publican's? (cheers) . . .

Mr. George Butcher was the next speaker, and he said that he had been sent into the fields at nine years of age, and at a salary of a "bob" a week (laughter) . . .

The farmers . . . set the labourers the example of having a union. They had been union men for a very long time. When two farmers met at the church door on Sunday, and had shaken hands with each other, it had been "Well, how are you getting on now. What are you going to give for mowing this time?". "Oh, I mean to give about 2s 6d; what do you intend to give?" "Well, I am only giving about 2s." "Then I will give the same as you." "Well, you must stick to it, and if any man leave me and come to you, don't you set them on." That was the sort of conversation which the farmers held . . . If they had said that the agricultural labourer made red herrings very dear he should not have been surprised (laughter), for many a time a man and his family had had to dine on a couple of them and a dish of potatoes . . .

He was the organisation secretary for the Luton branch. Two or three years ago there were 70 men out of employment in one village because they could not get work, but the union had provided places for these labourers, and now instead of there being a lot of men hanging their heads over the farmer's gate, he would, when he wanted any thrashing done, have to look round before he could find men to do it. Mr. Butcher next spoke of the increase which the union had been the cause of making in the men's wages, stating that when the first meeting was held the wages were 10s, and now they were 13s.; and when the cuckoo came, they intended to have 15s per week (cheers) . . .

Mr. George Allington, who was described on the placard as an associate of Mr. J. Arch, next delivered a very vigorous address . . . He granted that [the labourers] were ignorant, but at the same time let him say, with all due respect to the farmers of this country, that they liked to keep them in ignorance . . . He thought that their ignorance, seeing how it had been produced and continued, was a great insult to hurl at the agricultural labourers . . . He hoped that the Education Act would be brought to bear in our agricultural districts as well as in the towns. It was just as much needed, but the farmers would twist and twine a thousand ways rather than they would submit to it, if they could possibly avoid it. They wanted the children on the farm at an early age and then they could keep them in ignorance – keep them down . . .

Mr Thomas Ruffhead . . . begged to move "That in the opinion of this meeting it is desirable that a branch of the Beds. and Herts. Agricultural Union be established to-night at Bedford". Mr. Butcher seconded the proposition, which was carried unanimously.

Beds. Agricultural Society. The Cultivation of the Kohl Rabi. Mr. George Street read a paper before the members . . . on Thursday evening . . . Mr. C. Howard [of Biddenham] . . . advised that agriculturists should be careful in their statements as, thanks to the cheap press, the labourers now read the papers; and Mr. Street had given a certain price for planting the rabi, and had not included pulling up . . .

Bedfordshire Mercury 26 April 1873

Dunstable. The Farmers Association. A meeting of the farmers of this district was held at the Assembly-rooms of the Sugar Loaf Hotel . . . in response to the following circular: "Proposed United Bedfordshire Farmers' Association. The time has arrived when it is found necessary for the farmers themselves to form an association for their own protection. The need of such an association is based upon . . . the continued strikes among farm labourers, proved, beyond a doubt, not to emanate from the labourers themselves, but from paid agitators, who, either from motives of gain or popularity, are going over the whole country to disturb the minds of the once peaceful and honest labourers; who encouraged by false and flattering statements, first join the union, next rebel against their master, and finally demand increased pay and decreased hours of labour; ultimately claiming as their right a uniform pay, whether for skilled or unskilled labour . . . The farmers of Bedfordshire, therefore, seeing this on the increase, whilst sympathising for many of the misguided men, are not blind to the fact that they themselves have a very great responsibility resting upon them . . . to protect their capital invested; and seeing this placed at the mercy of paid agitators, have resolved to form an association to guard and protect their rights, considering that all questions in dispute, either as to pay, hours, etc., should be settled only between master and man."

The promoters of this association consider it therefore necessary for the farmer to make a firm resolve not to employ any man belonging to the labourers' union . . . Further, as Bedfordshire has hitherto been free from strikes . . . the farmers feel that the time has arrived for them to come forward and boldly dispute the false statements so freely bandied about as to pay, and also disapprove of the many foul accusations brought against them as to the treatment of their labourers. For the future this association will register every farm, the owner and landlord's name, the number of men and boys employed, and the pay of each. By this means, should any agitator make a statement detrimental to the farming interest, he will be called upon to quote names, facts and figures . . ."

Mr. Joseph Cook, of Sewell, Houghton Regis, was called to the chair, and Mr. W. H. Derbyshire, auctioneer, acted as secretary . . . Mr. Taylor, bailiff to J. S. Crawley, Esq., of Stockwood, Luton, proposed a resolution pledging the farmers not to employ a union man . . . At a later period of the meeting this resolution was adopted . . .

Mr. Ekins, of Sundon, did not think it advisable for farmers to discharge union men. Mr. Lousley, of Barton, said he could not join the Association if he was to be compelled to turn off every union man. He could not see the consistency of forming a union amongst themselves, and condemning a union amongst the labourers. He was assured that every labouring man in Barton, except one, belonged to the Union . . .

Agricultural Labourers' Union. A second public meeting in connection with the recently formed South Beds. and Herts. District of the National Agricultural Labourers' Union was held on Tuesday night at the Working Men's Institute [Bedford].

The Chairman [the Rev. A. McKenna] thought from observations he had made that the condition of the majority of the agricultural labourers was one that could and might be materially improved, for he noticed that many of the dwellings in which they lived were little better than a hovel, frequently built on the edge of a ditch, with two holes in the side for windows, and divided into two parts, in which the entire family had to live . . . He had recently been speaking to some of the farmers of Bedfordshire, and he was sure they were anxious to do the right thing . . . One of them said he did not object to giving a good man 3s or 4s a week more, but what he did object to was being compelled to give as much to a man who was not worth it . . .

Mr. Josiah Rickett Green . . . said that a few days ago the Duke of Bedford expressed a decided opinion that the farmers could afford to pay higher wages than they were now doing . . .

Henry Wright, Esq., of St. John's College, Luton, [said] they had no enmity to the farmers, and they did not like strikes nor locks-out, only turning to them as a last resort. Such things would never take place if we had boards of arbitration, composed of equal numbers of men and masters, and whose decisions would be final . . . He asked how any man, at the present time and rate of living, could bring up a wife and family on from 10s to 13s a week . . . At Luton, at a great meeting, a labourer said he had done so for 17 years . . . For speaking at a meeting that labourer was discharged, and more than that, nobody about there would employ him, not one of any trade; they completely black-balled him, . . . he got into a wretched plight, but, bye and bye, he was sent by the union to Derby, where he now gets 25s a week. And that was not all; for from that village of Sandridge, whence he went, 39 more men have gone north, and the lowest wage any of them get is £1 a week . . . A number of men enrolled themselves at the close.

Bedfordshire Mercury 10 May 1873
Dunstable. United Farmers' Association. The following are the rules and regulations of the United Farmers Association, agreed to at a general meeting held at the "Sugar Loaf Hotel", Dunstable, on Wednesday, April 23rd, 1873:—
1. That this Association be called the "United Farmers' Association", and is formed for the purpose of establishing a general system for regulating the rate of wages to be paid to Agricultural Labourers, to afford assistance to its members for losses sustained by reason of strikes . . .
6. That one or more members shall be appointed to represent the Assocation in every parish within the district, and that the rate of wages in every such parish shall be decided by the farmers resident therein, and that the member or members representing the Association as aforesaid, shall use his or their best endeavours to carry out this arrangement.
7. That no member of this Association shall knowingly employ any labourer who shall belong to what is called "The Agricultural Labourers' Union", or any kindred Society, other than and except those who shall be in his employ at the date of his becoming a member of this Association, upon pain of forfeiting the sum of £5 for each and every offence that shall be proved to the satisfaction of the Committee . . .

Bedfordshire Mercury 7 June 1873
Dunstable. The Farmers' Association. Mr. James Howard, M.P., has addressed the following letter to the secretary of the United Farmers' Association, at Dunstable:— I think the farmers composing your Association are right in uniting to stem unfair aggression upon their interests, but I fear they are going too far. In attempting to regulate wages they have undertaken a work for which they will find themselves, in the long run, powerless — no organisation of either masters or workmen can resist the operation of natural laws . . .

The master engineers and ironworkers . . . formed a masters' association to counteract trades unionism. I refused to join it, believing that the efforts would do far more harm than good . . .

Bedfordshire Times 24 June 1873

Bromham. Agricultural Labourers' Union. On the evening of Friday, the 20th inst., a public meeting in connection with the Labourers' Union was held on the Green, there being a large attendance of labourers, their wives, daughters, and even young children. The meeting had been specially convened in consequence of a notice to quit having been served on the mother of an intelligent young labourer named Mayhew, who had prominently identified himself with the Union, by taking the post of secretary to the local branch, while residing with his wife and child in the cottage occupied by his mother. Mr. Henry Wright of Luton took the chair . . . a platform having been placed in front of Mayhew's cottage, and he was supported by Mr. J. R. Green of Bedford; Mr. Butcher of Bedford, Mr. Cooper, treasurer; and a few other friends of the movement . . .

[The Chairman] had called upon Mr. Golding, the agent, in the hope that he would withdraw the notice and allow Mayhew's mother to remain in the cottage until the crops Mayhew had set there should be got in, but Mr. Golding was not at home . . . Seeing that Mayhew had married a young wife, and that a family was likely to spring up around him, he did not think the cottage was a desirable place of abode for them. There was a bedroom down stairs, on a brick floor, which it was not very desirable to sleep in, and it really was wonderful to see what a lot of agricultural labourers were afflicted with rheumatism . . . The apartment upstairs he thought it fit to be used only as a storeroom for potatoes . . . He thought that if the Hon. Miss Rice-Trevor, and other interested in the estate, knew the state of the cottages, they would not wish their labourers to live in them, and would pull them down and have better ones built. It was a pity these things were left in the hands of agents . . .

He had met Mr. Lavender [farmer at Biddenham] and [he] stated that he did not care one rap if all his men joined the Union. The men had a perfect right to meet together and combine to promote their own interests, and it was idle to try to prevent them . . . The speaker . . . described the case of a man 78 years of age who was compelled to break stones on the road, at 9d a yard, earning 9s a week for 13 years, after he had been incapacitated for agricultural labour.

Mr. Rust, of Pilcroft-street, Bedford . . . said that . . . if the men could thoroughly combine, and through it acquire bits of land for themselves, they could contribute their few halfpence to this society and so form a superannuation fund for old age, from which old men would receive something like 5s a week. If they had a couple of acres to cultivate they would not be compelled to apply to the workhouse for relief. Until working men entered the House of Commons the labourers would never get their rights . . . He moved "That Mr. Golding be requested to allow Arthur Mayhew's mother to remain in the cottage until at least her son be enabled to gather in his crops" . . . The resolution was carried unanimously, and the Chairman undertook to forward a copy of it to Mr. Golding and to the Hon. Miss Rice-Trevor.

Bedfordshire Times 28 June 1873

St. Neots. Labourers' Union – A meeting in connexion with the Labourers' Union was held on the Market-hill, St. Neots, on Friday, June 20, when about 400 persons assembled to hear the remarks of Messrs. Lane, Richardson, and several other well-known local agitators. The speeches were of the usual violent and one-sided character, the farmer being painted as a hard and bloodthirsty tyrant, and the labourers as down trodden sons of toil . . .

Bedfordshire Times 1 July 1873
Maulden. Agricultural Labourers' Meeting. On the evening of Thursday, June 26th, an open-air meeting was held under the well-known chestnut trees at the entrance of the village from Ampthill, with the object of forming a branch of the Labourers' Union. About 150 men, women and children were present, nearly all of them belonging to the agricultural class. The gathering was presided over by Mr. Aburn, secretary of the Ampthill branch, who introduced Mr. Haines, the district secretary . . . Some allusion having been made to the landlords, Mr. Aburn proposed three cheers for the Duke of Bedford, which were lustily given. At the close of the meeting it was concluded to form a branch, and a mechanic in the village was appointed secretary.

Bedfordshire Mercury 5 July 1873
Higher wages. At a meeting of the masons of Bedford, held on Saturday, June the 28th, it was resolved that the rate of wages proposed by the masters, viz., 6d per hour for 56½ hours a week, be accepted, to come into operation on the 14th of July. It was at the same time resolved that notice be given that a further advance of ½d an hour be the rate from the 1st of March, 1874.

Bedfordshire Mercury 12 July 1873
Leighton Buzzard. Agricultural Labourers' Union. A stormy meeting was held on Friday, after the wool fair. It had been announced that Mr. Taylor, general secretary of the union, of Leamington, and Mr. Tattam would address the meeting, but from "circumstances over which they had no control" they did not do so. Half an hour after time, the deputation arrived and sold a number of the Union Hymn-books; the crowd meanwhile increasing until about 2000 were present. A hymn having been sung in an orderly manner, Mr. Tattam addressed the crowd, but was repeatedly interrupted. These frequent interruptions led to a scene of the utmost confusion, and help of the police was requested to remove the disturbers; but, contrary to expectation, the superintendent informed the deputation that he should hold them responsible for any consequence that might ensue. Mr. Taylor, hereupon, commenced a violent tirade against the police and every one else, the crowd included, which was retaliated by upsetting the platform and a general attack on the speakers. The police saved them from the passions of the crowd, and escorted them to the railway station, where they were followed by the mob hooting lustily; but they have promised to return soon.

Bedfordshire Times 26 July 1873
National Agricultural Labourers' Union. Meetings in Bedford. On Monday afternoon . . . a meeting of local delegates from 22 branches of the above Union was held at the Working Men's Institute, Bedford, 1051 members being represented. Mr. J. Ricketts-Green presided, and amongst those present were – Mr. Henry Wright, of The College, Luton, and Mr. H. Taylor, general secretary, of Leamington. It was moved "That this meeting of delegates representing branch Unions of labourers in and around the vicinity of Bedford do agree to amalgamate and form a district of the National Agricultural Labourers' Union, to be called the Bedford District of the N.A.L.U." This was carried unanimously. The following officers were appointed: Chairman, Mr. Arthur Mayhew (Bromham); treasurer, Mr. G. Ward (Bedford); secretary, Mr. G. Butcher; executive committee, Messrs. Boston, Askew, Mothers, Myers, Redding, Allen, and Bryant – all to hold offices for six months.

In the evening . . . a large public meeting was held on the Market-hill, St. Paul's square, when about 3,000 persons were present, the entire area being occupied by labourers, mechanics, and other classes, including many farmers. Mr. James Howard, M.P., sat in his carriage on the border of the crowd for an hour and a half and we noticed

Mr. Charles Howard, Mr. T. F. Armstrong, Mr. Prole, Mr. T. Sergeant, and other agriculturists of the locality. At the commencement of the proceedings a farmer interrupted the Chairman who said if the interruption were continued he should call upon the men present to remove the offender, as they were not to be interfered with by the farmers as they were at Leighton Buzzard. After this somewhat plain intimation the meeting was a thoroughly harmonious one throughout, and the labourers manifested much enthusiasm, especially during the address of Mr. Joseph Arch, who is a man of remarkable ability as a speaker. Myers's van was occupied by the following amongst others: Mr. Arch, Mr. H. Wright (who presided), Mr. H. Taylor, Mr. J. Smith, Mr. M. Judge (Luton), Mr. J. Ricketts Green (Bedford), Mr. G. Butcher (agent of the Union), and Mr. A. Mayhew (Bromham) . . . The Chairman . . . said . . . There were respectable men . . . Arthur Mayhew and George Butcher, who had had notice to leave their cottages and gardens because they had joined the Union (cries of "shame"). Butcher had long held his cottage, but he was compelled to leave it because he chose to advocate the cause of his suffering fellowmen . . .

Bedfordshire Times 2 August 1873
The Beds. United Farmers' Association and Mr. James Howard, M.P. The following appeared in the *Mark Lane Express* of July 21:
Sir, I have not been well enough during the past two or three weeks to read the newspapers, but last night . . . I met with the letter of Mr. Derbyshire, Secretary to the above Association . . . Seeing that I have never lent the least countenance of support to the Labourers' Union, Mr. Derbyshire was clearly not justified in raising the doubt or insinuating that I was more in favour of the Labourers' Union than the Farmers' Association: because I objected to some rules of the latter it by no means followed that I approved of the former . . . In a leading article in the *Labourers' Union Chronicle* the editor denounced me and my letter in the strongest language . . . from the fact of my views being denounced, on the one hand, by the *Labourers' Union Chronicle* and on the other hand by the Secretary of a Union diametrically opposed to the Labourers' Union, I am led to conclude that the views expressed in the letter in question are moderate and sound — at all events I know that they have met with the approval of men of the highest standing as tenant-farmers, as well as of men of eminence in the political world . . . If three men are running after one master, wages — notwithstanding a hundred Unions — must fall, and the contrary condition of things — despite a hundred Farmers' Associations — will inevitably lead to higher wages . . . to my mind there is no greater evil than the practice of fixing a dead level of wages, irrespective of a labourer's powers or abilities . . . From the commencement of the movement I have held to the opinion that the wisest thing for farmers is to ignore the existence of the Union, as far as possible, for all experience in other branches of industry has proved that the efforts of masters to check Unionism have proved abortive. Above all, I am desirous that in dealing with the labour question, measures should not be adopted which would promote or invite an organised system of emigration; let this once set in, and we should see such an exodus of our best agricultural labourers as would make the stoutest heart quail. It should be rememberd that whilst our Colonies and the United States can only do with a limited number of factory operatives and artisans, the field of employment for ploughmen, shepherds, and the like is practically unlimited . . . This is quite as much a landlords' as a tenants question, if not more so, for the value of land in all countries depends upon the labour supply . . .
Ridgmount. Agricultural Labourers' Union — The village was all alive on Tuesday in consequence of its being the place selected for holding a tea festival on a large scale in connection with this Union. The place of meeting was in a field opposite to the Rose and Crown, and the tea was served to the people in groups . . . About 800 tickets were sold previously, and we did not hear of there being any absentees . . . The Eversholt Brass

Band was in attendance. Stalls were numerous, and well supplied with refreshments, toys etc. . . . Taking into consideration that the whole affair was managed by a committee of labourers themselves it was creditable to them throughout . . . After tea the band and members of the Union paraded the village, and at 7 o'clock a public meeting was held in the field, presided over by the Rev. Dr. Hillier. Addresses were delivered by the Chairman and Messrs Abott, Butcher, Haines, etc. Mr. T. F. Armstrong, a farmer of Marston, also was politely invited on to the platform, and for a time had a patient hearing, but was ultimately obliged to retire, the Unionists and some of the leaders evidently not relishing portions of his remarks. The meeting broke up about ten o'clock, the band playing "God save the Queen".

Bedfordshire Mercury 2 August 1873
Ridgmount. Agricultural Labourers' Meeting. Tuesday was a high day here for the labourers, the united committees for Eversholt, Lidlington and Ridgmount, having resolved to have a demonstration in the latter village in favour of the object of the Agricultural Labourers' Union . . . In the Ridgmount branch there are 141 members, in Eversholt 81, and in Lidlington 126, making a total of 348.
Cople. Labourers' Meeting. A meeting of labourers was held here on Monday night last, in connection with the Bedford District. Mr. Henry Wright, of Luton, occupied the chair, and delivered a most stirring speech . . . Mr. Nottingham, of Cople, followed with an earnest address to his own villagers, and urged them all to support the union, he being the secretary of the Cople branch . . . the Rev. H. E. Havergal gave the men some sound advice, both as regards the union and their social habits; he was loudly cheered. The meeting was one of the largest ever held in the parish, and was conducted in an orderly . . . manner.

Bedfordshire Times 9 August 1873
Cople. The Harvest is progressing fairly in and around this village. There was a difference between one or two farmers and their labourers at the beginning of the week, and in one case a "strike" occurred, but after further negotiations matters were satisfactorily arranged, the services of men regularly employed being preferred to those of strangers who could have been engaged. A short time ago the cottagers memorialized the Duke of Bedford for an enlargement of their allotments, and his Grace has acceded to their request, allowing them 40 poles additional. The rent is 3d per pole or £2 an acre annually.

The Labourers' Union Chronicle 16 August 1873
News from the Counties. Bedfordshire. South Beds and Herts District . . On Monday evening, August 4, a very large meeting was held at Gravenhurst. The chair was taken by Mr. Worsley of Luton, and addresses were delivered by Messrs. Smith and Haines of Luton . . . Mr. T. H. Haines . . . addressed the meeting, in which the objects of the Union was laid before them, the emigration question and the land question was considered, and after receiving some of the good effects the Union had already produced, the meeting was brought to a close with hearty cheering. On Sunday, August 3rd, Mr. T. H. Haines preached afternoon and evening at Eversholt, on behalf of the Protestant Evangelical Mission. As these services were held at the request of the Union men of that neighbourhood, it is hardly necessary to say they met on both occasions in large numbers, in the afternoon about 300, and in the evening about 500. The services were held on behalf of the above mission, which has for its object to retain an open bible and promulgate a free gospel, and to counteract the subtle and wide-spreading influences of "popery". . .
Employment of labour on large and small farms. At Willstead there is a Mr. T -, a farmer whose men began harvest on the 6th August. This Mr. T - holds about 200 acres at Willstead and 300 or 400 at Marston. The day the men began harvest he discharged them

all except the foreman, and the men got work at a farmer's in Willstead of the name of Markes. Mr. Markes holds about 50 acres of land, and it is said employs more men all the year round than Mr. T - does with his 500 or 600 acres. Mr. Markes is doing well, he pays his men well, keeps his horses and cows well, and all who work for him are perfectly satisfied; but I heard Mr. T - say himself that he would sell his own wheat crop this year, standing as it is, at 20 bushels per acre, to avoid the trouble of harvesting it.

Cople. On Monday, the 4th inst., the village of Cople was thrown into a state of excitement, in consequence of the men of that place having asked for 13s per acre for cutting, and carting, and stacking the corn. The farmers refused to give it, and consequently the men refused to work, but fortunately the Duke's steward having been called in to arbitrate between the two parties, the men agreed to accept 12s. per acre, and went back to work. It is to be hoped this system of arbitration will become more universal among farmers and farm labourers, for there is no doubt the farmers have ground down the labourers to a fearful extent . . .

Bedfordshire Mercury 20 September 1873
National Agricultural Labourers' Union – Bedford District . . . On Tuesday a public meeting was held at Stagsden . . . the chair being taken by Mr. J. R. Green . . . He said that because some men had been disappointed in their harvest operations they began to blame the Union for it; but it was not the Union that had done them any harm, it was those railway labourers that had left constant and good employment for the purpose of gathering in the harvest, thus assisting the farmers to get in the grain without the assistance of the bona fide agricultural labourers . . .

Bedfordshire Times 4 October 1873
Woburn. Agricultural Labourers' Meeting. On Thursday, Sept. 25th., a meeting was held in the Town Hall, Woburn, at which Mr. H. Wright of Luton, presided . . . and its result was the formation of a branch of the Union at Woburn in connection with the Bedford Association . . . Mr. Wright produced the following propositions as the present platform for the Union: 1. A good fair wage of 16s. a week, with allotments amply sufficient for vegetables, and good cottages. 2. The extension of the franchise to counties as well as boroughs . . . A Mr. Green of Bedford, the secretary for the district . . . congratulated the workmen on the Duke's estates on their appearance, which . . . contrasted favourably with their brother labourers in some parts of the county, and bespoke better wages and cottages. But this he urged as a greater reason why the Woburn labourer should by union help his more needy brother . . .

Bedfordshire Times 11 October 1873
Beds. Agricultural Society. At the conclusion of the annual ploughing match and show, a number of members and friends . . . dined at the Swan Hotel . . . . . Mr. Stimson [of Marston alluded to his] favourite subject of the Agricultural Labourer, on which I read a paper last February. There has been a great alteration since then, and perhaps I should now alter it in some parts. I said I was not at all afraid of the Agricultural Labourers' Union doing damage to the farmer, but I thought it would do so to the labourer, and I think . . . that opinion has been borne out . . . The fact of the labourers having joined the Union has made the farmers use machinery more extensively, and therefore the farmers have been benefited while the labourers have not. I was told by the stationmaster that at the beginning of harvest 40 men went from our station at Marston to the Fens, to get work, but that many of them came back because they could get nothing to do. Before the introduction of machinery that could not be the case . . . I think the Labourers' Union may be a good, and I will tell you why. It seems to me there will be a more extensive use of machinery and that labourers will not be so much wanted, so that there will be a surplus of labourers, and if the Union be the means of sending the labourers

where there is work for them it will be a benefit both to the masters and to the labourers themselves. Mr. Arch has gone to Canada, and if he can find an opening for labourers he may be doing good to the people . . . for . . . if there is a surplus of labourers it is important there should be an opening for them . . . I don't think it was proper to have a Farmers' Union at all . . . If the farmers talked to their men reasonably instead of uniting and creating a bad example, they would be able to stop the progress of the Union, whether for good or bad, in the parish they live in . . . I believe, on every farm in this county where piecework is done, there is the opportunity of getting 3s always within their reach for 6 months of the year. But when you let your piecework, instead of seeing the labourer there at 5 o'clock in the morning, when it is cool, you don't see him till six, and he is gone off again at half-past five or six, setting a bad example to your ploughmen and boys whom you expect to work . . . Some of the unwilling ones are satisfied to take £4 or £5 for the month, but other men will take double the amount, and such a man as this is the independent labourer, and worthy of the money paid by the master . . .

Mr. F. Street [Harrowden] . . . The grand object of steam cultivation was that more work could be done with it in a single day than with the old teams in a fortnight . . .

Dunstable. United Farmers' Association. It has been resolved to continue the institution on a permanent basis in consequence of the completely successful effect it produced during the recent feverish excitement of the labourers after the visits of Unionist agitators. Not a single case of difficulty with the labourers during harvest occurred to any member of the Association.

The Labourers' Union Chronicle 25 October 1873

Bedfordshire. Bedford District. Sir, just a line or two to be inserted in your valuable paper, the *Labourers' Chronicle*. They say we should not expose the faults of others. Well, we have had no wish to do so, but as an agricultural labourer, I think I for one have been silent long enough. I think it's high time to open my mouth when I know the misery to which the agricultural labourers class is subjected, and now, because many of them are trying to help themselves out of a little of their misery, some of the landlords, statesmen and farmers are trying to keep them in, or to plunge them further in yet. Just a word about the hamlet of Sharpenhoe. Mr. Smyth, of Quickwood, is landlord of much of the property, and the poor labourers of the place have hired some land allotments for 28 years. These allotments were laid out by Mr. George and John Smyth, of Stevenage, for the labourers, 20 poles each, but now he, Mr. Smyth, of Quickwood, is taking them away, or allowing the farmers to do so, and also some of the cottages, because the men have been so simple as to join the Union. One or two of the farmers of that place think of getting some labourers from other parts of the country to live in these old tumble down cottages, and then making them work for them at any price they like, and the landlord is allowing them to do so, but I would say to the labourers, don't go to Sharpenhoe, if you do you will have a pinching time of it. The non-Union men of that place have all the allotments now; even an old man of 75 may have one. A CORRESPONDENT.

Bedfordshire Times 20 December 1873

Meeting of Agricultural Labourers. On Tuesday evening another public meeting in connection with the National Agricultural Labourers' Union was held at the Working Men's Institute, Bedford. There was not a large attendance, it being late in the season for men to come in from country villages at night. The chair was taken . . . by Mr. Henry Wright, of Luton who said . . . a large number of men had joined the Union, so that now there were 25 or 27 branches in connection with the Bedfordshire district (cheers). They, for the most part, were in a healthy state, although in one branch, on account of the farmers or landlords not allowing Union men to hold any land, the labourers had ceased to belong to it (shame). With this exception there had been no sort of intimidation, and amicable relations existed between the employers and the employed . . . Their object was work with peaceable means, as they had no wish to come into collision with the employers . . . In some parts of this county they had some of the best cottages in England, but he regretted to say there were also some of the very worst . . . He had read in the county papers sanitary reports for this district . . . on the state of certain cottages at Thurleigh . . . Some . . . were not fit for human habitaiton (shame), and he maintained that the landlords ought to erect good cottages (hear, hear) . . . When they read that the men had to live in such wretched places, they need not wonder that they went to the publichouse, where they obtained something like comfort . . . In *The Times* it was stated that many of these miserable cottages belonged to the men themselves, but they paid a quit rent to the landlord, who was therefore the real owner, and Government ought to prevent him from allowing such buildings to exist. The name of the owner . . . was Mr. J. S. Crawley of Stockwood Park, Luton . . . He (the Chairman) was no great advocate for emigration, but he would rather see men leave the country than remain in a poor condition here. The Government of New Zealand . . . had offered facilities, and they must take away surplus labour, thin the villages, and then the men who remained could demand more money . . . When he first took up this question he had no idea that it would lead to a political issue, but he now saw that working men would never get their rights unless they fought for them inch by inch . . . Self-help was the best help, and they must demand the franchise — household suffrage, not rateable suffrage, as if it depended on rates the landlords would pay them and keep the men out of their vote . . . Mr. James Howard's Landlord and Tenant Bill . . . was withdrawn through the . . . illness of Mr. Howard . . . The clause respecting compensation for unexhausted improvements was most important, and if this were passed a vast amount of capital would flow in and the productive power of the country would be doubled . . . They must all help to get Mr. Howard's bill passed, and then they might succeed in getting rid of the iniquitous game laws . . .

Bedfordshire Times 28 March 1874
Lock-out of Agricultural Labourers. *To the Editor of the Bedfordshire Times and Independent.* Sir, I shall be obliged if you will publish in your next impression the enclosed copy of a letter to the Duke of Bedford with respect to the lock-out threatened on this estate. I am, Sir, faithfully yours, H. E. Havergal. Cople Vicarage, Bedford, March 24th, 1874.

"My Lord Duke, Permit me to plead for the numerous cottagers on your estate of Cople and Willington, who at this sad crisis are unable otherwise to represent their case. I beg your Grace to observe that the farmers are the aggressors and the labourers the aggrieved. It is not a strike but a lock-out that is threatened, and will take effect at the end of this week. Since the last harvest the men have been perfectly quiet and orderly. The rate of wages — 13s — has been below that of several adjoining parishes. When the wages of Cardington, about four or five weeks ago, rose to 14s, some individual labourers a fortnight afterwards naturally asked their masters for a similar advance. The request was made respectfully, and the refusal was taken in perfect good temper, there being no threat or intention of striking; they merely remarked that there was no harm in asking. Thus unprovoked the farmers broke the peace by arbitrarily demanding that the labourers should renounce their Union or quit their work and cottages; and it is with the greatest surprise and pain that I have learnt from Mr. Stephenson that your Grace will passively witness such interference with their liberty by giving the farmers a general power of enforcing their threats, that if the men will not work at the wages offered by the farmers, or if the farmers on any account refuse to employ them, though they are willing and even ask for work at the farmers' price, they must nevertheless leave for that your Grace will not interfere between master and man.

This policy is one-sided, and against the labourer. The men must accept the terms of the master irrespective of justice or arbitration, or be ejected. It would have been more fair to have said — Here are labourers, most of whose families have been older denizens of the estate than either the landlord's or the farmers'; they are a fair sample of English labourers. Agricultural competitions show their commensurate ability, the police and criminal statistics are favourable, poaching is unknown, their demands and their wages have lagged behind their neighbours. If, therefore, the farmer cannot arrange terms with his men, as others do, the fault lies presumably with the farmer . . .

Both political and Christian motives suggest that power, especially in respect of evictions from family homes, should be tenderly and discreetly exercised. Further, the labourers resent the demands of the farmers to give up the Union as an intolerable interference with their liberty. There appears to be great haziness about the National Agricultural Labourers Union. It has been unjustly saddled with the opprobrium of certain objectionable features of Trades Unions, and otherwise ignorantly objected to, when in reality it stands in favourable contrast with many of them. The tendency and interest of the N.A.L. Union is to prevent the strikes which the farmers dread and the public disfavours. Its procedure is fair and legitimate. It distributes labour from redundant to needy districts by deportation. This or emigration is beneficial to the community as well as to the class. In other words, it enables the labourer to take his labour to better markets. The effect is to raise the price where the market is overstocked or where the farmers are not astute enough to bid sufficiently high for its retention, and this tends to equalize wages, to the general benefit of the class.

It will be seen at once that a strike is against the interest of the Union, as it diverts the funds from these normal operations, and it is accordingly discouraged instead of being fomented. The rules enact in all cases of dispute between master and man that negotiation and arbitration shall be attempted . . . and 'in no case shall a strike be resorted to until the above means have been tried and failed' Rule 10. It is a further discouragement that men on strike receive only 9s a week. It is evident then that the N.A.L. Union is an inoffensive and useful association. It is without objectionable stipulations as to equality of wages; it neither dictates or suggests their amount. It is a purely defensive institution, whereas the farmers, while complaining of the Labourers' Union, inconsistently combine aggressively against this lawful endeavour of the latter to assist each other in taking their commodity to the best market.

Surely in the face of these considerations your Grace is not prepared to abnegate the duties of your position by delegating such irresponsible power to those who have shown insufficient tact, or to stand by while your tenants provoke the bitterness, and inflict the hardships of a lock-out, or evict, so lightly, with such a wrench of their feelings, families who for generations have been domiciled upon the estate, which is at present under the tenure of your Grace . . .

I am, my Lord Duke, most respectfully yours,

H. E. Havergal, Vicar of Cople

P.S. Considering that the matter is pressing, and of public importance, I shall consider myself free to publish this appeal."

Mr. Joseph Arch in Bedford. On Thursday evening, March 19, Mr. Arch, President of the National Agricultural Labourers' Union, again visited Bedford, a serious difference having arisen between the farmers and their labourers in the neighbourhood of Cardington, Wilshamstead etc. respecting wages. We learn that in most instances the wages paid to men during the winter have been 13s and a demand having been made for 2s additional, the farmers declined to accede to it, alleging that they would not be dictated to by the supporters of the Union. The consequence was that a large number of men and boys left work, and donning blue ribbons and rosettes, appeared in the streets of Bedford on the following market-day. Members of the Union have received 9s per week during the continuance of the "strike", and they declare that by great frugality and self-denial it is possible to subsist on the amount which a few years ago was paid to ordinary labourers in many parishes. Some of the younger ones are emigrating . . . while a few are seeking work in other parts of the country. Meanwhile the farmers are applying themselves to manual labour and at great inconvenience carry on the work of the farm with such assistance as can be obtained; while the landlords are in several cases acting in conjunction with them, especially with regard to the tenure of cottages, notice to leave which have been served upon many of the labourers, who with their wives have expressed indignation at such measures. The men have occupied their time in cultivating their allotments, the cropping of which they can sell if they are compelled to leave and . . . their general behaviour has been remarkably quiet.

The men assembled on the New Market-hill, near St. Paul's Church . . . and we noticed more women than were present at the meeting in the same place last summer. As many as 2,500 persons were collected together, a good sprinkling of farmers and the general public being noticeable. . .

The Chairman [Mr. Henry Wright of Luton] . . . said . . . This is not the first time . . . that I have occupied this post in the town of Bedford . . . Perhaps some little apology is due . . . The fact is this, gentlemen, on coming to analyse the matter, I find that one great reason why no one else is found to take the chair is that it is a somewhat difficult thing to find a gentleman in Bedford to do so (laughter and cheers). The fact is . . . there are very few men who have the moral courage to identify themselves with the working classes of this country . . . I believe that if [the agricultural labourers] would all take the advice given to them over and over again by those who take an interest in their welfare by joining themselves in union as one man, Bedfordshire would in less than a month be in a very different position than it is now (cheers). Many people say to me "How is it you go to speak for a lot of farm labourers? Look at them – what are they? A lazy, drunken, vagabond lot". I deny it . . . there are many of them as honest and sober men as any that can be found . . . If they were brought up in the way in which I maintain they ought to be brought up – if they were better clothed, better fed, had better wages, and had better cottages to live in, they would be in a higher position altogether than they are now (cheers). Many of the labourers live in cottages like those at Steppingley, where there are 20 or more cottages with only one bedroom . . . We have now come to a peculiar crisis in the agricultural labourers question in this part of the county – I refer to what has happened at Cardington, Cotton End, Wilshamstead and Lidlington, where a difference has arisen with regard to wages between the masters and the men. And what is this difference? The question is whether the wages shall be raised from 13s to 15s a week. I maintain, friends, that the request of the men . . . taking into consideration the high price of provisions, particularly of animal food and bread, and every production of farmers by which they profit, and also the price of coal – is a very moderate one indeed . . . [The men] went in many cases to the masters in a respectful manner and asked for more money, and some sent in written requests . . . In the majority of cases the farmers have said in effect, "We shall not raise your wages; if you do not choose to remain at the present rate you can leave your places and we dismiss you . . ." Some of the men have actually been dismissed by their masters on account of making their demand and others have had notice to leave their cottages (shame). Every effort has been made in this neighbourhood to harass, oppress and crush the poor agricultural labourer . . . Let me give a note of warning to those who have prophesied that the Union would soon be stamped out. All the landlords and farmers of Bedfordshire united will not be able to stamp it out

. . . Do not be persuaded to leave the Union under any consideration, and do not allow the greater part of the men on any farm to be discharged while two or three are left (hear, hear). If two or three are kept at work I would strongly urge them to say "If you discharge the others you must discharge the lot" (cheers). If nothing else will in a few weeks bring the masters to their senses, this will . . .

The land question lies at the very bottom of this. Taking into consideration the present high price of food, and that many farmers are not half cultivating their land, they do not employ the amount of labour they ought. There are many who do not produce enough . . . to pay £5 an acre in the year . . . and . . . some who do not produce even 10s worth of animal food to the acre. This is, therefore, a people's question . . . If farmers do not cultivate well whose duty is it to step in? (a voice "Everybody's") Why, the State (cheers). The more you investigate this question the more important does it appear, and it is evident that the land of this country is merely placed in the hands of some in trust for other people . . .

Mr. Arch . . . said . . . Tomorrow I shall attend before a Committee of the House of Commons, and I shall lay the case of the Bedfordshire landlords, farmers, and tenants, before that Committee . . . and I shall ask gentlemen who have more influence and intelligence than I have to look at the Conspiracy Act and say, if it deals with the workmen so severely, why it should not apply in a similar way in the other direction (loud cheers) . . .

You will before long be entrusted with the power of sending men to represent you in Parliament . . . If the Government of the past were pleased to guarantee to the cities and boroughs household franchise, we have equal right to ask that it should also be given to counties . . . If you had a vote now this nobleman or that squire would never have attempted to turn you out of your cottages . . . I say to you working men, rather than bind yourselves to live in cottages and be slaves to the farmer, leave the county, leave the country – yes, leave it! .
. . . Don't be anxious about having to quit your cottage, but stand firm . . . Now, gentlemen, let me tell you that the New Zealand Government want between now and the middle of April nine shiploads of labourers. Queensland is also bidding high, as not only a free passage and a ship kit are offered, but will also pay the railway fare from the port of landing. As to America, Senator Sumner said "Here we have got in America nine times more stuff than mouths to consume it." . . . Then as to Canada . . . the work has been found difficult in some cases, but you agricultural labourers are the very giants of agriculture in the world, and there is no class among the tillers of the soil whom the sun shines on that is better fitted for such a life than you . . . It has been customary for emigration certificates to be signed by the clergyman, farmer, or squire of the parish from which the emigrant goes and, in many instances they would not sign it (shame); but Government has consented to take every farm labourer, whether in the Union or out of it, with my signature (loud cheers) . . . Mr. R. F. Armstrong, farmer, of Marston, made his way through the crowd to the van . . . and was hailed with much hissing and jeers. Addressing the men as those with whom he has worked, he proceeded to take up various points . . . particularly arguing that as land was cheaper than labour, the farmer need not be inconvenienced by the state of the labour market . . . and that the farmer could not afford to pay more than the present rate of wages. . . Mr. Armstrong asked, "Has your Union done you real service or not?" and emphatically answered "No" (great uproar). He then asked whether it was not a fact that the wages of servant girls had been raised considerably during the last 10 or 15 years without any Union? (renewed uproar). Mr. Armstrong said he could give instances where labourers were better off than some farmers, and contended that it was unfair to the masters for the men to leave work after being kept all the winter. This excited considerable uproar . . . The Chairman . . . answered Mr. Armstrong . . . In Mr. Armstrong's own village the men had notice of an

Irishman's rise, viz., a reduction of 1s per week, but this was not carried out as a meeting of the Union was held. At Ampthill he was told that the masters raised the wages 1s on hearing that a meeting was about to be held . . .

Lidlington. Meeting of Agricultural Labourers. On Friday evening, a large number of labourers and others, variously estimated at from 3000 and 5000 persons, assembled in the Sandpit to hear an address from Mr. Joseph Arch . . . People flocked in from all sides for miles around, and not a few arrived by M.L.N.W. Railways. A large platform with lamps had been fitted up, and as the crowd stood tier above tier the scene was one of a striking character . . .

Bedfordshire Times 4 April 1874
The Lock-out of Agricultural Labourers. The subjoined letter from the Duke of Bedford and the Rev. H. E. Havergal's comments upon it have been sent to us for publication by the rev. gentleman:—

Dear Sir . . . I regret the present condition of relations between masters and men, but I cannot dictate to the labourers for whom they should work, neither can I dictate to the farmers whom they should employ. The cottages are built for the accommodation of those who work upon the farms, and their appropriation must follow that arrangement. Either party acting in union has great power and corresponding responsibility. Public opinion alone can control excess on either side . . .

Believe me, dear Sir, your very faithfully, Bedford.

Cople Vicarage, April 1, 1874

My Lord Duke . . . My contention is that terms *are* dictated to the labourer which are not to the farmer. The farmer has a *carte blanche* . . . The unwisdom of placing·more cottages in the hands of tenant-farmers may be shown by reference to those built as adjuncts to outlying farms . . . Although the higher wages of horsekeeper or herdsman be attached, there has been greater difficulty to get occupants for them than for those under the landlord . . . The first cottager who emigrated this week was from one of these houses, and the pair are now empty. I have had cognizance of cases where such occupants would have emigrated but for the farmer's interception, till at last a character from myself has been accepted without reference to the farmer . . . The condition of a farmer's tenant is precarious. He is liable to dismissal from his house without appeal . . . all chance of other neighbouring work is gone, for migration is a necessity. Not so with the landlord's tenant — an appeal must be made if eviction is desired: this gives time for cold reflection . . .

There is another injustice . . . There is no reciprocal provision that, if the labourer must work on the farm only, the farmer also must furnish him with continuous employment, and not turn him off to starve in the short and cold days . . .

I am, my Lord Duke, most respectfully yours
H. E. Havergal

To the Editor of the Bedfordshire Times & Independent
Sir, It was with surprise, amounting almost to astonishment, that I read the letter of the Rev. Mr. Havergal to the Duke of Bedford in your impression of last week. The singular estimation in which that reverend gentleman is held by the clergy, by his neighbours, and his parishioners, will . . . secure for his observations their just weight and value; but it is difficult to imagine a clergyman taking a more mischievous and perilous step than venturing, as Mr. Havergal has done, to interfere with the management of property with which he has nothing to do . . .; and to put himself at the head of an insurrection of labour against capital — for that is the proper designation of the proceedings of the "Labourers' Union". Mr. Havergal has not been content even with this: he has made his

pulpit the vehicle of his denunciations of the great landowner and all the farmers of his parish . . .

Mr. Havergal must know that he is setting all classes in his parish by the ears; that he is doing his best to fan the flames of discord . . . If he *must* interfere, he should do so in the character of a mediator and peacemaker, not as an angry partisan . . . From [Mr. Havergal's] own showing it appears that the labourers began this unhappy dispute by asking for an increase of wages! which request was refused. Mr. Havergal should have told us the real reason of this refusal. These labourers belong to the "Labourers' Union" . . . Mr. Arch says he has got plenty of thousands of pounds to distribute amongst all agricultural labourers who will strike for increased wages. They are to be supported in their idleness until they have brought their employers to submission . . [The farmers] know that the labourers are truly and merely the catspaws of hired agitators and their revolutionary paymasters . . .

I am, Sir, your obliged servant, Fair Play

Cople.Labourers' Meeting. On Monday evening a meeting of labourers and their wives in this and neighbouring villages was held on the lawn at the Vicarage, about 400 being present. The Vicar (Rev. H. E. Havergal) presided, and in his opening speech warmly espoused the cause of the labourers who are out of work, of whom there are some 60 at Cople . . . Farmers are advertising for men, as they are seriously inconvenienced . . . The Vicar has opened the school-room daily as a reading and recreation room.

Lidlington. The Labourers still refuse to resume work at the wages offered and also to leave the Union . . . Some of the labourers are migrating and others emigrating. The number out of work is about 70.

The Lock-Out of Labourers. The following appeal on behalf of the Agricultural Labourers of this county has been issued by Mr. Henry Wright, of Luton, who has forwarded us a copy for publication: "Many of the Agricultural Labourers in Bedfordshire . . . are endeavouring to obtain higher wages. In Bedfordshire they are trying to get 15s per week . . . The men, knowing there is not the slightest chance of getting any increase of wages single handed, have . . . joined the National Agricultural Labourers' Union. The masters see the power of the Union and are endeavouring to crush it. In this they are encouraged . . . by the Landlords, who have, in some instances, given the men notice to quit their cottages unless they give up the Union . . . Many of the men are bravely standing out, and they receive pay from Leamington; but as large numbers are locked out in other counties, additional help is needed . . . Do not stand by and see the weak oppressed. Come to the rescue. Every penny will be useful . . .

The Bedfordshire Times 11 April 1874
The Agricultural Labourer. From a number of reports from different counties of Britain published by the Agricultural Gazette we take the following:—

Bedfordshire — The ordinary day's pay of the agricultural labourer in this county is from 2s 2d to 2s 4d, but this by no means represents his average earnings for the year. Piecework on most farms is the rule, when men of ordinary skill and industry can earn from 2s to 4s a week extra, and even more for some work, such as draining, etc. The general custom is to double the usual day's pay for the harvest months, but as most of the work is let it is no uncommon thing for a man to earn from £6 to £6 10s during the month. To this must be added beer, costing the farmer at least £1. On many farms small beer is supplied the year through, and for a variety of operations ale is also. I think it may fairly be estimated that on a Bedfordshire farm the beer costs very nearly if not quite 1s 6d per man per week the year through. I may, therefore, safely say the earnings of the industrious agricultural labourer, including his hay and corn harvest, overtime and beer, will average fully 18s per week. Horsekeepers get from 15s to 16s per week; they are also paid for overtime after 6 o'clock, with an allowance for taking out corn of from 6d to 1s per day. Shepherds receive from 15s to 16s per week with generally an allowance of some 2s 6d per score, for raising lambs. Shearing is done by the piece at from 3s to 3s 6d per score. The average earnings of horsekeepers, shepherds, and stockmen, approach very nearly, if not quite, to £1 per week. On most of the larger estates the cottages of the labourers are good, and where they are not so, thanks to the rural sanitary authority, much improvement has already taken place. The rents are very moderate for the cottage and garden, from 1s to 1s 6d being paid. There are now but few villages without allotments, varying from 20 to 40 poles, at a rent of some 2½d to 3d per pole, free of taxes. Notwithstanding the great outcry there has been of late about the agricultural labourers' condition, there is no class more surely improving it; 22 years ago in this county he was paid 8s per week, he had now 14s – 75% increase. When it is taken into consideration the low rent of cottage, garden, and allotment, the freedom from all rates, the gleaning at harvest of his wife and family, the fruit and vegetables of the garden and allotment, the supply of wood for fuel, together with the assistance rendered by his employers and others to clothing, coal, and benefit clubs, the condition of the agricultural labourer not only far surpasses that of the labouring population in towns, but will compare favourably with that of many artizans. I regret to add many of the villages south of Bedford are in a disturbed state, by reason of the strike in some and a lock-out in others. It is felt the demand of the Union must be resisted, it is not likely men will be satisfied with an advance of 1s per week, when they are informed by paid agitators that they shall have very soon a greater increase and each man several acres of land. Such a prospect is too much for the needs of our agricultural labourers. It is perfectly useless for masters, who have hitherto been supposed for many years past to deal liberally and kindly with their men, to interpose any advice, it is utterly disregarded, and no wonder, when these deluded men have been taught to look upon their employers, who have been known to the labourers all their lives, as their greatest enemies and oppressors. Matters have not been improved by the visit of Mr. Arch and his allies to our county town, and one or two villages, during the past week . . . The farmers of Bedfordshire will require much grace and patience during the coming summer; it is earnestly to be desired the great Overruler of all events will so dispose the hearts and minds of employers and employed, that there may be a speedy and satisfactory conclusion to this unhappy strife. *Charles Howard, Biddenham.*

Correspondence To the Editor of the *Bedfordshire Times and Independent*
The Lock-Out of Agricultural Labourers
Sir, So far as your correspondent, under the misnomer "Fair Play", enables me, in controverting his errors, to give the public clear and just views . . . I need not recapitulate the facts adduced in proof in my first letter to the Duke, as they have not been impugned. But having been in the full confidence of the men, I can pledge myself that no strike was contemplated with respect to present circumstances. But the farmers having for months been concocting along with the Duke's agent a coercive scheme thought the occasion favourable for combined action, and seized the first specious excuse for striking their blow. They have delivered it, and are chagrined to find that instead of proving fatal it has aroused unexpected vitality . . . What does your correspondent mean by this astonishing and somewhat confused statement: "We learn that the men at Cople who demanded a rise of wages without effect struck work" . . . To this moment the "men at Cople" have been desiring to work at the unraised wages, but the farmers will not let them . . . The farmers in their agitation are blindly forcing up the price of labour in their own market by driving labourers away. The farmers will do well to regard . . . that the men who have left bettered themselves, obtaining wages and rent-free house equivalent to £1 a week. By the time these lines appear another . . . labourer, with a companion, will have mig-

rated in answer to an advertisement by a farmer near Leicester, who eagerly snapped him up at £1 a week, a good cottage with three bedrooms and a garden, besides travelling and removal money . . . In self-vindication let me reply that I have repeatedly taken occasion both in the pulpit and on the platform to explain how regretful and distressful is the situation. I have no interest to serve, no feeling to gratify in opposing the farmers. An overpowering sense of justice alone constrains me to become the partizan of the weak and the wronged. The nature of the case admits of no middle course . . . The farmers demand that the men shall renounce their Union, the men refuse to surrender their liberty. If the one party is right the other is wrong. To stand aloof is culpable indifference to right and wrong . . .

Cople Vicarage, April 6   H. E. Havergal

BEDFORD DIVISION PETTY SESSIONS, Saturday, April 4.
Present: Col. Stuart, in the chair; Rev. R. G. Chalk, Mr. Harry Thornton . . . Assault by a member of the N.A.L.U. – The Vicar and Squire of Cople – *Frederick Cambers* (20) labourer, Cople, who had been before the Bench on several occasions, was charged with assaulting William White, labourer, at Cople, on March 20. He admitted the offence, and offered no explanation. – Mr. A. Stimson, who appeared for complainant, informed the Bench that his client was not a member of the National Agricultural Labourers' Union, but defendant and his friends were. On the night in question complainant and a friend, named Hartwell, left a public-house not long before closing time, and outside they were met by a mob of persons, among whom was defendant. White and Hartwell, being alone, walked away as fast as possible, but unfortunately they stopped for one of them to light his pipe, and were overtaken by the mob. Defendant struck White with his fists on the side of the head three or four times without anything being said by complainant, who was called by the new name of "blackleg" . . . Mr Thomas Barnard, of Cople House, said that as defendant had nobody in court to speak for him he (Mr. Barnard) might perhaps be allowed to say that at the time the assault was committed defendant was temporarily in his employ, was so still, and would be taken back, as he was a good workman . . . He might remind the Bench that the assault arose out of a quarrel or dispute respecting the Agricultural Labourers' Union, and he might say a few words relative to the state of Cople at the present crisis. – Mr. Barnard wished to say that the parish of Cople was not under the good influence it might be. In the unfortunate circumstances of the dispute between the labourers and their employers it behoved persons of education and intelligence to try and do everything in their power to assuage the differences of feeling that naturally arise, but he was sorry to say that in his parish the vicar, Mr. Havergal, had alluded to the subject in church and made certain one-sided statements which there were no possible means of answering. . . Mr. Barnard observed that when there was any breach of the peace committed, those who incited it ought to be responsible. – The Chairman said that if information were laid on oath as to persons being incited to commit a breach of the peace, the magistrates could deal with it, but a mere statement was not sufficient . . . Mr. Barnard remarked that he mentioned the fact of the parish not being under those influences of which other parishes had the benefit in order that the magistrates might be induced to act leniently with the defendant. – The Chairman said this was a common assault, and . . . the Bench inflicted a fine of 10s and 6s costs, with the alternative of 14 days imprisonment . . . The money was paid. A number of Unionists, wearing blue ribbons, were in court . . .

Bedfordshire Times 25 April 1874
Correspondence The Labourers Union.
Sir, . . . I maintain that all a great proprietor can do is to let his farms at moderate rents to respectable and liberal tenants, to provide the labourers with comfortable dwellings

and large gardens, to take the rents direct himself and leave the farmers and labourers to settle their own differences.

As regards the lock-out and the strike I believe that victory will not accrue to either party along the whole line, but will vary according to local circumstances.

In this parish the battle was fought nearly two years ago and the Union defeated, owing to the local circumstances that female labour was pleasant, well paid, and in demand. The Union, to do it justice, sent the labourers to places where they could earn 5s to 6s a week in advance of existing wages, but the women would not leave and the men soon found that the advantage of an increase of wages vanished before two cupboards and bachelor lodgings – they came back and gave in. Some of the older men have never had regular places since. In like manner the prevalence of comfortable homes and allotments at low rates must operate prejudicially . . . I think moving a middle aged agricultural labourer as a rule does not answer, and he is rarely a happy man when transplanted.

If Clergymen, like Mr. Havergal, will turn their attention to the young and unencumbered – train the lads so that they may take situations on the railroads, in the police, etc., cultivate a spirit of adventure and emigration amongst them, the surplus labour will surely decrease, wages will rise . . . and the position of the labourers will be more surely, though less rapidly, advanced than by strikes or wholesale emigration . . .

H.S.

Sir, I find that there are persons in various parts of Bedfordshire who are making assertions respecting myself and the part I am taking in the Labourers' cause which are utterly false . . . I beg to inform the public in general and the "perverters of truth" in particular, that I have never received a fraction for anything I have ever done, and not only so, but my railway and other expenses incidental upon attending meetings at a distance from my own home have been defrayed by myself. What I am doing for the Labourers is from no other motive . . . than to do some good to a class of men who . . . ought to be in a very different position from that in which they are . . .

H. Wright

Maulden. Labourers' Union. On Sunday afternoon, the 19th inst., a meeting for Divine worship, convened by the supporters of this Union, was held in the Sand Pit, near the Black Horse Inn. About 1,000 persons were present, many no doubt from curiosity to witness the unique spectacle of a service in aid of locked-out agricultural labourers . . . There was a similar meeting in the evening, the sum collected at both services amounting to £5 10s 7d.

Bedfordshire Times 13 June 1874
Cardington. The Vicar of Cople and the Labourers. On the evening of Thursday, the 4th, a meeting of agricultural labourers was held on the Green, when there was not a large attendance. Mr. G. Butcher, Bedford, the district secretary of the Union, gave a short address, and called upon Mr. Askew, a labourer, to take the chair. The latter stated that the object of the meeting was to bid farewell to those who were about to leave this so-called land of freedom, and said he for one should very much like to go, but there was always something to hinder . . . Mr. Butcher . . . introduced Mr. Havergal in a short speech relative to the emigration of the men from Cardington to New Zealand . . . The speaker referred to the hope expressed by farmers of stamping out the Union in a fortnight, and said that it had done them good service for twelve weeks in that locality . . . Although he had had to send to Leamington for about £1,000 there was no complaining. He urged the men to stick to the Union and not give up, for if they did leave it the farmers would shortly take off a shilling from their wages and then another . . . The Rev. H. E. Havergal . . . complimented [the farmers of Cardington] for taking back the men

without asking them to give up their tickets, and he did not wish to crow over them, for he could not think they took them back just to get a little corn thrashed to send to market or some chaff for the horses. Indeed they were setting the Cople and Willington farmers a good example. The Cople farmers rode about at first to convert their Cardington brethren, but now he hoped the latter would send missionaries to convert the former . . . At the close of the meeting a collection was made for the emigrants, consisting of Messrs. Addington, Roberts, and Fuller, their wives and children.

Bedfordshire Times 20 June 1874
Labourers' Union. The number now on the funds is: Banbury, 30; Gloucester, 10; Dorset, 25; Luton, 50; Bedford, 91; Essex (North), 229; Essex (South), 100; Suffolk, 1,963; Cambridgeshire, 376; Swanton Morley (Norfolk), 20; Old Buckenham, 110; Wisbeach, 250; Market Rasen (Lincoln), 45; Spalding, 25.

Bedfordshire Mercury 4 July 1874
The March of the Locked-Out Labourers. The long-talked-of procession of agricultural labourers through the Northern and Midland Counties has at length begun. On Monday morning Mr. Taylor, the General Secretary of the National Union, selected about 70 men in the Newmarket district, and started from that town for Cambridge shortly after 1 o'clock, arriving there about 6 . . . The object of the march, as defined by one of the men, who, by the way, all appeared exceptionally quiet and respectable, is to "excite public sympathy and to collect subscriptions," to which may perhaps be added, "for the purpose of improving their moral and social condition, and that of their class generally." . . . The party . . . set out for Bedford, walking to Lord's Bridge . . . whence they went by train to Gamlingay. Here they again took to the road, and marched through Potton, where they stopped for dinner, to Sandy, the remainder of the journey to Bedford being accomplished once more by the aid of the railway, where they arrived about 5 o'clock . . . After about an half-an-hour's rest the party again started in procession through the principal streets of the town, headed by the Promenade Band, Mr. H. Wright, Luton, the Rev. H. E. Havergal, and Mr. Henry Taylor, General Secretary, of N.A.L.U. leading the men. All the men wore blue ribbon of the Union and many had cards on their hats describing their special duty. Some of the men carried flags and banners, bearing typical mottoes and initials . . . At the commencement of the meeting [on Market-hill] . . . there were probably not less than 1,000 persons on the square, and though many more came up during the speaking, the audience at the edges was of the usual shifty nature. Many farmers were in the outskirts listening to the labourer's grievances, and appeared to take considerable interest in the proceedings. The conduct of the crowd was all that could be desired save one farmer, who was politely informed that he had better be quiet or make himself scarce . . .

Bedfordshire Times 1 August 1874
The Bedfordshire Prize Farms. *The Agricultural Gazette* publishes the subjoined notices of the three farms, that of Mr. Richard Checkley, Brogborough, near Woburn, that of Mr. Thomas Crouch, Lidlington, and that of Mr Charles Howard, Biddenham, to which . . . prizes were awarded . . .

It is a noteworthy fact . . . that both [Mr. Checkley's farm] and that of Mr. Thomas Crouch . . . were deprived of their labourers by a strike during the two most critical months of this year. In April and May, when the seed must be sown, or there will be no crop, and when weeds must be hoed, or the crops will be smothered; and when cows must be milked, or there will be no profit; the labourers on this and some other neighbouring farms, who had been receiving generally 13s, struck work for 15s a week. After about ten week's absence, they were received back again for 14s a week. Mr. Crouch's ten men, who had meanwhile tried work in the North – in Nottinghamshire and York –

have all returned to him wiser and better, as he believes, and not very likely to strike again in a hurry . . . The farm is provided with an admirable farm-house, and there are many excellent cottages, in which the families of the truant labourers remained, while the discontented men went on their fruitless search after better circumstances . . .

The Agricultural Labourers' Lock-Out. At the weekly meeting of the executive committee of the N.A.L.U.at Leamington on Monday, Mr. Arch in the chair, the following resolution was passed: "That in face of the harsh and prolonged lock-out of the farm labourers in the eastern counties, this committee cannot feel justified in supporting them in enforced idleness indefinitely, nor can they seek the public support continually while the harvest is waiting to be gathered. The committee, therefore, resolve to place emigration and migration at the disposal of the labourers, or the alternative of depending wholly upon their own resources." A committee was appointed to carry out this resolution, and the executive committee voted £600 for relief of the lock-out unionists, whose numbers are now reduced by one-half . . .

Bedfordshire Times 15 August 1874

Statistics of the Lock-Out. Some interesting statistics respecting the recent protracted struggle in the Eastern counties have been collected by the National Agricultural Labourers' Union. The lock-out lasted for about 18 weeks, and for strike pay, migration, and emigration, cost the National Union alone about £25,000. The total number of men locked out was 2,400. Of these 400 migrated, 440 emigrated, and 870 returned to work without being required to give up their union tickets. Since the stoppage of lock-out pay 350 men have resumed work, some of whom have abandoned the union, and there are still 340 unemployed. The secretary attributes the failure of the lock-out to three principle causes — the want of union and combination amongst the men, the refusal of many of the lock-outs to migrate to places where work and better wages could be obtained, and the injudicious admission of old men into the Union, who apparently expected life annuities from its funds.

Bedfordshire Times 3 September 1874

Renhold. Harvest Home Celebration . . . Captain Polhill-Turner thanked them most heartily for thus drinking his health. They had heard a great deal of late about Unionism, but he felt they had reason to congratulate themselves on the happy bond and unionism they had at Renhold — unionism between landlord and tenant, master and men (cheers). . . . With regard to the Unionism of which they had heard so much during the past year it was unnecessary to go into the question, but he was extremely glad it was over, and now that the struggle had been fought out between employers and employed, labour and capital, he hoped the matter would be set at rest. There was a good deal to be said on both sides. He might say that many of the men who left their masters were glad to come back again to their work and their cottages. Doubtless there were grievances on the part of the men, and for the young and able emigration was a very good thing; but with all that, it behoved men to think twice before leaving their masters . . . No doubt there must be a different system of hiring. He also thought the allotment system should be carried out to a larger extent (loud cheers) . . .

Bedfordshire Times 10 October 1874

Mr. Joseph Arch in Bedfordshire. Meeting at Eversholt. On Saturday Mr. Arch, President of the National Agricultural Labourers' Union, arrived in this county, arrangements having been made for holding two demonstrations — at Eversholt on that day and at Marston on Monday. Mr. S. Sandys, of Eversholt House, near the church, entertained Mr. Arch, Mr. Henry Wright of Luton, and others, as well as allowed the use of his field for the gathering. A Committee, consisting of representatives from the branches of Eversholt, Woburn, Ridgmount, and Husborne Crawley, was formed to make the necessary preparations . . . At 4.45 the Eversholt Brass Band, under the leadership of Mr. Franklin, after playing on the lawn of Eversholt House, led the way to the field, with Mr. Arch, Mr. Wright, Mr. Sandys and party, Mr. W. Cockbill, Mr. G. Butcher (agents of the N.A.L.U.), and the Committee, wearing Union ribbons . . . Nearly 500 persons had tea, and many afterwards indulged in dancing . . . At 7 o'clock the platform was occupied by Mr. Arch, who was again cheered to the echo, Mr. Wright, who was voted to the chair with much cordiality, Mr Cockbill, Rev. W. Hillier (Ridgmount), Mr., Mrs and Miss Sandys, Miss Saunders, and others, and there must have been nearly 1800 persons present . . .

Mr. Arch was introduced with three cheers and one cheer more, and proceeded to address the meeting at length with astonishing effect, the cheering and homely ejaculations of the labourers being frequent . . . An earnest appeal was made to those present to remain united, as then they wielded a tremendous power, and they were urged to make themselves intelligent instead of muddling their brains with drink. With bitter sarcasm Mr. Arch spoke of the meanness of guardians of the poor in cutting down the out-relief and making the treatment in the house as rigorous as possible, although in most cases labourers were compelled to seek relief from no fault of their own. He said this wicked, blasphemous thing must be put a stop to, as it was a disgrace to Christian civilisation, and ministers of the Gospel would be called to account before God if they did not raise their voice against such a system . . . Dr. Hillier addressed the meeting on the importance of combination as the only means of raising the condition of the labourers . . .

On Sunday afternoon nearly 2,000 persons assembled at the tent to hear Mr. Arch, who preached an excellent sermon from John iv., 50. In the evening a much larger number congregated from all the villages around as well as from Woburn, and Mr. Arch preached with his accustomed point and clearness . . .

Bedfordshire Times 9 January 1875
National Agricultural Labourers' Union. The monthly meeting of the Executive Committee of this district was held on Tuesday, at the Rifle coffee-house, Bedford, and among those present were Mr. H. Taylor, the general secretary, who has just returned from Canada; Mr. H. Wright, of Luton; the Rev. H. E. Havergal, of Cople; and other friends. The Secretary reported that he had written to the Central Committee at Leamington forwarding a resolution of the district, urging them to devise a scheme for securing land for the labourers . . . Reports were brought in by members of the Committee that wages were being reduced in some parts of the district from 1s to 2s per week, and that others had been discharged after joining the Union. Mr Taylor referred to his Canadian tour and his scheme for colonisation . . . The Committee are of opinion that emigration is desirable and necessary, and are determined to push it the ensuing spring. The Secretary was instructed to assist those men to gain employment who had refused to submit to a reduction of wages.

Bedfordshire Times 16 January 1875
Cople. Death of the Vicar. In our obituary is a notice of the death of the Rev. H. E. Havergal, for many years Vicar of this parish. As he was found seriously ill on Sunday no services were held in the church, and he expired on Tuesday. Mr. Havergal was admired in the musical world as a composer and performer of merit. and he was conductor of the Bedford Harmonic Society now extinct. The living is in the gift of Christ Church College, Oxford . . .
DEATHS . . . Jan. 12, of apoplexy, at Cople Vicarage, in his 55th year, the Rev. H. E. Havergal, M.A., for 27 years vicar of Cople, Bedfordshire.

Bedfordshire Times 6 February 1875
Agricultural Labourers' Union. On Tuesday afternoon the annual meeting of the Bed-

fordshire Branch of the National Agricultural Labourers' Union was held at the Working Men's Institute, Bedford, when representatives from about 26 villages attended . . . Mr. Butcher [local secretary] reported that about 20 meetings were held each month in the district, and that about 347 men had migrated and 200 had emigrated during the past year . . . The Chairman [Mr. H. Wright of Luton] remarked upon the decease of the Rev. H. E. Havergal vicar of Cople, as a warm and sincere friend of the movement, pointing out that that gentleman was doubtless the means of preventing the ejection of several members from their cottages because they had joined the Union . . . At seven o'clock a largely attended and enthusiastic meeting was held in the large hall . . .

Bedfordshire Times 27 February 1875
Lidlington. Labourers' Meeting. A labourers' meeting was held in this village on Tuesday evening. Samuel Monk in the chair. Messrs. Butcher (of Bedford) and Cockbill were the speakers. Two letters were read, which had been delivered that day from New Zealand, written by labouring men who went out last year, and in which they speak very highly of the change in their circumstances. Within the past few days three other families have received papers to go to New Zealand. Our correspondent asks what is to be done to keep our best labourers at home? and he thinks it a mockery to offer them land at 6d per pole, and that they ought to be allowed to rent land at a fair price . . . sufficient to provide them with bread and food for a pig. He thinks they might then look forward to old age with pleasure, whereas their present prospect is anything but pleasing, the Union House or out-door relief being the alternatives before them. He says labour is short now, and asks what farmers will do when the best men have left.

Bedfordshire Times 10 April 1875
Lidlington. Emigration. On Tuesday another batch of 17 left this village for New Zealand. During the past year 59 persons have left Lidlington, and there are now nearly 20 cottages unoccupied.

Bedfordshire Times 3 July 1875
National Agricultural Labourers' Union. A special meeting of the Bedford District of the National Agricultural Labourers' Union was held at the "Rifle", Bedford . . . to hear Mr. Henry Taylor, General Secretary, with reference to the dispute between the Editor of *The Labourers' Union Chronicle* and the National Executive Committee. After the matter was deliberately and fully discussed, it was moved . . . that "This Committee desires to express its approval of the action of the Executive Committee in procuring another paper *The English Labourer*, and express its confidence in Howard Evans as its conductor" . . . The Branches and members will consequently understand that they must forward their Branch Contributions at once, in order to enable the District Secretary to place the District right with the Central Office; otherwise in case of anything occurring in the District we have no claim on the Central Fund.

Bedfordshire Times 10 July 1875
The Labourers' Union has been split into two sections, as was plainly foreseen would be its fate some time ago. *The Labourers' Union Chronicle*, the organ of the Union since its origin, called attention to certain discrepancies and deficiencies in the accounts of the Society at the recent conference, which swiftly led to hot personal encounters, and have now developed into rival factions. *The English Labourer* is the title of a new paper, started in the interests of the party who support the two secretaries whose accounts and conduct formed the original subject of disagreement. At present it is difficult to say on which side lies the balance of right. Mr. Arch is now being appealed to with all the pathos and frantic entreaty at command of each organ, but he appears to vacillate . . . His estimable personal character is the only satisfactory object in the pitiful squabble . . .

Bedfordshire Times 31 July 1875
Cardington. An Emigrant's Letter. "New Zealand, Oct. 22nd. Dear Brothers, I now send these few lines, hoping to find you all quite well. We are doing well, and you need not wonder at it, for we eat half a sheep in a week; and I think you must value your place to get up at five in the morning, but if I get up and have my breakfast by eight o'clock that is soon enough in this country. I have a good master; I have a cottage and garden. He got me a six-gallon boiler, a tea-kettle, a saucepan and frying-pan, two sacks of potatoes, six cwt. of coal, a peck of sugar, a tin of tea, and a grate and oven, and two hundred feet of boards to do what I liked with; and when he sent my wife and family to me he went to Christchurch and bought two hundred of flour, half a sheep, and bread, and some salt and hops to make yeast with to bake our bread; he also got tickets for my wife and family, and saw them safe in the train. I don't know how far I might have travelled in England to have found a master to have done that. I have not seen my master for over two weeks; he has over twelve miles to come to see me. He has two hundred acres of land where we are, and he bought it for fifty shillings an acre . . . our nearest neighbour is twenty chains off. We are fifteen miles from the Snowy Mountains and can see them quite plain . . . I wish I had come ten years sooner. I have this evening been potatoe setting. Remember us to all. We feel very thankful to those who helped us here. From your affectionate brother, George Addington, late of Cardington, Bedfordshire.

The Bedfordshire Times 11 Dec 1875
Cople. Labourers' Union. The labourers here have been in doubt as to which of the two unions, the old or the new, they should pay their subscriptions. They have now resolved to adhere to the Union managed by Henry Taylor.
The Late Incumbent. The labourers of this parish have raised £3 17s towards a tombstone for the late Mr. Havergal, in whom they lost a staunch friend.
Eversholt. A meeting of the Labourers' Union was held here on the 25th ult., but it was a failure.

The Bedfordshire Times 18 December 1875
Maulden. Labourers' Union. On the 1st inst. a meeting was held here . . . There was a fair attendance considering it was an outdoor meeting and snowing all the time.

Bedfordshire Times 12 February 1876
Ravensden, Labourers' Union. At a recent meeting Mr. Ezra Wiles (in the chair) gave the men some excellent advice. He asked the men to stick to him; he meant to go to the vestry meeting to try and get a resolution passed for the vestry to be held at such time in the day as the poor men can attend. Mr. Sletcher spoke of the hardships of bringing up a family of ten children with farmer's pay as he had done . . .

Bedfordshire Times 20 May 1876
Lidlington. National Agricultural Labourers' Union. On Tuesday the labourers met at the Royal Oak to hear an address by one of the delegates of the Union. He told the labourers the pay per day in Canada was 6s 8d and 10s. It is reported some more are leaving the country shortly.

Bedfordshire Times 7 October 1876
Silsoe. Labourers Union Strike. The labourers from the farms of Mr. Richard Eve and Mr. E. F. Squire are out on strike, owing to their wages having been reduced one shilling per week, pursuant to notice which had previously been given . . . On Tuesday, 3rd inst., a meeting was held on the subject near the Almshouses in the village, a labourer from Greenfield named Clark "in the chair" and the speakers were Messrs Butcher and Rich . . . The principal tendency of all the speeches was to congratulate the men upon having so boldly refused to succumb to their oppressors and to continue the strike even to the

end; and they would be paid by the Union at the rate of nine shillings per week, for how long a period did not definitely transpire, but the advantages of emigration were strongly advocated . . .

[Leading article] The general public have heard but little of late respecting the doings of the Agricultural Labourers' Unions. It will be remembered that a split occurred about eighteen months ago in the original Union, whereupon a new one was started, which owes such success as it thinks it has attained to the fact that Mr. Arch's services were retained on its behalf, and its organ is of a sensational order . . . The thoughtful labourer has at last been discovering, . . . that the bombastic harangues and magnificent promises . . . are not stuff on which children can be fed and rent paid . . . In the extracts from the reports of the local District Secretary of the New Union which we take from time to time . . . may be seen some indications of the decay of the society. Moneys are falling off, indifference to meetings is shown . . . Why should [labourers] rejoice at being advised to fly to worse ills than they now endure, with absolutely no chance of returning when once out in the bleak backwoods of Canada or the wilds of New Zealand? . . . The truest friends of the labourer are those who counsel him to beware of loose-tongued men retained in the interest of other countries and colonies, and urge him, instead of listening to such emigration agents, to combine in honest English fashion to secure fair play from their employers at home . . . If the men at Silsoe think they are treated with exceptional hardness or unfairness, in having their wages reduced by a shilling a week, their best policy . . . is to imitate the sensible custom of skilled artisans, and hold a conference with the farmers through a deputation from themselves – not a paid agitator. If friendly exchange of facts and opinions fail . . . arbitration before disinterested persons of standing would be the next course, and could hardly fail at arriving at a just settlement . . .

Bedfordshire Times 14 October 1876
The Agricultural Labourers' Union. To the Editor:
Sir, Your editorial remarks last week lead one to look at both sides of this question. As regards Unionism it has got into such bad hands that no persons of character can countenance the course they are now pursuing, but the cry for high wages and the depression in agriculture cannot go on long together. My farming friends tell me they are losing money . . . Some are paying rent out of capital, and some who have not much of that have had to succumb, and the number of sales advertised in your columns show that some are giving over from choice and some from necessity . . . In out-of-way districts labour is getting scarcer by the tendency of people to flock to larger centres: some get employment on the railway, others turn to bricklayers . . . those remaining command higher wages . . .

Bedfordshire Times 21 October 1876
Agricultural Labourers' Union. The District Secretary reports to his Society as follows. Meetings have been held in the following places: Houghton Conquest . . . A goodly number present . . . Silsoe, October 4th. The men are nobly standing out against their wages being reduced to 12s per week. They were all met by the District Secretary at Ampthill, who paid them the usual allowance; and a collection was made at Silsoe at the public meeting, and £1 1s was collected; then a nice little piece of money from the incidental fund was shared between them, so they did not suffer very great loss . . . Ridgmount . . . A few good Union men here, but many that are not in Union. Carlton . . . A public meeting was held . . . At the close three joined, and all paid up their contributions, and delivered to the District Secretary the sum of £1 0s 5½d. Odell . . . Seven joined and paid their entrance fees . . .

Bedfordshire Times 4 November 1876
Agricultural Labourers' Union. The District Secretary reports as follows: Renhold . . . the men seem very dull about Union. Wootton . . . This was once the very best branch in the Bedford district, but they are getting very low . . . Cranfield . . . Presided over by a lock-out labourer from Salford. This branch once numbered over 100, but has got very low . . . Five rejoined at the close. Pulloxhill . . . Presided over by a lock-out labourer from Silsoe . . . at the close thirty-three joined the Union . . .

Bedfordshire Times 6 January 1877
National Agricultural Labourers' Union. The District Secretary reports to his Society "Meetings have been held . . .: Renhold . . . In a house kindly lent by a good Union man and labourer. The company was not large, but we had a good meeting . . . We are much blamed for holding our meetings at public-houses by those who shut the chapels and schoolrooms against us. The fact is, we are obliged to be beholden to our public-house friends for shelter . . .

Bedfordshire Times 27 January 1877
National Agricultural Labourers Union. The District Secretary reports that meetings have been held as follows: Cranfield . . . One farmer is kind enough to give his men (no, that is a mistake: they are not men, or they would not allow it) 11s per week. This is a large village, and has only a few good members in the Union. Then men came in numbers to the meeting, and I hope they mean to join the Union and be ready, not for 11s., but 16s., when the sun shines . . . Barton . . . the sum of 2s 3d was given for the men with large families that are locked out . . .

The annual reports from the Woburn Park Farm Office include comments on the labour force, from which come the following extracts.

1872   The actual cost of work of all descriptions was very much increased by the frequent advances of materials and labour.

I have much pleasure in recording the fact that in the management of work of every description upon these Estates great regularity was maintained by slight and well timed advances in the rate of wage we continued to maintain a sound and healthy feeling with the Labourer and the work estimated to be completed within the year was finished by the time specified. . .

Nothing which has taken place in Country Parishes for many years has caused so much interest and criticism as the upward tendency of the rate of the Agricultural Labourer, this movement affects not only the Landlord and the Tenant but the whole community and I therefore hope that in the end everything may be arranged to the satisfaction and advantage of all parties concerned. In considering this movement the Duke cannot I think fail to be impressed with the way in which he is endeavouring to ameliorate the Labourers condition by improving their Cottages and 'thus affecting them means of health comfort and cleanliness: His Grace has, I am sure true pleasure in caring for their welfare and of placing in their way advantages which will tend to make them contented and shew them a reliance which is the surest way to the Well-being of their Families.

1873   **Labourers** The relations between the Farmers and their Labourers continued unsatisfactory throughout the year: it is to be hoped that not only the Farmers but their Labourers will in the end profit by present uneasiness. A superabundant population is doubtless a great drawback, for then the quality of the work is depressed by the supply being maintained at a low rate of wage: there is to my mind no doubt that the Labourers have been poorly paid, but it does not follow that they are paid less than they are worth to the Farmers who employ them. I regret to notice the Exodus of our best Labourers and this is occurring at the very time when their condition is receiving such material improvement: there is however no help for it, and it appears tolerably clear that, by and by, the Labourers must gain by the present agitation.

Woburn Park Farm. Labour.   The Accounts shew an increase of £46.6.6 for Labour in 1873 as compared with 1872, caused by the Increased rate of Wages. No advance however was given to the Men during the year the Wages as settled (14/- Per week) in the latter half of 1872 being deemed sufficient and the Men appearing satisfied.

1874   **Labourers** Some anxiety was caused by a lock out and strike of Labourers at Cople and Lidlington – The movement was incited by the Managers of the Agricultural Labourers' Union, and the Farmers accepted the challenge by declining to employ any man who would not withdraw from the Union.

For some months a good deal of feeling was shewn, but on the whole there was no great cause of complaint to be made against either the Farmers or the Labourers.

The Labourers have gained by the Strike – wages have advanced 1/- per week and there is full employment everywhere – migration and emigration have certainly assumed a more distinct form, and in many villages, not only are families leaving, but I notice that the young men are drawing away.

Woburn Park Farm

. . . The Farm Labourers, as also all the ordinary Labourers upon the Estate, were advanced from 14/- to 15/- per week on the 25th April . . . Horsekeepers and Cowmen 17/- per week.

1875   **Woburn Park Farm. Labour.** No alteration was made in the Rate of Wages during this year.

Beds. C.R.O. R 5/869

INDEX OF NAMES

Lee, Chas., Northill, 124
Lee, Jn., 124
Lefevre, Mr., 134
Leicestershire, 41; Leicester, 192
Leighton Buzzard, 146, 180-1; Hockliffe Road, Mr. Theobald's house, 145; Poor Law Union, 99
Lidlington, 14, 71, 74, 91, 182, 187, 189-90, 197-8, 201; Royal Oak, 198; Sandpit, 189; School and teacher's house, 161
Lincolnshire, 41; Market Rasen, 194; Spalding, 194
Littledale, H., 120
London, 45, 129
Long, R., jnr., Upper Stondon, 108
Long, Robt., Stondon Manor Farm, 106, 110, 161
Longuet Higgins, C., Turvey, 77
Lousley, Mr., Barton, 177
Lovell, Jos., Blunham, 132
Luton, 5-6, 9, 12-3, 45, 104, 171, 176, 178-80, 182-5, 187, 194; Lewsey Farm, 73; Poor Law Union, 20, 99; Water Street Plait Hall, 171
Macan, T. A., 168
McKenna, the Rev. A., 178
Macqueen, Col., 134
Markes, Mr., Wilstead, 183
Marston Moretaine, 92, 183, 195; School, 161
Matthews, Hen., Woburn, 29, 47
Maulden, 71, 75, 90, 92, 100, 154, 180, 193, 198; Black Horse Inn, 193; Sand Pit, 193; School, 161
Mayhew, Art., Bromham, 179-81
Melchbourne, 21; Park, 17
Meppershall, 71, 75, 106, 111, 161
Mercer's Company, 111
Middlesex, Harrow, 45
Millard, Jn., Aspley Guise, 34, 36
Millbrook, School and teacher's house, 161
Milton Bryant, 36, 39, 41, 135
Milton Ernest, 137
Mogerhanger *see* Blunham
Monk, Sam., Lidlington, 197
Moore, Capt., 120
Morley, Sam., 173
Morris, H. B., Caddington, 72
Mossman, Mrs., Battlesden, 133

Mossman, Robt., Battlesden, 35
Mothers, Mr., Bedford N.A.L.U., 180
Mountain, the Rev. J. H. B., Blunham, 72
Myers, Mr., Bedford N.A.L.U., 180-1
Musgrave, Geo., 80-1
Musgrave, Hen. M., 80-1
Nash, G. P., 120
Neall, Jas., Riseley, 135
Neve, the Rev. Fred. H., Southill, 77
New Zealand, 5, 129, 185, 188, 193, 197-9; Christchurch, 198
Newal, Jac., Bolnhurst, 138
Norfolk, Old Buckenham, 194; Swanton Morley, 194
Northamptonshire, 9, 41; Northampton, 129; Wellingborough, 99
Northill, 71, 76
Northumberland, 15; Glendale, 15
Nottingham, Jos., Cople, 182
Nottinghamshire, 41, 194
Oakley, 21-2, 135; school and teacher's house, 161
Odell, 162, 164, 199; feast, 164
Odell, Jas., Stagsden, 124
Odell, Wm., Eversholt, 140
Odell, Wm., Westoning, 97
Orlebar, Rich. L., 76, 121
Osborn, Mr., Flitwick, 95
Overman, Thos. Wm., Maulden, 4, 75, 90, 92
Oxfordshire, 41; Banbury, 194; Oxford, All Souls' College, 21, 37; Christ Church College, 196
Page, Sir Greg., 64-5
Palmer, Charlt., 94
Parker, Mr., 140
Parker, Rich., Harlington, 105
Partridge, Mr., Wellingborough, Northants, 172
Passy, Rev. Mr., Wilstead, 136
Pearse, the Rev. Thos., Westoning, 77, 159-60
Pearson, Mrs., 140
Peddar, Jos., Silsoe, 99-100
Peddor, Phil., and family, Cranfield, and Mellor, Derbys., 130
Peel, A. W., Eyeworth, 146
Peete, Dav., Maulden, 100
Pestell, Hen., Broughton, Bucks., 109
Pickering, Mr., Riseley, 134

INDEX OF SUBJECTS

Most subjects have been grouped under major headings.